THE MEANING OF GENERAL EDUCATION

The Emergence of a Curriculum Paradigm

THE MEANING OF GENERAL EDUCATION

The Emergence of a Curriculum Paradigm

Gary E. Miller

 TEACHERS COLLEGE, COLUMBIA UNIVERSITY
NEW YORK AND LONDON

Published by Teachers College Press, 1234 Amsterdam Avenue,
New York, NY 10027

Library of Congress Cataloging-in-Publication Data

Miller, Gary E.
  The meaning of general education: the emergence of a curriculum
paradigm / Gary E. Miller.
    p. cm.
  Bibliography: p.
  Includes index.
  ISBN 0-8077-2894-2
  1. Universities and colleges—United States—Curricula.
2. Interdisciplinary approach in education—United States.
I. Title. II. Title: General education: the emergence of a
curriculum paradigm.
LB2361.5.M55   1988
378′.199′0973—dc19   87-26739
                                                    CIP

Quotations from Algo Henderson and Jean Henderson,
Higher Education in America (San Francisco: Jossey-Bass,
1974) are reproduced by permission of the publisher.

Manufactured in the United States of America
93 92 91 90 89 88   1 2 3 4 5 6

This book is dedicated to Karen and Gregory

The author gratefully acknowledges the advice, support, inspiration, and friendship of Dr. Hans Flexner

Contents

Foreword

For the college and university faculty member, the academic administrator, the student of higher education—for anyone concerned with and about the improvement of the postsecondary curriculum—this volume provides an uncommonly penetrating and illuminating treatment. While it offers a much-needed historical and conceptual analysis of general education in the United States, it provides a good deal more than that. Much of the discussion surrounding the curriculum in past years has been focused on content rather than on the conceptual and theoretical foundations from which curricular alternatives and priorities are established and meaning and consistency in practice are derived.

Thus it is not surprising that the curriculum, notably but not solely at the undergraduate level, has been marked by confusion and inconsistencies, particularly over the past two decades. It is especially ironic that general education, which was originally formulated as a reaction to what were perceived to be the serious shortcomings of liberal education, should today be confused with the latter. Indeed, the two terms are often used interchangeably, despite the fact that the two forms of education have fundamental conceptual differences that lead in turn to important practical differences. The assumptions that underlie the curriculum and practice of liberal education grew out of the late nineteenth century liberal culture movement in the university, with its emphasis on the separate disciplines that have long served as the administrative and organizational basis of the university and as the structural foundation of its curriculum. General education, on the other hand, which was generated in the 1920s and 1930s solely as a curricular movement, is founded on pragmatic and contextual premises. It is interdisciplinary in character, as are the human problems and concerns that provide the basis of its curriculum.

Essentially, the liberal education perspective looks to the past for a sense of direction, for a pattern of meaning. Those who advocate excellence via a return to the glories of the past have in fact just this perspective in mind. Knowledge, historically viewed as a priori and universal, becomes an end in itself in this scheme; the curriculum is merely a vehicle for the acquisition of knowledge, most commonly in disciplinary segments. In the general education view, on the other hand, knowledge is hypothetical and should be regarded as a means to a desirable end: a fuller, more abundant personal life and a richer, freer society. To achieve that goal, knowledge from various sources, past and present, is utilized as and when it is needed, often in the solution of human problems. Indeed, general education is fundamental to the quality of life in a democratic society and has, in fact, been conceived in that context.

In spite of these and other important distinctions between liberal and general education—and the quite different curricular choices and educational practices these distinctions imply—it has become common practice to attempt to combine in a single program or curriculum the goals and objectives of the one with the means and procedures of the other. But since the underlying assumptions of the two are not only different but frequently incompatible, the resultant mix is more often than not dysfunctional.

These current trends need very much to be corrected, and in offering this splendid analysis of general education in the United States, including its important and potentially vital relationship to forms of professional, continuing, and adult education, Dr. Miller has provided an invaluable service to all those concerned with curriculum formulation and construction in higher education. Since general education increasingly has come to serve as the foundation of higher education in colleges and universities throughout the country, this book should be warmly received by members of curriculum committees, faculty, higher education administrators, and higher education professionals everywhere.

Comprehensive in scope and scholarly in interpretation, this exceptionally insightful and instructive book is also remarkably readable. In addition to offering a serious and penetrating analysis of the roots and sources of general education, it provides a conceptual framework, a nexus of assumptions for analyzing and revising the higher education curriculum, that will be welcomed by the increasing number of individuals interested in and concerned with educational reform. It is the most important book on the meaning and development of the concept and practice of general education available, and with its publication Dr. Miller and Teachers College Press have made a major contribution to the improvement of the quality of American higher education.

Hans Flexner

THE MEANING OF
GENERAL EDUCATION

The Emergence of a Curriculum Paradigm

CHAPTER 1

Transformation
and the Search for Meaning

American higher education is going through a period of massive change. Depending on one's perspective, it is a time of exhilarating innovation or of crippling crisis, a time of challenge or of collapse. It is certainly a time of self-examination, self-criticism, and reassessment of some of the basic assumptions and organizing principles on which higher education is established.

The change (and the prospect of even more change) in higher education reflects what may be a fundamental change in the broader society with which our colleges and universities are inextricably intertwined. In times of social transformation, it becomes almost unnecessary to be reminded of just how flawed is the myth of the ivory tower and of how much the mission of higher education is defined by the needs of society. In an age of stability, the ivory tower protects and conserves the basic assumptions and principles that form the bedrock of society. But what are the assumptions and principles that must be upheld by higher education in an age of transformation, an age when, to use Toffler's (1970) phrase, we have seen the death of permanence?

The Industrial Revolution, itself less than two centuries old, has already given way to the Technological Revolution, whose tide has moved much faster than our institutions' abilities to adapt. We find ourselves playing a game whose economic, political, and social rules no one knows quite how to teach. Like the Industrial Revolution before it, the Technological Revolution involves a paradigm shift. It is not just the technology that is changing; it is the intricate fabric of society, the collection and organization of shared assumptions and principles that are the common stock of thought and action in daily life, that are only too quickly being transformed.

The current confusion of purpose and program in higher education reflects a search for meaning within this new paradigm. The

1

depth of the problem is stated eloquently in the 1986 report of the Carnegie Foundation for the Advancement of Teaching:

> The undergraduate college, the very heart of higher learning, is a troubled institution. . . . [Educators] are confused about how to impart shared values on which the vitality of both higher education and society depend. The disciplines have fragmented themselves into smaller and smaller pieces and undergraduates find it difficult to see patterns in their courses and to relate what they learn to life. . . . Colleges appear to be searching for meaning in a world where diversity, not commonality, is the guiding vision. [p. 16]

What the Carnegie Foundation found, says its report, was "on most campuses a disturbing gap between the college and the larger world" (p. 17). The gap reveals itself in almost every facet of academic life: increased reports of faculty stress, concern that university researchers are being outdistanced by the private sector, a scramble for new students in the wake of a much-ballyhooed drop in the traditional student population, demands by business and industry for tailored programs, and an unexpected, though much belated, new respect for continuing education among faculty and administrators alike.

The National Commission on the Role and Future of State Colleges and Universities (1986) warns of "a storm brewing" in public higher education: "The storm warnings are unmistakable: our society is troubled, our economy endangered, our democratic values jeopardized, our educational system embattled" (p. 29). Among the warning signs noted by the commission are an increase in the high-school dropout rate, a decade-long decline in minority students as a percentage of the total college population, growing adult illiteracy, a growing "underclass" of children who live in poverty, cutbacks in remedial programs, increased college costs, shortages of teachers, and poor understanding by college students of international issues.

These and other concerns have caused many educators to ask if the curriculum has become irrelevant for a generation of students facing a rapidly changing, increasingly dangerous and complex world. Thus it is not surprising that it is in the curriculum—especially in the undergraduate curriculum—where the issues underlying the call for reform all come together. It is also only natural that so-called general education would come to be seen as a catalyst for innovation as colleges and universities try to deal with these changes. For many, general education is the conscience of higher education, the part of a university that is concerned most directly with the individual student's responsibility to society at large. Many, including the authors of the key commission reports of the 1980s, have called for a reexamination of general education.

Indeed, serious discussion of general education should be an urgent item on the higher education agenda; however, it has been hampered by a pervasive sense of confusion over the meaning of the term *general education*. Thus we hear advocacy of one particular subject area or another, such as advocacy of international education as a component of general education or of computer literacy as a component of general education or of science and mathematics as components of general education. Advocates see the issue from the narrow perspective of their own disciplines and thus see the solution within the same context. How the parts might fit together into an integrated, comprehensive curriculum is rarely discussed.

Part of the problem for those who seek to cultivate general education is the lack of a definition that (1) is widely accepted (even within the academic community of a particular college or university) and (2) is specific enough to have more than rhetorical value as the basis for establishing the content and methodology of a curriculum and to provide a basis for evaluation. For the past century or more, higher education has moved steadily away from an ability to reach agreement on such issues. Faculty—the final determiners of any curriculum—have become firmly rooted in the research ethos, thanks in large part to the reward system that colleges and universities have created. The emphasis on research has bred a vast array of academic specialties and fostered the professionalization of the curriculum at all levels. In this environment, faculty members are given neither means nor encouragement to communicate effectively across disciplines in order to find innovative answers to new instructional problems. As a result, while there is much serious, concerned talk about general education, each person brings to the discussion a definition of the term that is colored by his or her own perception of purpose. Agreement about general education objectives reached in conference dissipates in the classroom; the vagueness of the term *general education* almost inevitably results in teachers succumbing to the temptation to focus on specialized, professionally oriented, discipline-ordered knowledge.

What does *general education* mean in this environment? Active definitions cover a wide spectrum. At one end is Arthur Levine's (1978) simple statement that general education is "the breadth component of the undergraduate curriculum" (p. 3). This definition is most notable for what it leaves out. It suggests no goals for general education other than "breadth" and confines it to the undergraduate curriculum. It is simply instruction that leaves a person generally educated but sets no other goals. Such a general education might have no relationship to the remainder of a student's academic career or to the student's daily life.

But there are other definitions along the spectrum that testify to a more specific role for general education within the totality of postsecondary education. One example is an eight-objective approach summarized by Algo Henderson and Jean Glidden Henderson (1974) that "attempts to analyze the functions of [humanity] in life today and the aspects of knowledge that should facilitate the performance of those functions" (p. 33). A variation on this theme is struck by Earl J. McGrath (1974), who writes that general education is "the thread that ought to weave a pattern of meaning into the total learning experience" (p. 2). McGrath defines general education as "that which prepares students for the common life of their times and kind, regardless of their calling; including that fund of knowledge and belief and those habits of language and thought which characterize and stabilize a social group. It is the unifying element of a culture" (p. 2).

Clearly, it is *possible* to make a distinction between the goal of being "generally educated" and that of receiving a "general education" that has specific objectives. Still, confusion remains over what, specifically, distinguishes a general education curriculum from other curricula. Here, the question becomes not only one of goals but one of means—the content and method of the curriculum which are, in practice, what ultimately give reality to the goal. For instance, the term *general education* is often used interchangeably with *liberal education*. However, as later chapters will reveal, there are important differences between the two, which are revealed most clearly in the assumptions about content and method that one brings to the curriculum. The nature of these distinctions is central to this book, the thesis of which is that there is a fairly specific set of assumptions and organizing principles which, taken together, constitute the *paradigm* that defines general education. These assumptions and principles have been consciously developed since early in this century.

The first step in the search for the meaning of the term *general education* is to identify the origins of the general education paradigm. Halliburton (1977), borrowing from Thomas Kuhns, defined a paradigm as an intertwined collection and organization of assumptions that are shared by a group of people and which provide a basis for thought and action among members of that group. If one understands the general education paradigm, then one can compare and evaluate specific curricula to see which fit into it and which do not. This is a basic activity to be undertaken if discussion of general education is to take on practical meaning.

A survey of higher education in the past century reveals that there is, indeed, a paradigm of general education that is fundamentally different from other conceptions of the curriculum. Like a river running through the terrain of higher education, our concept of general education has been fed by several sources, its course shaped by pressures of the times. Briefly, the general education paradigm can be described as follows:

> General education is a comprehensive, self-consciously developed and maintained program that develops in individual students the attitude of inquiry; the skills of problem solving; the individual and community values associated with a democratic society; and the knowledge needed to apply these attitudes, skills, and values so that the students may maintain the learning process over a lifetime and function as self-fulfilled individuals and as full participants in a society committed to change through democratic processes. As such, it is marked by its comprehensive scope, by its emphasis on specific and real problems and issues of immediate concern to students and society, by its concern with the needs of the future, and by the application of democratic principles in the methods and procedures of education as well as the goals of education.

The idea of general education has been evolving for almost a century. It started as a reform movement following World War I. Today, however, one must seriously consider whether the goal can be reformation or, given the scope of change facing higher education, whether there must be transformation into a new context for discussing educational goals and methods. The nature of that context can be glimpsed by a comparison. The Carnegie Foundation report (1986) notes that "a balance must be struck between two powerful traditions—*individuality* and *community*" (p. 18). But there is another way to look at the question of balance. In *The Aquarian Conspiracy*, Marilyn Ferguson (1980) argues, "The person and society are yoked, like mind and body. Arguing which is more important is like debating whether oxygen or hydrogen is the more essential property of water" (p. 190). General education represents a continuing effort to create a third option in the curriculum, one that recognizes and builds on this inseparable relationship between the individual and community. After almost a century of experiment and, often, of quiet failure, it offers a way of articulating a curriculum that can meet the challenges facing postindustrial society.

To understand this third option, we will look at the history of higher education, tracing how pressures inside and outside education helped shape the curriculum over the past two centuries and how these pressures led to the development of a specific general education paradigm. Many general education curricula have been tried over the years. Some have been radically different from the others. This book will focus less on their differences than on their commonality—the assumptions and organization of ideas that make these curricula *general* education rather than some other kind of education.

Throughout its development, the concept of general education has been especially sensitive to forces and events both inside and outside higher education. To understand how and why general education has evolved as it has, one must also understand these forces and how they shaped and were shaped by the curriculum. This book draws upon a variety of resources to put general education into a broader institutional and social context. It should be stressed, however, that, while it uses the work of many historians to put general education into perspective, this book is not a history in the strictest sense; instead, it is an attempt to reestablish an understanding of the meaning of general education as it applies to the challenges facing higher education today.

While general education is primarily a twentieth-century phenomenon, it is in some ways a continuing response to the experiences of the nineteenth century, which, to a large degree, still define the practice of higher education in the United States. The next chapter therefore focuses on the nineteenth century, to set the backdrop against which general education appeared.

In the first four decades of the twentieth century, general education grew around the contributions of two competing philosophies, which are outlined in chapters 3, 4, and 5. One is a humanist approach, articulated by Alexander Meiklejohn and others who inherited the anti-research, pro-aesthetic culture movement of the nineteenth century and redirected it to meet twentieth-century needs. The other is an instrumentalist philosophy associated with progressive education and with the work of John Dewey. The two philosophies made essential contributions to the general education paradigm and set it apart from the classical ideal of liberal education advocated during the same period by Robert Maynard Hutchins.

Chapter 6 summarizes the definition of general education that evolved from the interplay of the humanist and instrumentalist approaches. By the beginning of World War II, the line separating general education and liberal education had been drawn. That line would become confused and in some cases lost in the decades after the war.

Chapter 7 is devoted to World War II and the Cold War, when higher education responded to a rapidly changing postwar society and to a concern with basic democratic processes, and chapter 8 to the 1960s and 1970s, when higher education adapted to an increasingly diverse—and volatile—society. The experiences of these periods illustrate how, within the basic themes of general education, the emphasis has shifted to meet the specific needs of a specific time and place. Both periods contributed to the common perceptions of general education and to the current confusion surrounding the term.

Finally, in chapter 9, current applications of general education are explored, some conclusions are drawn about the general education paradigm, and ideas are culled from the historical analysis for describing general education curricula.

This broad, integrative approach is the only way to tell the story of general education and to reveal its meaning as it has evolved over the century. The goal throughout is not simply to document what happened to general education in the twentieth century, but to gain insight into the meaning of general education that will guide curriculum planners today.

CHAPTER 2

The Classical Curriculum Confronts Democracy

When Alexis de Tocqueville wrote the account of his 1831 visit to the United States, one of his first observations was the unusual state of education in the young democracy. "I do not believe there is a country in the world," he wrote, "where, in proportion to the population, there are so few ignorant and at the same time so few learned individuals. Primary instruction is within the reach of everybody; superior instruction is scarcely obtained by any" (1840/1980, p. 51).

The observant Frenchman had captured an accurate image of higher education in ante-bellum America. What he could not know was that higher education was on the verge of a metamorphosis that would radically transform the role of colleges and universities in the nation. At the end of that metamorphosis, higher education would be almost as accessible as primary and secondary education, and yet there would remain some truth to the notion that, in America, there are few ignorant and few truly learned among the citizenry.

While Tocqueville could not have foreseen the changes that were about to occur in American education, he did observe and report on a basic fact of American society that would help fuel the engines of change:

> In America there are but few wealthy persons; nearly all Americans have to take a profession. Now, every profession requires an apprenticeship. The Americans can devote to general education only the early years of life. At fifteen, they enter upon their calling and thus their education generally ends at the age when ours begins. If it is continued beyond that point, it aims only toward a particular specialized and profitable purpose; one studies science as one takes up a business; and one takes up only those applications whose immediate practicality is recognized. [Tocqueville, 1840/1980, p. 51]

How American higher education would respond to the practical and professional educational needs of young people was already a controversy when Tocqueville visited the United States in the 1830s. It is a controversy that has continued into the latter decades of the twentieth century. At issue is the role that colleges and universities should play in preparing Americans for a profession or vocation. But also at issue is the responsibility of higher education to prepare Americans for all those other things that a democracy asks of its citizenry, such as voting and participation in the formulation of public policy, living as responsible members of a community, and, certainly not the least, pursuing individual happiness. A knowledge of how this controversy evolved and how colleges and universities responded to it is a key to understanding how and why general education emerged as a reform movement in the twentieth century.

Democratic Pressures on the Classical Curriculum

When the Puritans set out for their new world, they carried with them a belief in learning. An educated elite was necessary to the survival of a religious community whose entire structure was centered around the words in a book. Once arrived, however, they soon discovered the fear that their community might pass to "an illiterate ministry to the Churches, when our present Ministers shall lie in the Dust" (Hofstadter, 1961, p. 83). They founded Harvard College with the primary objective of insuring a literate ministry and an educated leadership who would preserve the religious purity of the Puritan community. It was an essentially *conservative* objective, the means to which was the classical curriculum of the medieval universities of Europe.

But the growing community soon found other uses for its college. As Boston and the other emerging colonial communities diversified, a growing class of merchants, traders, shippers, and other professionals began to send their children to college; their aim was not to train young men for the ministry, but to ready their sons—both socially and academically—for careers in business, law, and other secular pursuits. Increasingly, college came to be, in Phyllis Vine's phrase, "an institution which was best suited to inculcate virtue and promote social sponsorship among the privileged" (1976, p. 409). By early in the eighteenth century, graduates bound for the clergy were in a minority; by the end of the century, 80 percent of all graduates were going into other vocations (Hofstadter, 1961).

For almost two centuries, American colleges resisted—successfully for the most part—pressure to make the curriculum more responsive to the vocational and social aims of their students. But, early in the nineteenth century, the pressure became overwhelming in the face of two revolutions—the continuing aftershocks of the American Revolution, which gave ever-increasing power to the common people, and the Industrial Revolution, which was just beginning in the textile mills of New England and the iron furnaces of Pennsylvania. As Algo Henderson noted, the profound changes of the American Industrial Revolution began just "as the wave of democracy, spirited by Jefferson and brought to a crest during the Jacksonian period, swept over the nation" (1960, p. 3). Together, these two forces would re-form American higher education.

Thomas Jefferson had been looking for ways to apply his meritocratic view of democracy to higher education since the early days of the republic. Jefferson's view of education was based in the belief that "there is a natural aristocracy among men. The grounds of this are virtue and talents" (quoted in Malone, 1981, p. 239). He asked his old friend and sometime adversary John Adams, "May we not even say that that government is the best which provides most effectually for a pure selection of these natural *aristoi* into the offices of government?" (p. 239). Toward that end, Jefferson had sponsored bills for "the general diffusion of knowledge" that would have provided free primary education for all and government support for the further education of young people of exceptional merit (Malone, 1981).

Jefferson's energies would focus on the creation of the University of Virginia. In 1818, Jefferson served on the Rockfish Gap Commission, which had been appointed by the state legislature to pick a site for the University of Virginia. Its report, which embodied many of Jefferson's ideas, laid out the following purposes for higher education: "To expound the principles and structure of government. . . . To harmonize and promote the interests of agriculture, manufactures, and commerce. . . . To develop the reasoning faculties of our youth. . . . To enlighten them with mathematical and physical sciences. . . . And generally to form them to habits of reflection and correct action" (Rockfish Gap Commission, 1818/1961, pp. 194–195). The university's original curriculum in 1824 centered around eight schools: ancient languages, modern languages, mathematics, natural philosophy, natural history, anatomy and medicine, moral philosophy, and law (Hofstadter & Smith, 1961). The range of courses reflected Jefferson's goal of training "natural *aristoi*" for professional and civic leadership. The availability of choice among eight programs of study reflected Jefferson's faith in the virtues and talents of the individual. His insistence on the study of law and politics reflected his belief in the importance of an educated populace to the success of the republic. These two concerns were to remain important to American higher education; they would become central to general education in the next century.

The curriculum plan for the University of Virginia attracted the attention of educators throughout the South (Brubacher & Rudy, 1958), but Jefferson's program also influenced several northern educators. Most notable among these was George Ticknor, a Boston Brahmin who traveled to Europe armed with a letter of introduction from Jefferson (Malone, 1981). Ticknor became one of the first four Americans to receive a Ph.D. from a German university (Brubacher & Rudy, 1958). Profoundly influenced by the German system, he returned to Harvard, where, as a faculty member, he began to advocate a free elective system that would guarantee the student's freedom of study by doing away with prescribed courses. He also maintained a correspondence with Jefferson, informing him of developments at Harvard and at the German universities during the time Jefferson was designing the program for the University of Virginia (Malone, 1981).

While the combined influences of Jefferson's meritocratic approach to education and the German ideal of student freedom were shaping a more student-oriented, utilitarian curriculum philosophy at Virginia and Harvard, another kind of democratic spirit was spreading on the frontier. This spirit was embodied by Andrew Jackson, who became President of the United States in 1829. The ensuing 12 years, known as the Jacksonian era, had a lasting effect on the national consciousness. Before the Jacksonian period, democratic rhetoric tended to speak of Americans as "a sovereign people." The emphasis was on the national polity itself, and in this context colleges would comfortably justify their role in training an elite leadership for that polity. Jacksonians, on the other hand, talked about democracy in terms of "real people"—the planters, farmers, and mechanics on whom the Industrial Revolution and the settling of the frontier depended and who were fast becoming a force in national politics (Meyers, 1968).

The Jacksonian view of democracy was much different in spirit from that of Jefferson, but it, too, focused greater attention on the educational needs of the individual. This time, however, it was not the "natural *aristoi*" but the common person whose needs were in the forefront. This concern would shortly give rise to the land grant movement and to a great surge in vocationalism in higher education. Ironically, Jacksonian democracy also stimulated some aspects of vocationalism for another, quite different, reason. Henderson notes that educators, alarmed by the extension of the vote to "illiterate workers, saw the solution in universal literacy. In turn, compulsory education created a need for teachers and teacher training institutions; along with this came public acceptance of its responsibility for meeting educational needs" (1960, p. 162). Beginning with the Jacksonian era, education at all levels began to lose its strictly conservative function as it was called upon to deal with the immediate needs of a fast-growing country (Brubacher & Rudy, 1958). The stage was set for a confrontation between two visions of education. One, the classical curriculum, looked to the past for enduring truths to guide students in the present. The other, still to be born, would look more to the present to find the tools needed to shape the future.

The Yale Report

The Yale Report of 1828, written four years after the University of Virginia opened its doors and in the same year that Andrew Jackson was elected President, stands as the most articulate defense of the classical curriculum against the pressures for curricular change. It challenged the basic social issues head on:

> It is said that the public demand that the doors should be thrown open to all; that education ought to be modified, and varied, to adapt to the exigencies of the country, and the prospects of different individuals, that the instruction given to those who are destined to be merchants, manufacturers, or agriculturists should have special reference to their prospective professional pursuits. [Yale University Faculty, 1829/1961, p. 285]

The Yale faculty accepted the assertion that "our republican form of government renders it highly important that great numbers should enjoy the advantages of a thorough education" (p. 287), but they emphasized "thorough" and defined a thorough education as being embodied in a prescribed curriculum that would provide for the "discipline and furniture of the mind" (p. 278). Specifically, the Yale Report called for these curriculum goals:

> Those branches of study should be prescribed . . . which are best calculated to teach the art of fixing the attention, directing the training of

> thought, analyzing a subject proposed for investigation; following, with
> accurate discrimination, the course of argument; balancing nicely the
> evidence presented to the judgment; awakening, elevating, and control-
> ling the imagination; arranging, with skill, the treasures memory gath-
> ers; rousing and guiding the powers of genius. [p. 278]

The Yale faculty responded to demands that education address itself
to the varied needs of individual students by offering a curriculum
that gave the *same* education to *all* students. Yale did not deny the
need for professional or vocational studies. Instead, its faculty
argued, "our object is not to teach that which is peculiar to any one
of the professions, but to lay the foundation which is common to
them all" (p. 281).

In arguing for the classical curriculum, the Yale faculty was
appealing to a different vision of American democracy—that of a
homogeneous republic in which a common education would prepare
all citizens (or at least the leadership) to respond to the requirements
of citizenship. However, the wind would soon turn in the direction
of diversity, the goal being to prepare many different people for
many different walks of life. Increasingly as the century wore on,
higher education would be called upon to prepare growing numbers
of citizens for an increasingly greater variety of tasks in an industrial
society. The relationship between higher education and the rest of
American society was beginning to change.

The innovations of the 1820s did not catch on right away;
neither the times nor the economy was right. However, the social
pressures continued to build throughout the period leading to the
Civil War. The effect of those pressures on the antebellum college
can be seen most dramatically in two reports by President Francis
Wayland of Brown University. In the first report, written in 1842,
Wayland argued forcefully for the maintenance of curriculum standards. He recommended, for instance, that the college should admit
only students who were candidates for degrees and that the number
of students be limited so that "whatever is taught may be taught
thoroughly" (Wayland, 1842/1961, p. 357). He also argued that other
subjects should be added only if the degree program itself were
expanded. These were arguments very much in the spirit of the Yale
Report.

However, by 1850, Wayland was arguing for a much different
approach. He now urged the Brown Corporation to "carefully survey the wants of the various classes of the community in our own
vicinity, and adopt our courses of instruction, not for the benefit of

one class, but for the benefit of all classes" (Wayland, 1850/1961a, p. 478). Specifically, he urged Brown to eliminate a fixed term of study; to permit a student to choose as few or as many courses as he liked; to permit the student, within some limits, to "study what he chose, all that he chose, and nothing but what he chose" (p. 479); and to free students to decide for themselves whether or not to pursue a degree. "The object of the change," he wrote, "would be to adapt the institution to the wants not of a class, but of the whole community" (p. 480). Such a change, he argued, was not only expedient but necessary in light of his recognition that "a great and progressive change has taken place" (p. 484).

The change in Wayland's philosophy of education foreshadowed the profound and rapid changes in higher education that came in the aftermath of the Civil War. For the remainder of the century, the curriculum of higher education would be shaped and reshaped by two forces: the utilitarian movement and the influence of the German university, especially in the rise of a research ethos that would come to dominate academic life.

The Utilitarian Curriculum

By the time America emerged from the Civil War, it was well on its way to becoming an industrial power, with a growing urban population and a social environment that reflected its fascination with technology (Rudy, 1960). The rush to the western frontier had started an economic boom and fostered what Daniel Boorstin (1974) called a "go-getter" mentality. Charles Francis Adams, Jr., looked at the United States of 1868 and saw "the curious hardness of a material age" and "an incalculable force . . . precipitating upon us novel problems which demand immediate solution; banishing the old before the new is half matured to replace it" (quoted in Boorstin, 1974, p. 3). This era of great and rapid change and of stiff competition generated many new vocations and made many old ones more technical. Americans began to look to higher education to provide the training needed for young people to take advantage of the new age (Rudy, 1960). The pressure mounted for a curriculum that was more vocational, more diversified, and, ultimately, more utilitarian in its mission. A broader role for higher education in society was developing.

It was against this background that Charles Eliot assumed the presidency of Harvard in 1869. In his inaugural address, Eliot redefined the role of college instruction:

With good methods we may confidently hope to give young men of twenty to twenty-five an accurate general knowledge of all the main subjects of human interest, beside a minute and thorough knowledge of one subject which each may select as his principal occupation in life. . . . For unless a general acquaintance with the many branches of knowledge, good so far as it goes, be attainable by great numbers of men, there can be no such thing as an intelligent public opinion; and in the modern world the intelligence of public opinion is the one indispensible condition of social progress. [1869/1978, p. 563]

The "good method" that Eliot had in mind was the free elective system, which his uncle, George Ticknor, had advocated a generation before. The goal of the system was to allow individual students to define their own courses of study, with the advice of faculty, thus giving students the opportunity to prepare themselves freely for a place of their own choosing in life. This was revolutionary in an educational community still dedicated to the prescribed curriculum, but, Eliot argued, "This lack of faith in the prophecy of a natural bent and in the value of a discipline concentrated on a single object, amounts to a national danger" (1869/1978, p. 567). The elective system would allow individual students to discover and develop their "natural bent" through a free choice of courses. Eliot was, in many ways, a Jeffersonian meritocrat; the key element in his curriculum philosophy was individual students' freedom to choose their own paths and to develop along the lines of their own strengths and merits. For this individual freedom, Eliot was willing to set aside the old idea of a closely knit collegial community (Veysey, 1965).

It is important to note, however, that the purpose of the curriculum was not simply to feed the students' self-interest. The ultimate objective of the elective system, as Eliot stated it, was to insure "an intelligent public opinion," that "indispensible condition of social progress." This combination of individual and social goals was right in step with the mood of the times. Spurred on by the westward movement, the recent advances in technology, and, not the least, the revelations of Charles Darwin, the United States was having a love affair with progress. Eliot proposed to put the curriculum into the service of society and, moreover, into the service of the idea of progress, while recognizing that, in a democratic society, the individual was the key to progress. In this sense, Eliot was one of the first pioneers in what Laurence Veysey called "the utilitarian university" (1965, p. 113), an institution that was accessible to large numbers of

students and which, among other aims, encouraged vocational specialization.

As the example of Francis Wayland will attest, the idea of social
utility as the rationale for a university curriculum was not new.
Wayland had been slightly ahead of his time, but during the Civil
War the idea began to catch on. Probably the single greatest stimu-
lant was the Morrill Act of 1852, which provided a funding mechanism by which states could create at least one college designed to
"promote the liberal and practical education of the industrial classes
in the several pursuits in life" (quoted in Levine, 1978, p. 558). One
of the early successes of this movement was Cornell University,
where the mission was "to fit the youth of our country for the
professions, the farms, the mines, the manufactures, for the investigation of science, and for mastering all the practical questions of life
with success and honor" (Ezra Cornell, 1869/1978, p. 560). Cornell
President Andrew White led a revolution as far-sweeping as the one
Eliot started with the elective system. He built a curriculum based in
divisions and departments. A division of special sciences and arts
offered nine departmental programs in agriculture, mechanical arts,
civil engineering, commerce and trade, mining, medicine, law, education, and public service. A second division of science, literature, and
the arts offered five general courses of study that did not lead to a
vocation (Rudolph, 1977).

The idea of a curriculum geared to social utility saw its fullest
expression at the University of Wisconsin toward the end of the
nineteenth century and in the early years of the twentieth century.
Here, not only was the curriculum oriented toward the vocations, but
the university encouraged its faculty to serve as experts for state
government and operated a statewide extension program to insure the
university's utility to all of the people of Wisconsin (Veysey, 1965).

The combination of a more diversified curriculum—accomplished either through free election or through a departmental
structure—with a mission to serve society had a far-reaching effect
on higher education. For one thing, it encouraged greater emphasis
on professional education and greater specialization; faculty expanded the scope and, eventually, the number of professional programs by creating specialized courses in new areas. It also fostered
graduate instruction: business at Harvard, medicine at Johns Hopkins, pharmacy at Cornell. The emergence of the graduate school
put undergraduate instruction into a new context. Graduate-
oriented faculty began to design undergraduate programs whose main
purpose was to prepare students for graduate school; undergraduate

instruction tended to become preprofessional instruction. Finally, the utilitarian university's emphasis on social expertise encouraged research into the new social sciences, creating a fertile field for a second wave of influence from the German universities. Along the way, the university movement began to create some new attitudes within education: the idea, for instance, that a college or university could be a progressive force for change in society rather than a preserver of traditions. This, in turn, encouraged a view of the student not simply as an individual in the classical liberal education view, but as a member of a community who would, upon leaving school, assume a specific role in society.

The utility movement began with a missionary zeal; however, with its great success, it lost much of its enthusiasm for reform. The concept gradually became merged with the research mission and with purely administrative, rather than instructional, initiatives (Veysey, 1965). The utilitarian reform movement had established an ongoing public service mission for higher education, but it also had contributed to the fragmentation of the curriculum, a problem that would be complicated further by the overwhelming influence that research would have on higher education.

Research, Culture, and the Emerging Curricular Crisis

Hand in hand with the growing popularity of the free elective system came a force of unexpected power: scientific research. By the turn of the century, the research ethos would totally dominate university life in the United States.

Research and the elective system had much in common. Both were imports from Germany, although the idea of research underwent change in translation. Both encouraged increased specialization of knowledge. Both benefitted from a departmental organization. But there were striking differences, as well. Where the elective system was designed to give students more freedom of choice in instruction, research was concerned more with the freedom of faculty. Where the elective system was clearly oriented to the vocational needs of society, research tended to be distant from the immediate needs of the community. Despite the differences, the two concepts coexisted rather nicely and in some ways fed each other; however, this was more by accident than by design.

The American concept of academic research grew out of the experiences of a second generation of American students who had gone to study in Germany. There they discovered *Wissenschaft*, the German ideal that true understanding is achieved through scholarly research and inquiry. In Germany, *Wissenschaft* was permeated with the Hegelian philosophy of idealism; there was a spiritual quality associated with the search for truth and enlightenment through scholarship. The German concept was also tied closely to the teaching function of the university. "Working in the vineyard of knowledge side by side with his master, the student learned the method of his discipline and undertook his own investigations," wrote Metzger (1961, p. 99) of the spirit of the time, adding, "The joining of teaching and research gave the four-part German university a distinctive purpose and character" (p. 99).

But American scholars brought back only a partial understanding of *Wissenschaft*. They placed emphasis on scientific proof and on the search for certainty rather than on the kind of transcendental understanding that was the original goal of *Wissenschaft*. Gradually, the spirit of inquiry became associated with the search for an objective, measurable reality and the unearthing of scientifically certifiable fact. The American researcher also placed a high value on the intellect as a reliable instrument of investigation. These factors all led to an ever-increasing specialization in research—and ultimately in teaching—and to the celebration of the intellect for its own sake (Veysey, 1965).

Initially, the research ethos warred with the concept of a utilitarian university. While utilitarian educators fought to increase enrollments and thus serve increasingly larger numbers of students, research-minded faculty complained that the universities were already overcrowded. Research faculty welcomed the elective system for the freedom it gave them to explore new specialty areas, but they saw teaching simply as a means of reaching research goals, not as an end in itself. In fact, the research ethos would lead faculty away from the teaching function; spending time with immature and often mediocre students could be seen as a waste of time for someone who saw investigation as the primary aim of a university (Veysey, 1965).

The research ideal included an element of service to society via the generation of new knowledge and insights, but it was contrary to the general concept of service as it had been defined and practiced by the utilitarians. While faculty at utilitarian institutions like the University of Wisconsin offered their expertise in service to the state government, the research ethic would have no faculty member speak outside of his area of specialization. Pure research, noted Metzger (1961), fostered a decided neutrality as an aspect of academic freedom, along with a suspicion of popular sentiment. The research movement was an essentially ascetic, inward-looking movement.

Ultimately, pure research became a profession unto itself. The graduate school became another professional school that specialized in the training of new academic researchers in a wide array of specialized fields. The concept of utility was kept alive by those other professional schools—agriculture, engineering, and education, for instance—that received their research inspiration from the social problems to which their professions were directed and that received their funding from social institutions (Metzger, 1961).

The effect of the research ethos on the curriculum was overwhelming. On the positive side, the German influence that had brought research into higher education also helped create higher standards of instruction, along with new methods such as the laboratory, the seminar, and the lecture (Veysey, 1965). But in many other ways, the research ethos turned universities away from teaching. The growth of specialized departments contributed to the fragmentation of the curriculum and to increasing competition among the various disciplines (Rudolph, 1977). Perhaps most important to the curriculum, research-oriented faculty took a *laissez-faire* attitude toward students (Rudolph, 1977), with the result that the students were forced to take charge of campus life through the extracurriculum. The students created a campus environment in which the curriculum mattered little, if at all.

The growth of an institutional bureaucracy, the development of an inwardly directed intellectual purpose, and the professionalization of the faculty all contributed to a university that was insensitive to the human needs and "natural bent" of all but the best students (Rudolph, 1977).

The Culture Movement

In the late nineteenth century, a small but vocal band of counterrevolutionaries arose on campus carrying the banners of "culture" and "liberal culture." These faculty were opposed to the materialistic vocationalism and to the social scientists who had come to dominate the utility movement. They also were opposed to the narrow intellectualism they felt had become associated with scientific research. They offered themselves as an alternative. As one English instructor wrote in 1897, education was becoming divided into two parties, "the party of those who seek fact, and the party of those who seek inspiration through fact" (Veysey, 1965, p. 181). This was to be the crucial difference between culture and research; in seeking inspiration, the advocates of culture were taking an idealistic, emotional, and essentially anti-intellectual stance.

The culture movement grew and flourished in the smaller liberal arts colleges and in some of the larger universities along the eastern seaboard, where the tradition of the classical curriculum still had a foothold (Veysey, 1965). It was strongest in departments of modern languages, English literature, philosophy, and the arts—in short, in those areas of academia where research and utility had not yet been able to establish a power base (Rudolph, 1977). The culture movement tended to be concerned most with aesthetics, ethics, and a response to art that drew upon an intellectual framework that was more spiritual and emotional than it was logical or scientific. While the scientific researchers were setting standards for gathering facts, the culturists were reconfirming canons of literary and artistic taste and appreciation.

In many ways, the culture movement reflected the mood of the times. It was, after all, the *fin de siècle*. The American painter James MacNeil Whistler was in England making his reputation and preparing the artistic world for the modernists, while fellow aesthete Oscar Wilde was touring the mining towns of the American West, bringing aesthetic sensibility to audiences who could hardly be expected to know what they were getting. But the late nineteenth century was also a Victorian society, with a strict moral code. If the culture movement provided students with an emotional release, it also gave them a strong moral training, even if it had to be at the expense of aesthetic feeling (Veysey, 1965). Charles Eliot Norton of Harvard expressed this moral side of the culture movement when he wrote, "It is the final result of intellectual culture in the development of breadth, serenity, and solidity of mind, and in the attainment of that complete self-possession which finds expression in character" (Veysey, 1965, p. 186).

The aesthetic and moral aspects of the culture movement were accompanied by a social code, for, in the end, the culture movement was *really* directed toward the civilization of well-bred young men. As Veysey (1965) reports, a "cultured" gentlemen was one "'whose manners are the natural doings of a free character.' He was someone willing to 'accept trusts,' even when personally disadvantageous. He would subordinate his own desires 'to a social code' and do so of his own will" (p. 190).

Unlike the utilitarians, the advocates of culture did not identify themselves with a Jacksonian view of democracy. Unlike the researchers, they did not see themselves as ascetics removed from the general run of society. Instead, the culturists set about to transform what they saw as a boorish society; their tools were idealism, the development of aesthetic appreciation, and, above all, the study of humanity rather than the study of nature.

At first, the aesthetic sensibility of the culturists was at odds with the empirical intellectualism of the research scientists. But over time, the culturists came to believe that appreciation of literature, art, music, or philosophy could be enhanced through careful and considered analysis not unlike that of science. As Hans Flexner (1979) noted, "The intellect gradually became associated with liberal culture itself, to the point at which the basic aim of the liberal arts faculty was precisely to elevate intelligence above all else" (p. 109). With this, the culture movement faded. As faculty turned to more and more specialized areas of intellectual investigation, the unity of the liberal arts curriculum collapsed, liberal arts faculty became professionalized, and the liberal arts became subjects of specialized research and professional training.

The culture movement has been described as a secular reincarnation of the mental-discipline philosophy that had dominated the classical curriculum. As Frederick Rudolph (1977) noted, the culturists "discovered that the old values, the enduring questions, the challenges to judgment and morality, inhered in the new subjects quite as readily as they had in the old ones" (p. 188). While they were based in the modern languages, literature, and philosophy, some culture faculty advocated a return to the study of ancient Greece and of Greek and Latin languages, and celebrated the absolute values that were held to be fixed in the classics. Moreover, the culturists maintained that the humanistic thought of ancient Greece had a peculiar relevance to students in the beginning of the twentieth century (Veysey, 1965).

The culturists and the classicists also shared a common view of the *structure* of the curriculum. The culturists were very concerned with the unity of study. This focus was in part a reaction against the popularity of the elective system and the proliferation of specialized areas of research-based knowledge. This led to an active support for a prescribed curriculum. The culturists argued that the goal of creating a cultivated mind was incompatible with free elective choice and vocationalism (Veysey, 1965).

Seen in this light, the culture movement is accurately described as a counterrevolution that hoped to turn the tide against curricular fragmentation. Although it failed, its failure would stimulate, in the years following World War I, a more progressive type of reform: the general education movement. This movement, in its humanist incarnations, would trace some of its roots to the curricular philosophy of the culturists.

Other Early Attempts at Reform

The elective system had been an honest attempt to make college education more meaningful, more relevant to students, and more democratic by allowing students to concentrate on those subjects that interested them. The free elective approach did operate as a system. Internal safeguards (course prerequisites, for instance, and the natural safeguard of peer pressure) insured that most students got a balanced education. Students chose their own courses but with the advice of faculty. However, as the research ethos grew in strength and as some institutions began to concentrate more on graduate and professional education, faculty paid less attention to undergraduate education. Specialization brought with it an ever-growing array of ever-narrowing courses; the expanding knowledge base of higher education made it difficult for the free elective system to work. At the same time, the student body was changing (Brubacher & Rudy, 1958). By the beginning of the twentieth century, it was apparent that all was not well. New reforms, directed specifically to the structure and methods of the curriculum, were begun in response to what many perceived to be abuses of the elective system.

As early as 1886, David Starr Jordan, then at Indiana University, had suggested the concept of a major subject as a way of bringing coherence to a curriculum torn between liberal education and vocational studies. But this kind of structural change could not happen without there first being a movement away from free election (Rudolph, 1977). In 1901, Yale took a step in that direction by introducing a system of concentration and distribution, which combined a major field of study with courses chosen from groups that were defined by their intellectual style. Similarly, Cornell abandoned free electives in 1905 and required that 20 percent of a student's work be distributed across four subject areas. Wesleyan adopted concentration and distribution requirements in 1908 (Rudolph, 1977).

Nowhere was the movement against free election more visible than at Harvard, where free electives had been introduced by Charles Eliot in 1869. Forty years later, Abbott Lawrence Lowell, a culturist and bitter opponent of Eliot, succeeded Eliot and, in his own inaugural, attacked the system. Lowell called for the university to be more sensitive to its role in society. "The objective of the undergraduate department," he said, "is not to produce hermits, each imprisoned in the cell of his own intellectual pursuits, but men fitted to take their place in the community and live in contact with their fellow men" (quoted in Brubacher & Rudy, 1958, p. 323). His strategy was not to abandon free electives publicly but to "go forward and develop the elective system, making it really systematic" (p. 329). A systematic elective system was, in effect, a distribution system, which Harvard adopted the following year (Brubacher & Rudy, 1958).

In the early 1900s, the culture movement made its own contribution to structural reform: the honors program. It began at Swarthmore. As a later Swarthmore president, Frank Aydelotte, described its philosophy, "Liberal knowledge is not a formula; it is a point of view. The essence of liberal education is the development of mental power and moral responsibility in each individual. It is based on the theory that each person is unique, that each deserves to have his own powers developed to the fullest possible extent" (quoted in Brubacher & Rudy, 1958, p. 329). Using the same argument that Eliot had used to advocate free electives, but working from an entirely different set of assumptions, Swarthmore created an alternative to both free electives and distribution formulas: honors programs that would allow especially qualified students to explore topics in a structured way. By World War I, honors programs would be adopted at Harvard, Yale, Princeton, and Columbia.

The major subject, distribution formulas, and honors programs demonstrate how far the reformers had gone in accepting the basic intellectual premises on which the departmentalized curriculum had developed. But in 1905, Princeton University President Woodrow Wilson attempted a more extreme reform. Wilson had a radical view of what a college should be, one that extended the assumptions of the culture movement. Princeton, he said, was "not a place of special but of general education, not a place where a lad finds his profession, but a place where he finds himself" (quoted in Rudolph, 1977, p. 235). Wilson was concerned with the total experience that a student had in college. He was especially worried about the effects of extracurricular activities—football, Greek-letter fraternities, and the like—that had come to dominate a largely anti-intellectual student culture. Further, he believed that a college education should represent an unbroken internal unity (Veysey, 1965). His response was to create the "preceptor" system. He identified about 45 preceptors, usually young instructors, each of whom was assigned responsibility for four to five students. The preceptor would meet with the students at his home or over drinks to discuss their reading and to give informal encouragement to their intellectual growth (Rudolph, 1977).

The preceptor system did not find many imitators, but the honors program did, thanks in part to $4 million provided by the General Education Board (Rudolph, 1977). It seemed that effective reform would have to take place within the limited arena of teaching rather than through broad institutional change.

Thus far, curriculum reform had been primarily *structural*. It had served to help balance the competing forces within the university. As the twentieth century got under way, however, other institutions began to experiment with the *content* as well as the structure of the curriculum, in an attempt to respond to a rapidly changing student profile and to changes in American society. Reed College took a major step in this direction in 1911 with the introduction of a general course designed to orient freshmen to the college and to give them some sense of the humanistic tradition that they were expected to follow. That same year, the University of Rochester introduced a freshman course that covered the broad areas of knowledge, major social problems, and the institutions of contemporary interest. By World War I, similar courses could be found at many other institutions (Rudolph, 1977).

These attempts at reform were the precursors of a second wave of curricular revolution that would soon hit higher education. The general education movement would build on many of the themes introduced in these early reforms: a concern for the total student and for broadly defined intellectual development, a search for curricular unity and for a coherent educational experience over several years, and a desire to focus on the issues facing contemporary society.

The general education movement would involve a new organization of assumptions about education. Within the context of these assumptions, the general education movement would fuse together elements of all three major forces that had shaped higher education in the nineteenth century. From the culture movement, it would draw an overriding interest in teaching and, in some cases, a humanistic orientation. From the utility movement, it would draw a deep concern for the role of education in a democracy and for the development of the individual student. And from the research movement, general education would draw an intense interest in inquiry as a tool for learning and insight. But this fusion would await the heat of a world war.

The Social Context

The cultural and economic transformation that marked the culmination of the Industrial Revolution was already well under way at the beginning of the twentieth century. Gertrude Stein captured the magnitude of this transformation when she called the United States the oldest country in the world because it had been in the twentieth century longer than any other country. Nor was the significance of the times lost on the country's academic and political leaders. Woodrow Wilson noted,

> There is one great fact which underlies all the questions that are discussed on the political platform at the present moment. That singular fact is that nothing is done in this country as it was done twenty years ago. We are in the presence of a new organization of society. Our life has broken away from the past. [1913/1962a, p. 226]

Urban Culture and Rising Expectations

One of the most telling examples of this transformation was the changing ratio between rural and urban population in America. For most of the nineteenth century, the western frontier had helped shape American institutions and culture. In 1890, the frontier officially closed; the Superintendent of the Census declared that the frontier line had ceased to exist (Heffner, 1962). Frederick Jackson Turner had credited the frontier as the source of the "perennial rebirth, this fluidity of American life" (1893/1962, p. 179), but with the closing of the frontier and the simultaneous expansion of industry, the rapidly growing cities became the new "frontier" of opportunity for many Americans, including the new wave of immigrants from Eastern Europe.

The speed with which the cities—and an urban culture—grew can be seen in how the definition of *urban* changed over the years. The U.S. Government first distinguished between rural and urban populations in 1870; this itself was a sign that these differences had become significant. Initially, an "urban" person was someone who lived in a town of 8,000 or more people. After 1900, though, an urban person was one who lived in a town of 2,500 or more (Boorstin, 1974). This reduction in the size of towns considered to be urban suggests two things: (1) many towns were springing up around new industries and (2) a perceptibly urban culture was spreading, even in smaller communities. In 1890, one in four Americans could be considered urban; by 1910, the ratio was nearly 50:50; and by 1930, two of every three Americans lived in an urban community. It was, as Boorstin wrote, "a great internal migration" (p. 267).

The growth of the cities is remarkable in itself, but it is also a testament to another change: the rapid development of new technologies. Hand in hand with the urbanization of America came a wave of invention that transformed the daily culture and social landscape in ways that can be described only as revolutionary. Edison's invention of a practical system for citywide electrical lighting; the invention of the telephone and of a cost-effective communications network to make it practical; and, certainly not least, the transformation of the automobile from a toy of the very wealthy to a necessity for the working man helped make urbanization possible by making residential suburbs practical. The invention of techniques for mass production of goods not only brought more people to the cities to work but also helped to spread the emerging urban culture.

In 1908, Theodore Roosevelt had created the Commission on Country Life and charged it with finding ways of improving the living conditions of farmers, "to do away with the disadvantages which are due to the isolation of the family farm, while conserving its many and great advantages" (quoted in Boorstin, 1974, pp. 133–134). In the case of the latter goal, it was already too late. The long battle over Rural Free Delivery had ended a decade before; by 1906, the basic routes were in place and farmers were less and less isolated from the mainstream of American life. Newspapers and the new advertising-supported periodical magazines touted the advantages of urban life, speeding up the movement of Americans from the farm. As Boorstin notes, "While the isolated farmer may have been an unhappy farmer, the unisolated farmer often ceased altogether to be a farmer" (p. 133).

Americans began to see themselves in new ways. American culture had long been materialistic (Commager, 1950), but, with the mass production of what formerly had been luxury goods and with the national advertising of merchandise through magazines like *The*

Saturday Evening Post, social expectations of "the good life" began to change. Frederick Lewis Allen (1965) put it this way:

> Through this five-cent magazine, and others like it, millions of Americans were getting a weekly or monthly innoculation in ways of living and thinking that were middle class, or classless American (as opposed to plutocratic or aristocratic or proletarian) and . . . through the same media they were being introduced to the promised delights of the automobiles, spark plugs, tires, typewriters, talking machines, collars, corsets, and breakfast foods that American industry was producing, not for the few, but for the many. [pp. 104–105]

The Spirit of Reform

The raised expectations of many Americans were accompanied by a self-consciousness that saw its best articulation in a spirit of reform. Just as the triumph of industrial standardization and mass marketing over individual craftsmanship marked the passing of the old America (Commager, 1950), so a new sense of social responsibility marked the beginning of twentieth-century America. To some degree, it flowed from the feeling of national purpose that had grown out of the victory of the United States over the Spanish Empire in 1898 (Robertson, 1980). The war's hero, Theodore Roosevelt, invoked that spirit in a 1910 speech: "My fellow citizens, each one of you carries on your shoulders not only the burden of doing well for the sake of your own country, but the burden of doing well and seeing that this nation does well for the sake of mankind" (1910/1962, p. 220).

The reform movement made the *individual* responsible for the welfare of the entire country and the government responsible for the welfare of each individual. As Roosevelt declared,

> I do not ask for over-centralization, but I do ask that we work in a spirit of broad and far-reaching nationalism when we work for what concerns our people as a whole. We are all Americans. Our common interests are as broad as the continent. The national Government belongs to the whole American people, and where the whole American people are interested, that interest can be guarded effectively only by the national government. [1910/1962, p. 223]

A few years later, Woodrow Wilson wrote a similar message in *The New Freedom*:

We are facing the necessity of fitting a new social organization . . . to the happiness and prosperity of the great body of citizens; for we are conscious that the new order of society has not been made to fit and provide the convenience or prosperity of the average man. The life of the nation has grown infinitely varied. It does not center now upon questions of governmental structure or of the distribution of governmental powers. It centers upon questions of the very structure and operation of society itself, of which government is only the instrument. [1913/1962, p. 226]

Roosevelt and Wilson were not alone. The sense that the nation and its citizens must look out for the interests of all the people, not just the needs of "special interests"—a sentiment inherent in Roosevelt's reforms as President—resulted in the election of reform mayors and governors (notably Robert LaFollette in Wisconsin); in the establishment of charitable trusts by Rockefeller, Carnegie, and other barons of industry; in the creation of the General Education Board, the first of the great social improvement foundations; and in the movement of thousands of men and women into the new social service professions (Allen, 1965).

Meanwhile, the expectations of individual Americans continued to grow. The production of goods for mass markets, the boom in advertising that sold Americans on a new standard of living, and the growth of an urban culture all created an expectation that the best in life should be within the reach of all. Equality came to be seen as social, cultural, psychological, and economic, rather than simply political. "Economic equality," wrote Commager (1950), "was the assumption, and the poor took for granted their right to luxuries and privileges [that were] elsewhere the prerogative of the rich" (p. 14).

These expectations—combined with the pervasive spirit of reform and the insistent reality of poor working and living conditions among the working people of the cities and farms—led to new social movements, such as the women's suffrage movement and the labor movement. Within these movements, radical ideologies developed. There was a real concern that the nation would become polarized around dogmatic ideologies. For instance, one of the most radical labor organizations of the times, the Industrial Workers of the World, stated flatly in its constitution that "the working class and the employing class have nothing in common" (Allen, 1965, pp. 88–89). While there was violence, ideological conflict did not lead to class war or to political revolution. To some degree, this was because Americans had little patience with abstract ideas. Americans, commented Commager (1950), were incurable utilitarians, even when it came to philosophy: "Pragmatism triumphed over conflicting philosophies not so much because of its superior logic as because of its superior relevancy and utility" (p. 408).

The reform spirit was at its height when the United States entered World War I. In fact, many Americans came to believe that the country's involvement in the war was the fulfillment of its national mission—a crusade for international freedom and democracy (Robertson, 1980). Woodrow Wilson, who had been elected president on a reform platform, called upon this sentiment in his war message to Congress:

> We are glad . . . to fight thus for the ultimate peace of the world and for the liberation of its peoples, the German peoples included; for the rights of nations great and small and the privilege of men everywhere to choose their way of life and of obedience. The world must be made safe for democracy. [1917/1962, p. 242]

By the end of the war, however, the tide of idealism had ebbed. American soldiers returned disillusioned with the crusade on which they had been sent (Allen, 1965). While the popular image of the "Roaring Twenties" is one of spiraling prosperity, the years immediately following the war saw large-scale unemployment, industrial disarray, and agricultural depression. These events led to widespread disillusionment with the wartime ideal of making the world a better place in which to live (Robertson, 1980). The sense of national purpose had faded. While Theodore Roosevelt had promised a "square deal" and Wilson a "new freedom," postwar president Warren Harding was elected on the promise of a return to "normalcy" and his successor, Calvin Coolidge, brought to the presidency what Allen (1965) called "a genius for inactivity" (p. 117).

With national purpose went national unity. The war had been accompanied by vicious campaigns against "hyphenated" Americans. After the war, the same impulse brought about the end of free immigration in 1924 (Robertson, 1980).

The country found itself in something of a cultural void. The old order had been demolished, but in the aftermath of war there was nothing new to replace it. Religious skepticism spread, as did fascination with the new science of psychoanalysis; it became fashionable to have an identity crisis. The search for new cultural moorings stimulated a renaissance in the arts. While the Lost Generation of poets, artists, and writers sought new meanings in postwar Europe, others looked to jazz, film, and other popular arts to create a particularly American, particularly modern culture.

In general, the period saw a movement from certainty to uncertainty, and from order to disorder on almost every front. For the individual, finding one's way could be a particularly difficult challenge. As Commager noted at mid-century, "All that can be said with certainty is that twentieth century civilization was more complex than nineteenth and that even partial mastery of it required both intellectual maturity and moral integrity" (1950, p. 407).

The prewar reform movement was not without a legacy, however. It left behind it a new, pragmatic approach to dealing with social problems, and this, too, required intellectual maturity and moral integrity. According to Allen (1965), "It was the idea . . . that when the ship of state was not behaving as it should, one did not need to scrap it and build another, but could, by a series of adjustments, repair it while keeping it running—provided that the ship's crew were forever alert, forever inspecting it and tinkering with it" (p. 94). The need for expert tinkerers would place a great demand on education.

The Challenge to Higher Education

If World War I had meant the decline of reform in society in general, it had just the opposite effect on American colleges and universities. By and large, American educators had joined the war effort with some enthusiasm (Kolbe, 1919). They emerged from the war conscious of a new social mission for higher education.

The extent of this self-consciousness can be seen in speeches and articles by colleges and university presidents during the period right after the war. For instance, shortly after the war, liberal culturist Nicholas Murray Butler (1919) of Columbia University asserted, "The war has distinctly helped us. . . . It has laid to rest some rather widespread illusions and it has burned up many sources and causes of intellectual, moral, and social waste" (p. 8). J. H. Kirkland (1922) of Vanderbilt University called for a new social mission for the college: "The demands of peace are no less exacting than those of war. Knowledge should be not only enjoyable, but useful for promoting human needs, for building character, and for making a new world in time of peace as we were then trying to destroy the world in time of war." (p. 60). President Hopkins of Dartmouth College sounded a similar note: "The objective and ideal of the college can be nothing else than the objective and ideal of a society which wishes to promote and improve itself" (quoted in Kirkland, 1922, p. 71). William Guth, president of Goucher College, put the need for a social consciousness into a broad perspective in a 1921 speech: "Education may soon find that its problem is not the post-war curriculum at all, but the democracy that was forced into the open and brought under trial by the war" (p. 135).

This surge in the reform spirit among higher education institutions reflected not only the state of American culture after the war but a new pressure that was beginning to be felt in colleges and universities: a rapid growth in the number of students demanding a college education. In 1890, only 3 percent of the U.S. population was of college age; by 1920, that figure had doubled to 6 percent; by 1930, it had doubled again to 12 percent (Brubacher & Rudy, 1958). Moreover, an increasing number of these young people were high-school graduates: Only 7 percent of young people attended high school in 1890, but 33 percent attended by 1920 (Boorstin, 1974). These two factors created an unprecedented pressure on higher education, and the problem became even greater in the 1930s when millions of young people turned to college as an alternative to the unemployment line.

In the long run, Guth's prediction turned out to be accurate. Beginning in the postwar years, it became increasingly difficult to separate curriculum issues from the issues facing democracy itself. For their immediate future, colleges and universities faced two not-unrelated challenges. One was how to deal with rapidly increasing numbers of students who wanted a college education but whose backgrounds and ambitions were much different from those of the traditional student. The second, which must be seen in light of the social responsibility implied in the first, was how to apply the resources of the college to, as Kirkland (1922) put it, "make a new world."

One response was structural: the creation of a new type of postsecondary institution—the junior college—which helped absorb the many new students entering higher education (Brubacher & Rudy, 1958). Another response was academic: the development of new ways of using the curriculum to articulate the mission of the college and to respond to both social needs and the needs of the student. This response was the *general education* movement. It grew in the 1920s and 1930s along two lines: a humanist approach that evolved from the classical tradition and the culture movement, and an instrumentalist approach that emerged from the progressive education movement and from the philosophy of pragmatism. These two approaches started from very different assumptions about the nature of knowledge and the needs of students. By World War II, they had begun to represent two aspects of a new curriculum concept that was concerned specifically with the contemporary needs of students and American society. The next chapter will deal with the humanist approach to general education; the instrumentalist approach will be examined in chapters 4 and 5.

CHAPTER 3

The Humanist Approach
to General Education

The Philosophy of Humanism

Like the term *general education*, the term *humanism* has meant different things to different people at different times. The term was used first in the early Renaissance, shortly after the rediscovery of the classics of ancient Greece. The original humanists preferred the ancients' emphasis on life in this world and on the problems of being human to the emphatic other-worldliness of the medieval writers (Babbitt, 1930). These became essential elements in the definition of humanism. The classic works of ancient Greek and Roman writers continued to influence humanistic thought well beyond the Renaissance, although the emphasis shifted with the times. In the eighteenth century, for instance, the humanists' concern for the values of this world was reflected not only in the poetry of Pope and the satires of Swift, but in a generalized social concern for "gentlemanly" behavior. Humanists became concerned with the development of a sense of proportion—a moral and social equivalent to the aesthetic golden mean—that gave one poise and balance in one's relationships. This application of Aristotelian ideals became a lasting part of the humanist tradition and played an important role in shaping liberal education.

Humanism has been an essentially European phenomenon, although it has had a great effect on American thinking. During the Enlightenment, for example, the humanists' belief that reason could guide them to ultimate truths about nature and humankind and thus to the solution of human problems helped spark Thomas Jefferson's notion that "men, habituated to thinking for themselves and to follow their reason as guide, would be more easily and safely governed" (Commager, 1978, p. 44). In the nineteenth century, the Hegelian ideal of history as "the progress of the consciousness of freedom" and of freedom as "the sole truth of Spirit" (quoted in Mourant & Freund, 1964, p. 437) greatly influenced the American transcendentalists. Of course, traditional humanism also provided the basis for the culture movement, but very early on in the United States, humanistic ideas would be associated with notions of freedom and progress.

Meanwhile, other humanists were evolving a "naturalistic" humanism that attempted to reconcile humanistic thought with science. Reviewing the development of naturalistic humanism, Corliss Lamont (1949) distinguished between its basic elements and those of traditional humanism. The latter was comprised of the search for a "reasonable balance" in life, the study of polite letters, freedom from religiosity, and a responsiveness to human passions. The naturalistic philosophy, on the other hand, placed human beings at the center and made personal responsibility the moral force behind behavior. This philosophy Lamont defined as "joyous service for the greater good of all humanity in this natural world and according to the methods of reason and democracy" (p. 18). In this context, humanism ceased to be a secular reference point that looked to the past to provide a model for civilized life and became, to Lamont, "a way of thinking and doing for average men and women seeking to lead happy and useful lives" (pp. 18–19).

Lamont (1949) listed several central propositions that had become associated with naturalistic humanism by mid-century. The first was that nature is the totality of being and operates independently of any "mind or consciousness," that is, independently of any god. The second was that human beings are both product and part of nature, with no "supernatural" survival; reasoning and thinking are seen as natural phenomena rather than gifts that set humankind apart from the rest of nature. Another key proposition was that men and women can solve their own problems through reason and science; this proposition assumes the existence of free will. It is this proposition, Lamont noted, that leads humanists to believe in an ethic or morality that grounds all human values and that guides people in their experiences and relationships. Finally, Lamont stated that naturalistic humanism calls for the widest possible development of art and appreciation of beauty and for a far-reaching social program based in worldwide democracy. Thus, naturalistic humanism involves the development of *individual values* as a means to achieve *social ends* of a sort much broader than those of the traditional humanists. The naturalists also abandoned the classical authors as the sole authority for those values and became more concerned with the present. The goal of naturalistic humanism was not to create cultured gentlemen, but to empower people to solve social problems.

Higher education would draw upon both schools of humanism in the period between the two world wars. Traditional or academic humanism would lend itself to the rationalist Great Books curriculum developed by Robert Maynard Hutchins in the 1930s. But the seminal general education programs at Columbia University and the University of Wisconsin would draw upon the naturalist approach and, at the same time, contribute to the further development of this humanistic vision.

The Contemporary Civilization Program at Columbia

The Contemporary Civilization program introduced at Columbia College in 1919 was one of many attempts by faculty in American colleges and universities to confront the increasing professionalization of the liberal arts and to move into new directions after World War I. Columbia had long been committed to the liberal arts, but the war and its aftermath caused Columbia's faculty to take a fresh look at undergraduate education. Because it embodied this new perspective, Contemporary Civilization became something more than simply an innovative liberal arts program; what emerged from the application of a humanistic vision to the postwar issue of curriculum reform is now widely recognized as one of the first true programs of general education.

Contemporary Civilization grew out of what was essentially a utilitarian episode, but one that required a humanistic response. In 1917, before World War I ended, the United States War Department requested that Columbia create a War Issues course to be taught at Student Army Training Corps Centers at colleges and universities around the country (Buchler, 1954). The purpose was to help officers-in-training to understand better the background and meaning of the war, that is, to develop the set of values that would be needed to deal with the complex relationships that underlay the war. Soon after, while both the war and War Issues course were still in progress, a group of faculty began to develop the idea of a Peace Issues course that would help the student make the transition from war to peace. The course, Contemporary Civilization, was introduced in the fall of 1919. It was required of all freshmen and met five days each week. The course was described in the 1919–1920 college course catalog as follows:

The aim of the course is to inform the student of the more outstanding and influential factors of his physical and social environment. The chief features of the intellectual, economic, and political life of today are treated and considered in their dependence on and difference from the past. The great events of the last century in the history of the countries now more closely linked in international relations are reviewed, and the insistent problems, internal and international, which they are now facing are given detailed consideration. By thus giving the student, early in his college course, objective material on which to base his own judgment, it is thought he will be aided in intelligent participation in the civilization of his own day. [quoted in Buchler, 1954, p. 100]

The following year, the important last sentence was revised to read:

To give the student early in his college course objective materials on which to base his own further studies and his own judgment will, it is believed, aid him greatly in enabling him to understand the civilization of his own day and to participate effectively in it. [quoted in Buchler, 1954, p. 100]

These goal statements are remarkable for several reasons. One is that they make no reference to the need for students to master subject matter in the traditional discipline areas; instead, the emphasis is squarely on the development of a student's ability to *apply* learning to current *problems* and to make more informed *judgments*. This orientation of education for the development of values rather than for the acquisition of knowledge *per se* is important in the development of the general education paradigm. Equally important is the emphasis on contemporary issues and problems rather than solely on the western cultural heritage. Perhaps even more important is the fact that the means of the program—a highly interdisciplinary approach—matched the stated ends. This was a new and consciously taken direction on the part of faculty in two departments, history and philosophy. Their commitment to an interdisciplinary approach is illustrated by the fact that, with the establishment of the Contemporary Civilization program, traditional undergraduate requirements in history and philosophy were dropped from the curriculum.

Contemporary Civilization was developed at a time when Columbia was in the midst of a ferment of curriculum reform, and this, too, contributed to its long-term success. The changes were the work of Nicholas Murray Butler, who had become president of Columbia in 1902. Butler was a controversial and sometimes autocratic president, but he had long been concerned with curriculum matters. He had helped introduce manual training into the New Jersey public schools as early as 1886 and was the first president of the Industrial Education Association in New York in 1887. From a Saturday morning course for teachers that he offered at Columbia, he created Teachers College and, a few years later, a model school. He worked with Harvard's Charles Eliot and others on a historic report on secondary education and, with Eliot, established the College Entrance Examination (Coon, 1947).

Butler was firmly committed to the humanistic ideals of the culture movement. Like Eliot, he was concerned with the individual student; but, unlike Eliot, he argued against the elective system, which made the student, in his words, "a kind of cow grazing in the grass, munching on what pleases the eye" (quoted in Coon, 1947, p. 105). A curriculum that "turns education into a merely mechanical process, with a purely gainful end, is nothing short of treason to the highest, most uplifting, and most enduring human interests," he said in 1919 (quoted in Coon, 1947, p. 11).

Butler did not limit his ambitions to education. He was active in state and national politics and well known in progressive political circles. Theodore Roosevelt dubbed him "Nicholas the Miraculous" for his fund raising acumen, and he ran for vice president on William Howard Taft's losing ticket against former Princeton President Woodrow Wilson in 1912 (Coon, 1947). In short, he had a perspective on the curriculum that combined a culturist—or traditional humanist—outlook with the reform spirit that was afoot in the larger pre–World War I society.

That combination shaped Butler's educational philosophy, which centered around three fundamental human values that he traced to ancient Greece. These were ethics, or the doctrine of conduct and service; economics, or the doctrine of gainful employment; and politics, or the doctrine of the reconciliation of the first two. These three elements, he wrote in 1919, "Must lie at the heart of an effective education which has learned the lessons of the war. To these all other forms of instruction are introductory and ancillary or complementary and interpretive" (p. 12).

This attitude on the part of Columbia's president created a sympathetic environment not only for the Contemporary Civilization program but for other curriculum innovations that lasted well beyond Butler's tenure. For instance, the same year that Contemporary Civilization began for freshmen, an honors program emphasizing the great books approach began at the upper division. In the

1930s, an interdisciplinary humanities course was added, and some faculty experimented with survey courses in science. Not all of these innovations could be classified as general education; in fact, some were quite contrary to the basic ideas that later came to be associated with general education. However, this creative environment helped protect Contemporary Civilization from the initial criticism it received from other faculty.

Because it was not seen as a threat to other programs, faculty involved in it were able to experiment and refine the program over a number of years. Between 1919 and 1946, the Contemporary Civilization program was revised completely at least six times (Coon, 1947). From the beginning, the course used textual material that was prepared by Columbia faculty specifically for the course and that helped avoid the temptation to fall back upon the disciplines. The first was Irwin Edman's *Human Traits and their Social Significance*. The second book, John Storck's *Man and Civilization*, reflected a growing tendency to look further into the past in search of the meaning of the present. The third book, John Randall's *The Making of the Modern Mind*, became a staple of the course for years to come (Buchler, 1954).

In 1929, the program underwent a significant revision. A full year was added, so that Contemporary Civilization (now CC-A and CC-B) became a requirement of all freshmen and sophomores. The expansion, on one hand, reflected the success of the freshman program, but it also reflected the needs of the still-growing student population and the rise of the "student personnel" movement. As John Coss (1931), a faculty member at Columbia, explained,

> the breakdown of close family ties and the rise of great communities have left uncared-for certain elements of training and discipline once fairly adequately provided outside the schools, and as a consequence the college has needed to add to its academic functions the human responsibilities which have come to be called personnel work. [p. 4]

Coss was speaking of higher education in general, but in the same book Columbia College Dean Herbert Hawkes stated that increased student demand "inevitably places the welfare of the student in the center of the picture" (p. 8). He added that "the first year or two of the American college, or Columbia College at any rate, must be devoted to the discovery of the interest of the student, to himself, to his instructors, and frequently to his parents" (pp. 8–9). A sense of responsibility to the student pervaded the expansion of the

Contemporary Civilization program. Justus Buchler (1954) described
that responsibility this way:

> Greater responsibility on the student's part in the last two or elective
> years (the Upper College) entailed greater responsibility by the College
> in the first two years (the Lower College). Greater latitude in elective
> choice could be made far more significant if the student's fundamental
> equipment were sharpened and perfected. [p. 71]

The division of the undergraduate college into an upper part and
a lower part made it possible for faculty to develop to a greater
degree two entirely separate approaches to the curriculum that involved two entirely different approaches to the student. In the lower
college, a two-year prescribed program could be put into place without concern for the many different vocational interests of the students. In the upper college, a system of "maturity credits"—essentially a free elective system—replaced the old major system, and the
General Honors course was withdrawn.

The new lower-division Contemporary Civilization program,
required of all freshmen and sophomores, was given cooperatively
by the philosophy, history, economics, government, and sociology
departments, under the administration of a Committee on Instruction. Hawkes (1931) noted that it had two purposes: 1. to give "an
adequate and desirable survey of present-day civilization in the light
of its origin, for those students whose primary interest is in other
fields than the social studies" (p. 23), and 2. to provide a broader base
of intellectual understanding for students wishing to pursue social
sciences in the upper college.

As the two-year program developed, the relationships between
CC-A and CC-B became clear. The freshman year came to deal
primarily with the *making* of the present, while the second year came
to deal primarily with the *character* of the present. Gradually, CC-A
developed into an examination of the institutions and ideas of Western civilization, while CC-B became focused on contemporary economic and political problems in the United States (Buchler, 1954). As
the Great Depression hit the country in the 1930s, more attention
was paid to CC-B. Faculty felt that raising and examining problems
was not enough; there was a danger that the student would perceive
the selection of problems as arbitrary and that the program would
lose its sense of unity as a result. In the late 1930s, faculty tried to
give CC-B a new framework by centering it around one large,
contemporary problem: economic security. This was added to a field

trip component that had been with the program since 1930 (Buchler, 1954).

The organization of the Contemporary Civilization program revolved around three guiding questions and around the answers that an examination of the past and present could give to those questions: How have men made a living? How have they lived together? How have they interpreted the world they have lived in? In answering these questions, the program used a historical approach, but within the context of a philosophical technique in which, as John Randall said, students were "critically aware of . . . assumptions and methods" (quoted in Buchler, 1954, p. 104). This emphasis on *method* and its direct tie to the course's *objective* is one of the features that distinguished Contemporary Civilization from a traditional liberal education program; the unity of means and ends would become a defining characteristic of the new idea of general education.

Another consistent characteristic of Contemporary Civilization that became a bedrock assumption of the general education paradigm was its student-centered approach. Students, said Hawkes, (1931), "are our junior partners in the education project that we are discussing. . . . They may lack experience, but they do not lack intelligence, or freshness of point of view, or willingness to help when they see the chance" (p. 18). Columbia gave students a formal opportunity to help develop Contemporary Civilization. In any given year, there were 20 or more sections of the course, each of which had an elected student representative who met with all the other representatives several times during the year to share ideas about the course. Each was supposed to be given guidelines by his "constituents" in the course section but was free to make personal contributions (Hawkes, 1931).

Rudolph (1977) reports that, between 1920 and 1940, at least 30 colleges and universities adopted programs that were influenced by the Contemporary Civilization course and by an orientation program at Reed College. It is difficult, however, to pinpoint the direct influence that the program exercised nationally. There were, to be sure, many courses and programs on the general topic of contemporary civilization, and the program's readings were widely used by other colleges and universities. But what made Contemporary Civilization remarkable was not simply the title of the course but the methods that were developed for reaching the program's objectives and the relationship that evolved between instructor and student in the process of education. It is unlikely that many other schools were able to achieve the unity of Contemporary Civilization. Hawkes

(1931) had the habit of calling Contemporary Civilization a "survey" course, but it was far from that (Buchler, 1954). It was not a survey of the subject matter in history, economics, government, and philosophy; instead, it applied the inherent perspectives and methods of these disciplines to reach a new goal: helping the student understand his present-day world so that he could more effectively develop values, make judgments, and participate in the world. These elements—along with the student-centered approach and the unity of ends and means—moved Contemporary Civilization from the tradition of liberal education and into the new paradigm of general education.

Alexander Meiklejohn and the Experimental College

Alexander Meiklejohn's ideas and work at the University of Wisconsin offer a good illustration of how some of the major assumptions of the old liberal education paradigm were redirected and reorganized as the humanistic approach to general education developed in the years between the two world wars. Meiklejohn was eclectic in his curriculum reforms. Throughout his career, he remained loyal to some of the basic assumptions of the classical curriculum, such as an acceptance of formalism in the curriculum. In other areas, he modified or redirected classical ideas—the role of logic in the curriculum, for instance—as he turned to a more naturalistic approach. He also brought to the curriculum new ideas and assumptions that were unique to the emerging concept of general education and that would further differentiate between this new approach and the tradition of liberal education. As a result, his ideas sometimes seem inconsistent and self-contradictory, but they represent a major step in the building of a general education philosophy directed toward humanistic ends.

Meiklejohn began his career as a staunch supporter of rationalism and of the classical curriculum. In 1908, for instance, he wrote an article entitled "Is Mental Training a Myth?" The article came at a time when the methods of psychology were beginning to be felt in educational research and when the broad issue of how one learns was being explored experimentally for the first time. Meiklejohn, however, argued that, while mental discipline—the philosophy underpinning the "discipline and furniture of the mind" concept of the Yale Report—was generally accepted as false, its "lineal descendent of the present age is true" (1920, p. 116). He proposed that educators "turn from the field of psychology into that of another empirical science which deals with consciousness. . . . I mean the science of logic" (pp. 121–122). He continued to develop this rationalist argument over the next decade. In 1920 he wrote,

> Logic, modern as well as ancient, confirms the statement that the most important single judgment which can be made about the thinking process is that which singles out the form or method from content. If this be true then formal discipline in some very real and important sense must be at the very heart of all intellectual training and development. [p. 107]

In short, Meiklejohn believed that education should be directed toward training the individual's mental "faculties," through exercises or "discipline." The *form* of education—the methods and exercises that a student underwent—he saw as separate from the content or subject matter of education. If the end of education is to be mental discipline, content is simply a means to that end. Formalism, with its implicit separation of ends and means, was basic to the classical curriculum.

That Meiklejohn accepted these and other traditions of classical liberal education early in his career is illustrated in his 1912 inaugural speech as President of Amherst College. His description of the purpose of the liberal arts college is reminiscent of the Yale Report:

> The liberal arts college does not pretend to give all the kinds of teaching which a young man of college age may profitably receive; it does not even claim to give all the kinds of intellectual training of the liberal type, whatever that may mean, and to that mission it must be faithful. [1920, p. 31]

Meiklejohn, however, would soon move from the rationalist position to one based more in the newer naturalistic humanism. One reason for this shift was that, in addition to its base in logic and its separation of ends and means, there was something else about the classical curriculum that appealed greatly to Meiklejohn and that was to become increasingly important to him. It was that "the old curriculum was founded by men who had a theory of the world and of human life. They had a knowledge of human experience by which they could live and which they could teach to others engaged in the activities of living" (1920, pp. 42–43). This idea that education could focus on human experience and its value in helping students in the contemporary "activities of living" would become the dominant assumption in Meiklejohn's educational philosophy. His early ideas about logic and mental discipline would be redirected toward serving as a means to this educational end.

The idea had immediate, practical implications for Meiklejohn, for he believed that the United States had failed to achieve what he called a "national mind" (1920, p. 6) and that this was a dangerous situation for a democracy in the years following World War I. He called for the creation of a uniquely American national culture. "This nation, like an individual mind, must seek to understand itself; to feel, to will, to appreciate the part it has to play, must play its part with understanding. . . . This nation needs a mind with which to play its part" (p. 64). The purpose of having a theory of the world was not, to Meiklejohn, to root everything in the ideals of the past, as the traditional humanists would assert, but to create the future. Meiklejohn stated his goal dramatically:

> We, thus far, have been in cultural ways a dependent people, [dependent upon] the culture we have received from others; we have not made it for ourselves. But now the time has come when we must win our freedom, must be ourselves, must master our spirit—when feelings, beliefs, and actions must be our own as they have never been before. We are, I think, in this next century destined to make a culture and to cease from merely taking one which others made. [1923, p. 109]

The task of the liberal college, he said, was "the making of minds" (Meiklejohn, 1920, p. 4). He saw this as a largely intellectual task, but not one that was restricted to training in logic or in a survey of Western culture. Instead, the goal became to give the student some experience with how the intellectual processes are applied to the problems of daily life. The role of instruction, he said, was "to take human activity as a whole, to understand human endeavors not in isolation but in their relations to one another and to the total experience which we call the life of our people" (p. 38).

With this, Meiklejohn set aside the universalist world view of the classical curriculum and of the traditional humanists for a more naturalistic humanist goal: the development, within individual students, of social values and predispositions to social action that, taken together and applied to daily life, would comprise a new American culture. At the same time, he was confronting the growing specialization and fragmentation that had accompanied the acceptance of intellectual research by scholars in the liberal arts. His concern was not for the study of the humanities for their own sake, but for a holistic understanding of the relationships that are involved in a human community.

However, Meiklejohn's means of achieving these ends remained rooted in the classical paradigm of the separation of content and method that had marked the Yale curriculum. Like the culturists, Meiklejohn had attacked the elective system, saying that such a range of student choices reflected a lack of world vision on the part of faculty (1920). Similarly, he would have rejected a prescribed curriculum such as the Great Books that was based in the assumption that specific content was essential for every student. Meiklejohn proposed instead a prescribed curriculum that would provide a unity not of content but of *context*, a prescribed curriculum whose goal was the creation of a *community*.

Meiklejohn began to put some of these ideas into practice at Amherst College in the years surrounding World War I. In 1914, for instance, he created a freshman course (an elective course, ironically) in social and economic institutions. Its purpose was to make students "aware of the moral, social, and economic schemes—the society—of which they are members; and to provide (1) a sane, searching, revealing of the facts of the human situation, and (2) a showing of the intellectual method by which these situations may be understood" (1920, p. 135). In 1918, he recommended that Amherst be divided into a junior college and a senior college. The philosophy behind the recommendation was that the liberal college had two functions, the first being to give students a "general apprehension of the culture of one's race" and the second being to develop the "actual process of the mind by which that culture has been made and still is in the making" (p. 150). By separating the two aspects into the two colleges, he said, the two goals could be kept in focus: "Two aims, two sets of examinations; hence two colleges—that is the program" (p. 151).

These early programs were only the first, tentative steps that Meiklejohn was taking toward rethinking the college curriculum. In 1926, he left Amherst at the urging of Glenn Frank, who had just assumed the presidency of the University of Wisconsin. The two had worked together earlier on the idea of an experimental program, and Frank felt that an experimental college could be established at Wisconsin. While neither had much experience with a large state university, they decided to move ahead. Meiklejohn joined the philosophy faculty and became director of the Experimental College, which Frank established as a temporary unit of the university "to re-examine and re-adjust its traditional procedures in the interest of greater educational effectiveness on the lives of its students" (quoted in "Experimental College," 1930, p. 834). It was, in essence, a curriculum laboratory in which Meiklejohn and his staff of advisors (as the teaching faculty were called) would have the freedom to try out admittedly radical ideas. It offered Meiklejohn the opportunity to carry his ideas to their logical conclusions.

Meiklejohn continued to build upon ideas that he had developed while at Amherst, but he redirected some of them to the goals of his new curriculum concept. For instance, the goal of "making minds" grew into the goal of "teaching of general intelligence" (1932, p. 14). He defined intelligence as "readiness for any human situation; it is the power, wherever one goes, of being able to see, in any set of circumstances, the best response which a human being can make to those circumstances" (p. 8). The goal of the new experimental college curriculum, he said, was to develop intelligence by providing students with a sense of human values and by developing their capacity to judge situations. Meiklejohn's definition of intelligence was not that far from the classical concept of disciplining the "faculties," but a new emphasis on readiness for dealing practically with immediate social situations had replaced the rationalist emphasis on abstract logic. It is this basic shift in emphasis that made the Experimental College experience relevant to the development of general education.

The Experimental College focused on the first two years of the undergraduate program. Its stated goal was to prepare students to assume the various kinds of personal responsibility that would be theirs later in their careers. Meiklejohn emphasized, however, that the goal was *not* preparatory in the sense of simply readying students for the scholarly work of the last two years of college. Instead, he said, the goal was "the building up of self-direction, . . . trying to create or cultivate intelligence, capable of being applied in any field whatever" (1932, p. 10). While using the methods and results of scholarly work, "its primary task is not the education of scholars; it is the education of common men," with success being measured not by the standards of what scholars do, "but in terms of the kind of thinking which all men are called upon to do in the enduring relations of life" (p. 169).

One of Meiklejohn's goals was to avoid the reliance on discipline-based knowledge that pervaded most undergraduate instruction. He hoped to overcome what he saw as the "permanent problem" (1932, p. 66) of general education: how to identify the material that would be taught in order to help students reach the goal of a "scheme of reference" (p. 46). It was, in short, the problem of means versus ends, which he had carried with him from the classical curriculum.

The material that Meiklejohn chose to help students develop their scheme of reference at Wisconsin involved the study of two civilizations. Initially, the freshman year centered around Athens in the fifth century B.C., while the sophomore year focused on nineteenth-century America. The idea was that, by looking at two civilizations, students would gain a better understanding of what constitutes a civilization and learn to apply these insights as "an instrument of intelligent human living" (1932, pp. 68–69).

Certainly, the choice of ancient Greece as one of the civilizations to be studied reflected Meiklejohn's continued attachment to traditional humanism, as did the program's tacit assumption that the study of the past held the key to understanding the present and future. However, in practice the emphasis began to shift rather quickly. The freshman year's focus on ancient Greece expanded to include the fourth century B.C., while the sophomore year expanded to include contemporary America. With these shifts—not remarkable in themselves, perhaps—came an important change in the objective. The curriculum shifted from an objective study of ancient Greek and nineteenth-century American cultures to the analysis of how people at different times and in different situations dealt with the problems that confront all cultures. *Problem-solving* emerged as the real *content* of the curriculum, with the readings in Greek and American culture serving to provide the *context* for study. In the freshman year, for instance, the readings were expanded to include the dramatists and historians of ancient Greece, along with Plato, in an attempt to show how people living in the Greek culture tried to analyze their contemporary situation. As Meiklejohn observed in the final report of the college, "The shift in the freshman year has come from the perception that what we wish our students to get is not primarily an acquaintance with the Greek situation, but an acquaintance with the Greek mind, a sense of Greek intelligence at work on its situation" (1932, p. 73).

Similarly, the focus of the sophomore year shifted away from the objective study of a second situation. By the second year, "preparation" was over, and the job of the student became "to study now the modern, the American mind at work upon the situation in the midst of which he is to live" (Meiklejohn, 1932, p. 74). The second year ceased to be historical; instead, it centered around social problems "as they are set and modified by the peculiarities of value and circumstance which determine in the present age and country the special issues with which it must deal. Human problems must now become local and contemporary and specific issues" (p. 121).

The concern for the present and for local and specific issues in the curriculum can be seen in some of the eight written assignments given to sophomores in the 1930–1931 school year. One was an essay on "The World Picture Given by Modern Science." Another asked the student to describe "the expansion into your home region of the culture of Western Christendom." A third presented the student with this situation: "You have just been elected President of the United States or Governor of your state. Prepare your inaugural address, dealing with the current industrial depression" (Meiklejohn, 1932, p. 85).

Meiklejohn had begun with a fairly typical culturist curriculum rooted in traditional humanism, a curriculum that surveyed the cultural heritage of ancient Greece and the development of American civilization in an attempt to help students understand the essential qualities of civilization. But it very shortly evolved into a general education program that used the past as a kind of case study to help students develop the skills and attitudes needed to solve problems of contemporary significance. This was not simply a change in course content. Instead, the Experimental College program had made new assumptions about the objectives of education, about the relationship of education to the individual student and to contemporary society, and about the reason for studying the past. It is in these respects that Meiklejohn's curriculum represented a major departure from the paradigm of liberal education.

However, Meiklejohn's attempt to integrate these assumptions with those of the classical curriculum resulted in tension between the intellectual and social ends of the program. While the primary goal of "making minds" was, to Meiklejohn, intellectual, there were also social and behavioral components to the goal. As he wrote in 1932, "We wish our students to reach a certain level of self-direction. You can train a student for freedom only by building up more and more his freedom in all your relationships with him" (p. 121). Social relationships within the college—relationships between student and advisor and among students themselves—were to Meiklejohn essential to the success of the curriculum. One of Meiklejohn's definitions of a college was "a group of people, all of whom are reading the same books" (1932, p. 40). One function of the prescribed curriculum, accordingly, was to lay down the conditions for membership in this community. This set up a paradoxical relationship between the ends of the curriculum and the means of instruction, since the goal of the curriculum was to build up individual freedom, but the means toward that end was prescribed for all students.

Meiklejohn did attempt to provide for *some* individual freedom. This was mainly visible in what he called "a free and unhindered opportunity to decide whether or not they wish to be educated men" (1932, p. 125). Tests, required attendance, and other "secondary inducements" to study were played down in favor of self-motivation. However, the lack of inducements often led to student decisions that ran against the grain of the university as a whole. Some attendance requirements were finally instituted around holidays, for instance, and faculty debated several times the idea of requiring attendance at common class sessions.

There was also an attempt to individualize study to some degree. The curriculum combined class sessions that met five times a week with individual conferences and smaller group sessions that met weekly. The classes were not lectures, but "talks" that left the primary responsibility for interpreting the week's reading to the individual student. The personal conferences offered a mix of what Meiklejohn (1932) called "personal friendliness and impersonal criticism," and the advisors were charged to "have constant regard for the interests and peculiar capacities" of their students (p. 133).

Meiklejohn's goal of creating a tightly knit community was not realized, however. Common readings and intellectual activity proved to be not enough to sustain a sense of community. Students split between fraternity members and independent students, between political liberals and conservatives, and between Jews and Gentiles. The same tensions that tore at the community outside the college turned Meiklejohn's attempt to build a social community into what he called a "bitter disappointment" (1932, p. 316).

The Experimental College curriculum ended at the conclusion of the 1931–1932 school year. Meiklejohn submitted an extensive report (1932) that included a statement that "Our report is not that we have a scheme of teaching whose merits have been demonstrated, but that we have a plan which seems worthy of consideration by an American college of liberal arts" (p. 158). A faculty committee refused to endorse the recommendations, however, and the program was not renewed.

There are many reasons why the Experimental College curriculum failed to become institutionalized. Certainly a major reason is the scope of the "experiment." Neither Meiklejohn nor Glenn Frank had any prior experience with a major state university. Perhaps this lack of experience led Meiklejohn to try to create, within the institutional, social, and academic environment of a state university, a self-contained liberal arts college with a curriculum and extracurricular program much different from that of the larger institution. The program failed to achieve a sense of community in large part because it failed to take into full account the factors other than intellectual that contribute to a community. In addition, the curriculum was at best partial, since students had to go outside the college to meet university degree requirements in areas such as foreign languages ("Experimental College," 1929). Faculty carried general teaching responsibilities in addition to their Experimental College responsibilities. Under the circumstances, the constant movement of students and faculty to and fro between an experimental curriculum and a traditional university curriculum made unity impossible and helped fuel controversy about the program.

The Experimental College project was undertaken very early in the presidency of Glenn Frank. From its inception, it attracted suspicion and resentment from faculty. In an especially bitter postmortem on the college, faculty member Grant Showerman (1931) noted that "the Experimental College was not a professional, but a presidential project" (p. 482) that never had general faculty support. Another observer suggested that the low student-teacher ratio and the pressures of a radically different curriculum overworked the faculty, who were expected to "advise" on the entire range of the curriculum; he argued that the faculty tacitly sabotaged the program ("Why the Wisconsin Experiment . . . ," 1931).

In short, the Experimental College became a case study in the failure of institutional innovation. Because (1) it tried to establish a small-college educational milieu within a larger institution of a very different sort; (2) its main initiative and support were from the president and an outside expert (Meiklejohn) rather than from the faculty itself; and (3) it ultimately attracted too many out-of-state students, it had no support from the faculty, students, or legislature (which slashed its budget drastically in 1931).

During its short existence, however, the Experimental College curriculum moved steadily away from the rationalist assumptions and traditional humanism that marked Meiklejohn's early work and toward a much different and quite new approach. Had the environment for innovation been as supportive at Wisconsin as it was, for instance, at Columbia, additional change may have resulted. Nonetheless, the essential concepts of the Experimental College had an effect that went well beyond the four-year experiment. These included the idea that education should give students a frame of reference for dealing with contemporary problems, the emphasis on developing students who could re-create their culture, the vision that this kind of education was for everyone, and the present-oriented and situational nature of the instruction. The college attracted national attention, largely through Meiklejohn himself. The program helped shape the 1929 revision of Columbia's Contemporary Civilization program, through which naturalistic humanist assumptions would become fully integrated into the general education paradigm.

"General" vs. "Liberal" Education: Robert Maynard Hutchins

The extent to which the experiments at Columbia and Wisconsin represented a new and distinct curriculum rather than a reform within the traditional structure of liberal education can best be seen by comparing them with another major innovation in undergraduate education in the 1930s: the curriculum reforms undertaken by Robert Maynard Hutchins at the University of Chicago.

Like Meiklejohn and the faculty at Columbia, Hutchins was deeply concerned about the role that higher education should play in a society wracked by social change and economic depression. Hutchins summarized his view of the situation and his response to it in a classic book from the period, *The Higher Learning in America* (1936a). In it, he focused on three issues which, he felt, were at the heart of the problems facing higher education. The first of these was "the love of money," a passion that had fostered what he considered to be an unhealthy vocationalism in education, as institutions turned from the ideal of universality that underpinned liberal education and instead tailored curricula to meet the personnel needs of business and the professions. His concern was not with the basic goal of colleges in preparing graduates to enter into professional careers, but with the means, or with questions of how best to prepare professionals. Hutchins believed that colleges had, in emphasizing professional preparation, abandoned intellectual training in favor of vocational training. This, he said in 1936, leads to triviality, "which, with it close relatives vocationalism and mediocrity, is the greatest enemy of the higher learning in America" (1936b, p. 169).

Hutchins's second major concern was with "a confused notion of democracy," which, he said, had made higher education too responsive to social opinion and too vulnerable to economic conditions. This, too, threatened the intellectual foundation of education as Hutchins saw it and required a basic change in the total educational system. "Economic conditions," he wrote, "require us to provide some kind of education for the young, and for all the young, up to about their twentieth year. Probably one-third of them cannot learn from books. This is no reason why we should not try to work out a better course of study for the other two-thirds" (1936b, p. 61).

The third issue was what Hutchins called "an erroneous notion of progress," which had evolved from the reform movement earlier in the century and from the philosophy of pragmatism, which, as we shall see in the next chapter, was at the heart of the instrumentalist or progressive approach to general education. In Hutchins's view, progressivism had contributed to anti-intellectualism, resulting in a negative impact on the curriculum: "Our erroneous notion of progress has thrown the classics and the liberal arts out of the curriculum, over-emphasized the empirical sciences, and made education the servant of any contemporary movement in society, no matter how superficial" (1936b, p. 65).

In summary, Hutchins believed strongly that a love of money, a confused notion of democracy, and an erroneous notion of progress had resulted in an "anti-intellectual university" (1936a, p. 27) and an anti-intellectual attitude toward education that "reduces the curriculum to the exposition of detail" (1936b, p. 37). His reforms were designed to reverse that situation and to return education to what he saw as its primary mission: "the cultivation of the intellect" (Hutchins, 1936a, p. 67). The key to the reform was "general education."

Hutchins's response to the problem as he saw it resulted in two important innovations: new approaches to the structure and content of the curriculum at the high school and college levels, and a new approach to the content of the curriculum designed to reinvigorate the intellectual quality of liberal education. Both innovations rested on basic assumptions about education in general and about general education in particular.

The first assumption is that higher education is, first and foremost, an *intellectual* process. Universities, Hutchins said, "are founded as places where scholars and their students may develop or exercise their intellectual powers. . . . [They set] a standard of intellectual attainment that can only be achieved through those qualities that are commonly called 'character'" (1936a, p. 20). He described the object of education in one article as "the training of the mind" and "the production of intelligent citizens" (p. 20). "My thesis," he stated, "is that in modern times we have seldom tried reason at all, but something we mistook for it; that our bewilderment results in large part from this mistake; and that our salvation lies not in the rejection of the intellect but in a return to it" (p. 25).

The second basic assumption, which is his definition of general education, grows out of his commitment to an intellectual base for education: "General education is education for everybody, whether he goes on to the university or not" (1936b, p. 62). Its purpose is to "cultivate the intellectual virtues," by which Hutchins means the classical virtues of induction, demonstration, philosophical wisdom, art, and prudence. "In general education, we are interested in drawing out the elements of our human nature; we are interested in the attributes of the race, not in the accidents of individuals" (p. 62).

Hutchins also had a *structural* definition of general education—a vision of where the cultivation of intellectual virtues fit into the total educational system. Hutchins believed that the high school (and the junior college, which he saw as an extension of the high school curriculum) could not decide whether it was preparing students "for life or for college" (1936a, p. 1). His solution to this dilemma was that the four years between the sophomore year of high school and the beginning of the junior year of college should be devoted to general education. Secondary school would prepare *all* students for general education. University education would be "limited to those who had demonstrated in the period of general education that they were capable of scholarly and professional work" (1936b, p. 125). In this way, Hutchins hoped to deal with the social demands on higher education that had grown out of postwar notions of democracy and the economic conditions of the 1930s.

Hutchins's first important curriculum innovation at the University of Chicago was structural and was designed to provide a haven in which his general education could operate without interference from vocationalism. Thus, he created a self-contained undergraduate college which would accept students who had completed their sophomore year of high school and which had a four-year common curriculum—a general education—leading to a bachelor's degree.

The second innovation dealt with what Hutchins called "the serious, the difficult, the important questions about education" (1936b, p. 128), namely, the content of the curriculum. The goals were, first, "the recognition, application, and discussion of ideas" and, second, training "in those intellectual techniques which have been developed for the purpose of stating and comprehending fundamental principles" (p. 30). The means to these ends, eventually developed to its fullest extent at St. John's College, was the Great Books program, which Hutchins described as a "permanent studies" program based in classic books. It was selected because "it is impossible to understand any subject or to comprehend the contemporary world" (1936a, p. 79) without understanding the ideas contained in the great books. The complete general education would be "a course of study consisting of the greatest books of the western world and the arts of reading, writing, thinking, and speaking, together with mathematics, the best examples of the processes of human reason" (1936a, p. 85).

The Parting of the Ways

With Hutchins and Meiklejohn we come to an important fork in the road to general education. Today's confusion between liberal and general education can be traced back to this fork in the road. Hutchins's work is often called an important experiment in "general education," and, in fact, Hutchins used the term consistently. However, Hutchins was essentially conservative. His goal was to undo what he saw as the damage of the past generation and to reestablish a true liberal education. Meiklejohn and the followers of John Dewey, on the other hand, were attempting something brand new. To understand the distinction between general education and liberal education, one must go beyond the simple use of the terms and understand the fundamentally different assumptions that had begun to emerge.

In retrospect, Hutchins's innovations were based in the long-established paradigm of liberal education. Meiklejohn at Wisconsin and the Contemporary Civilization program at Columbia represented the beginnings of a new paradigm that was growing out of the social cataclysm of the period between the wars. Both the classicist, represented here by Hutchins, and the emerging general educationists, represented by Meiklejohn and the Columbia program, used similar language to define the problem. However, they were approaching. it from much different sets of assumptions. The results reflected two paradigms at work. One, the classical liberal education paradigm, was long-established. The other, the general education paradigm, was just beginning to emerge. Many of its assumptions and organizing principles were shared by progressive educators whose origins were not in the humanities, but in the instrumentalist philosophy of John Dewey. Their work would further define the new concept of general education in the 1930s and would result in the general education movement.

The comparison reveals something about the nature of curriculum change: When a new paradigm emerges, it tends not to disregard entirely the old paradigm but to incorporate into the new idea some of the assumptions and language of the older vision, but in a new context. General education and liberal education would stand as quite separate curriculum concepts by the end of the 1930s, but their common terminology and their sharing of several assumptions would be a constant source of confusion for later academics who understood only superficially the historical and philosophical underpinnings of either general or liberal education.

CHAPTER 4

Pragmatism, Instrumentalism, and Progressive Education

The Philosophy of Pragmatism

Pragmatism is often seen as a uniquely American philosophy. John Childs (1956), for instance, felt that pragmatism was the philosophy that best reflected the realities of the American experience, especially the frontier experience of the nineteenth century. The relationship between pragmatism and the American experience cannot be overemphasized. Pragmatism was born in the latter decades of the nineteenth century. It was shaped by the same forces that were re-forming American life at the end of the Industrial Revolution; pragmatism reflected the vitality in American life and, at the same time, made an active contribution to that vitality. As such, pragmatism owed little allegiance to the rationalist tradition of Europe; in fact, it is rooted in opposition to that tradition. Its founders were very conscious of a direct relationship between pragmatism and the American brand of political and social democracy. They wanted a philosophy that would help insure that the vitality of American culture was maintained.

Childs (1956) suggests that the all-pervading experience of the American frontier paved the way for the development of pragmatism. That idea had a precedent in Frederick Jackson Turner's classic history of the frontier experience. Writing at the same time that the pragmatists were beginning to form their ideas, Turner (1893/1962) noted,

> The pecularity of American institutions is the fact that they have been compelled to adapt themselves to the changes of an expanding people. . . . American social development has been continually beginning over again on the frontier. This perennial rebirth, this fluidity of American life, this expansion westward with its new opportunities, its continuous

touch with the simplicity of primitive society, furnish the forces domi-
nating American character. [pp. 178–179]

Applying this basic vision to pragmatism, Childs (1956) observes
that, in the life of the pioneer,

> ideas were literally instruments of adjustment and the test of conse-
> quences was prompt and decisive. Nor could life on the frontier be
> conceived as given. Pioneer America was seeking to lay the foundations
> for a new civilization, and these foundations could be lain only as the
> surroundings were transformed so as to release new possibilities for
> human living. . . . The general tendency of the pioneer experience was
> to strengthen the circumstances of life. [pp. 6–7]

If the frontier experience predisposed Americans to a new kind
of philosophy, the Darwinist revolution and the explosion of scientific and technological thought that transformed America as the
frontier closed provided the intellectual soil in which the philosophy
would grow. The advent of Darwinism had opened new and not
entirely welcome frontiers for philosophers. While humanists centered the world on humanity, evolutionary scientists focused on
nature itself and saw humankind as part of the fabric of nature.
Darwin's vision of nature made it impossible to separate humans
from the rest of nature; at the same time, it became impossible to
separate human thought and human values from the total environment—physical and otherwise—in which human beings had evolved
and lived and from the circumstances to which they had to adapt.
Many philosophers felt compelled to leave behind the dualism implicit in the classical humanist and rationalist philosophies of Europe
and to strike out in search of new understandings that better fit the
model of the world provided by the new science.

The new science also had other manifestations that directly
affected the development of pragmatism. For instance, Darwinism
stimulated the development of the social sciences. Psychology,
anthropology, and sociology were new areas of inquiry that used
the methods of science to explore the human mind and human
society, areas previously the exclusive domain of the humanities.
These new sciences reinforced an integrative and process-oriented
view of the world that emphasized the interrelatedness of things and
that was one of Darwin's legacies. They also built upon the idea that
mental and physical life were essentially inseparable. The relationships that constitute human experience were the raw materials of

the social sciences and were also at the very heart of the pragmatists' philosophy.

Pragmatism can also be seen as part of the general revolt against formalism that pervaded Western culture at the turn of the century and which itself owed much to the new sciences. The revolt manifested itself in many ways, from impressionist painting, which turned away from representational realism to celebrate the basic qualities of light and paint, to a similar self-consciousness in literature, to new political theories that disavowed the authority of tradition in favor of a new dialectic. Pragmatism was one typically American contribution to the revolt. It argued against the doctrine that knowledge and ideas could be distinct objects in reality that were separate from the social space within which they existed.

These forces all contributed to a sense that law and "social arrangements" were the natural products of a society in which institutions were constantly created and re-created. As a result, the society was oriented to the future rather than to the past (Childs, 1950). The pragmatists helped shape a new philosophy that asserted that individuals could change the future of their society, just as they could transform the frontier; that knowledge and action were essentially inseparable; and, thus, that action was as worthy a goal as understanding. As Israel Scheffler (1974) described it, knowledge, to the pragmatist, "arises in a biological and social context as a result of experimentation; that is, an active transformation of the environment directed toward the resolution of the problems of life" (p. 6). This was a paradigm shift of major proportions and one that would have a profound effect on American education.

Charles Sanders Peirce and the Pragmatic Maxim

Charles Sanders Peirce is generally credited with founding pragmatism. The son of one of the nation's leading mathematicians, Peirce had worked as a surveyor and earned a degree in chemistry from Harvard. During the 1860s, he lectured on the philosophy of science and on the logic of science and induction. In the 1870s, he was part of a group called—partly out of irony and partly in defiance of the popular agnosticism of the day—the Metaphysical Club. The club counted among its members William James and Oliver Wendell Holmes, Jr. It was to this group that Peirce presented a paper that contained the essential ingredients of pragmatism. Peirce's pragmatic maxim, as later published, was stated as follows:

Consider what effect, that might conceivably have practical bearings, we conceive the object of our conception to have. Then, our conception of these effects is the whole of our conception of the object. [quoted in Smith, 1978, p. 15]

This simple statement was a radical departure for philosophy. Peirce cut deeply into the rationalist assumptions about the absolute objectivity of reality and of truth. The pragmatic maxim rejected the basic rationalist vision of a clearly defined and differentiated universe governed by fixed laws. This paradigm—the old clockwork universe of Newton—had guided generations of philosophers who believed that there was an objective reality that needed only to be observed to reveal its universal, ineluctable truths (Scheffler, 1974). Peirce, however, was interested not simply in collecting and describing objects of truth. His goal was to find a new, clearer way of determining the meaning of an idea, proposition, or phenomenon, and this required that the idea be considered in terms of its *effect*—its *practical* bearings.

Peirce replaced Newton's clockwork, not with a new central object but with a central method: the process of inquiry and experiment based in scientific logic. This process, as outlined in the pragmatic maxim, became the force that brought sense and unity to the universe for the pragmatists (Scheffler, 1974). Peirce believed that serious thinking began with a problem; that is, with a doubt that calls into question one's old habits and one's old assumptions (Childs, 1956). Inquiry—the application of a logical, scientific method to a situation—is the tool that the pragmatist uses to overcome doubt and attain belief. Peirce wrote, "The sole objective of inquiry is the settlement of opinion. When opinion is settled . . . genuine inquiry cannot arise" (quoted in Scheffler, 1974, p. 32). Experience, belief, and meaning, were, to Peirce, inseparable aspects of inquiry. Something has meaning only to the extent that one can believe that it will behave in a predictable way, that its effect will be the same across time. Peirce maintained that action can have no meaning without a purpose and that neither ideas nor action can be described without referring to something general that is neither a fact nor an act (Smith, 1978) but can probably best be described as a relationship between the individual and the idea or action. "Education," for example, is meaningless as a concept except as it exists as a relationship between a learner and a goal.

Peirce put the basic elements of pragmatism into place as aspects of a philosophy. William James applied Peirce's basic concepts to individual behavior and to the pursuit of religious and moral beliefs.

John Dewey transformed pragmatism into instrumentalism, in the process giving the basic elements of pragmatism a distinctly social meaning and applying them to education.

William James and Instrumental Truth

William James, a member of the Metaphysical Club who shared in the development of pragmatism, brought to the philosophy an intense interest in the individual and a concern for establishing the nature of religious and spiritual truths. In doing so, he introduced the concept of *instrumentalism* into the philosophical vocabulary, setting the stage for Dewey's social philosophy.

James was not only a philosopher; he was one of the great early psychologists. In his *Principles of Psychology* (1890), he applied scientific Darwinism to the study of the mind (White, 1973) and stressed how an individual's behavior was inseparable from the individual's physiology (Scheffler, 1974). Applying the basic elements of Peirce's maxim to the study of human behavior, James founded experimental psychology, but he was also influenced greatly by Darwinian thought in the development of functional psychology. Here, he was concerned not only with describing *what* happens in human behavior, but with *how* and *why* that behavior happens. In short, James was concerned with the causes and purposes that underlie human behavior (Scheffler, 1974). To James, cause could not be defined without looking at the "total mind-body organism" (Scheffler, 1974). (The awkwardness of that phrase shows how difficult it is to articulate a holistic philosophy in a dualistic cultural tradition.) To do so required that one look at the individual and his experiences rather than at abstract doctrines of behavior.

While James accepted some of the basic elements of the pragmatic maxim, he was above all an individualist who did not agree with Peirce's stand that the meaning of a concept did not depend at all on the individual's reaction to the environment in which a concept developed. James went on to construct his own version of pragmatism. This outraged Peirce, who eventually repudiated James's version and afterward referred to his own doctrine as "pragmaticism," in an attempt to distance himself from James (Schneider, 1946).

Important to James's psychology is the idea that thought and thing are, in the final analysis, the same. There is, in his view, no such thing as an objective thought and no such thing as an objective idea that exists apart from a physical reality that to one degree or another shapes that thought or idea. The distinction that people make between the two—between an idea and the physical environment—is, in this view, a contrast formed by experience (Scheffler, 1974). This is the basis of James's principle of personality: "Every thought tends to be part of a personal consciousness" (quoted in Scheffler, 1974, p. 131). With this principle, James put the pragmatic maxim into psychological terms.

James the psychologist often struggled with James the philosopher. While he sought to unify thought and individual experience, he was also concerned with "truth" in the religious sense of the word. Religious truth implied the existence of absolutes, the very kind of abstracts that his psychology seemed to disavow. In the process of dealing with this apparent contradiction, James added to pragmatism new definitions of belief and gave a moral dimension to the philosophy that would be important to Dewey's instrumentalist approach to education.

The problem facing James was clear. If one's mental life—one's thoughts and ideas—is inextricably bound to one's physiology and environment, then absolute truths that are universal for all people and that exist apart from any individual's personal experience cannot exist. Yet, belief in such absolutes is a positive experience in the lives of many people. The pragmatic maxim held that it is the *effect* of a phenomenon that defines our conception of it. Therefore, if an idea *functions* effectively as an absolute in the sense that people believe in it and act upon that belief, it *is* an absolute for the community of people who believe it.

James was willing to accept absolutes as true to the extent that belief in them gives the believer satisfaction (Scheffler, 1974). However, it is not simply a matter of letting people live in self-justified illusion based on unsubstantiated beliefs. To James, beliefs must go through a process of verification; they can be held as true only if they are not overridden by other beliefs that have a greater ability to satisfy the believer. In brief, the settling of opinion on a belief does not absolve the individual from continuing the process of inquiry. Belief, to James, became the acceptance of a model that works within the experience of the believer and that can withstand constant comparison with other models. Inquiry, in this view, is necessary not only to establish belief but to maintain it. Inquiry thus becomes an ongoing process.

Truth, then, is not something that *exists* the way a book exists. Instead, it is a quality that is ascribed to an idea on the basis of inquiry and experience. In scientific terms, a hypothesis—such as a model of the atom—is treated as real as long as experience offers no conflicting model. James wrote, "Truth *happens* to an idea. It becomes true, is made true by events. Its verity is, in fact, an event, a process" (quoted in Scheffler, 1974, p. 110). Truth, in the pragmatic sense, has no objective reality but takes its value from the process of relating one experience to another. "Any idea which we can ride, so to speak; any idea that will carry us prosperously from one part of our experience to any other part," said James, " . . . is true for just so much, true in so far forth, true instrumentally" (quoted in Scheffler, 1974, p. 104).

James's ideas on the interdependence of physiology and behavior and on the relation between the pathology of belief and metaphysical truth caused an uproar that continued to grow in volume as the debate over his "will-to-believe" concept spread. After receiving a caution from John Dewey on the issue of "truth," James decided that what he had seen as merely a "method of conducting discussions" had gone too far and that he would leave the making of a philosophy to Dewey and others (Schneider, 1946). Meanwhile, however, Dewey had discovered in James's work the key to his own theory of instrumentalism.

John Dewey and the Transformation of Experience

It fell to John Dewey, who had been a student (although a reluctant one at the time) of Peirce (Dykhuizen, 1973), to develop the social and ultimately the educational implications of James's statement. Dewey recalled his early ideas this way:

> I became more and more troubled by the intellectual scandal that seemed to me involved in the current (and traditional) dualism in logical standpoint and method between something called "science" on the one hand and something called "morals" on the other. I have long felt that the construction of a logic, that is, a method of effective inquiry, which would apply without abrupt breach of continuity to the fields designated by both of these words, is at once our needed theoretical solvent and the supply of our greatest practical event. This belief has had much more to do with the development of what I termed, for lack of a better word, "instrumentalism," than have most of the reasons that have been assigned. [quoted in Childs, 1956, p. 108]

Dewey combined Peirce's concern with inquiry and meaning with James's emphasis on individual action and truth and gave pragmatism a new dimension: the use of inquiry to achieve individual and social transformation. This he called *instrumentalism*. Dewey believed that the central test of any philosophy was how it affected the intellectual and moral quality of daily life (Scheffler, 1974). Like earlier pragmatists, Dewey rooted his philosophy in science, because he felt that the natural sciences had a closer relationship to actual life than did other ways of knowing: "It is not too much to say that science, through application in invention and technologies, is the greatest force in modern society for producing social change and shaping human relations" (1946/1975, p. 82). But, unlike scientist Peirce and psychologist James, Dewey's ultimate goal was not the creation of scientific knowledge but the use of scientific processes to create social change. Morton White (1973) has noted that Dewey was a lifelong critic of political passivity who believed that one cause of passivity was the individual's skepticism that he or she could establish any general truths about society: If one cannot establish general truths, then it becomes very difficult to predict the outcome of any individual's effort to change society. Dewey's instrumentalism was designed to help the individual overcome this passivity by creating plans of action that would empower the individual to solve problems by transforming the environment.

While Peirce used inquiry to "settle opinion" and James used it to arrive at instrumental truths, Dewey saw inquiry as an instrument of personal and, ultimately, social transformation. His concern was less with the fixing of belief than with the transformation of situations to achieve a more satisfactory environment. Scientific inquiry, to Dewey, required the transformation of everyday objects and ideas which, when examined and shorn of their cultural associations, would reveal insights of general value (White, 1973). He wrote that "experience in its vital form is experimental, an effort to change the given; it is characterized by projection, by reaching forward into the unknown; connection with a future is a salient trait" (quoted in White, 1973, p. 85). In short, the purpose of a philosophy is *to help people solve problems.*

Dewey also refined the pragmatic idea of how knowledge is developed. To him, knowledge sought by science could not be gained by the pure intellect of the classical logician. Instead, it required the use of all the senses and, equally important, action as well as observation. The senses and the individual's participation do not interfere with or distort one's apprehension of knowledge; instead, they help define knowledge in very real, very practical ways. The essential factor in acquiring knowledge, to Dewey, is the individual's perception of the relationship between her or his actions and the observed consequences of how action changes the environment (Scheffler, 1974).

Of course, action can be planned or random, and this distinction is important to Dewey. Passive experience, to him, is simple random action and reaction; it has no *meaning*. But Dewey recognized another kind of experience, which he called *reflective* experience, in which action is taken with a purpose: to find out the relationship between the action and the environment. Reflective experience involves thinking and planning. Like Peirce, Dewey saw the process as beginning in a state of confusion about something. The individual first imagines an end in view, takes action anticipated to create that end, elaborates or revises the projected end in view, and then takes a stand: she or he defines something as being true. At the end of the process, the original confusion is gone; the situation has been transformed; the problem has been solved. The process applies to broad social problems when a community of individuals arrives at the same solution, when a common belief or faith develops through social inquiry.

Dewey did not see pragmatism as a philosopher's philosophy— something to be studied, elaborated upon, and debated among technical specialists in journals. As he put it, "Understanding, by its very nature, is related to action" (1946/1975, p. 49). Dewey's instrumentalism was a way of helping people create personal plans of action that would help them solve problems and transform their personal and social situations. As a result, Dewey saw a close connection between pragmatism and American democracy. On one hand pragmatism required a democratic society in which individuals were free to inquire, to hypothesize, and to take individual action. At the same time, he felt that pragmatism was vital to the maintenance of democracy.

> The very idea of democracy, the meaning of democracy, must be continually explored afresh. It has to be constantly discovered and rediscovered, remade and reorganized; while the political and economic and social institutions in which it is embodied have to be remade and reorganized to meet the changes that are going on in the development of new needs on the part of human beings and new resources for satisfying those needs. [quoted in Scheffler, 1974, p. 86]

As Dewey made clear, the pragmatists were prospectors. Perhaps building on assumptions about reality that derived from the American frontier experience, as Childs (1956) suggested, they had turned their backs on tradition as the authority for life and looked to the present to provide the tools for building a more satisfactory future. It was a radical shift in the basic philosophical assumptions on which Western culture had operated and on which most education had been based. For the most part, education had been a way of preserving the best traditions of a culture. The pragmatists looked to the future. If there was a tradition they sought to preserve through education, it was the American willingness to change society to fit the needs of individuals. The role of pragmatic or instrumentalist education came to be that of training people to transform themselves and their society to meet the future.

John Dewey and the Instrumentalist Philosophy of Education

Education was rarely far from the inquiring minds of the pragmatists. Peirce, for instance, believed that the purpose of education was no different than the purpose of life: "We are not simply striving for familiarity with ideas, or for verbal facility to be exhibited by giving proper definitions or correct answers to test questions. We are forming active systems of habit and expectation" (quoted in Scheffler, 1974, p. 82). Peirce was adamant that education could produce individual welfare only to the extent that it was focused primarily on larger goals.

Dewey moved education to the very center of pragmatism. In the process, he fathered the progressive education movement, revolutionized schooling in the years between the world wars, and greatly influenced the general education movement. "The philosophy of education," he wrote, "is not a poor relation of general philosophy; . . . it is ultimately the most significant phase of philosophy" (1946/1975, p. 165).

Dewey also saw a significant relationship between education and democracy: "Democracy is itself an educational principle, an educational measure and policy" (1946/1975, p. 34). Knowledge, especially scientific knowledge, was to Dewey a form of social behavior that could be effective only in a democratic society. At the same time, democracy depended on a citizenry educated to think freely, to be able to change their environment and build a future. The two ideas were inseparable parts of the instrumentalist vision.

The instrumentalist viewpoint recognized no separation between philosophy and education or between education and democracy. Given its central role, education could not be isolated in any way from the basic processes that defined pragmatism and (at least to some pragmatists) that defined democracy itself. Education was not a preparation for a profession or even a preparation for life in society. Instead, it was a continuous process of growth, whose only goal was the capacity for additional growth (Dewey, 1916/1944). Dewey defined education as "that reconstruction or reorganization of experience which adds to the meaning of experience" (p. 76).

The importance of this idea to the instrumentalist approach cannot be overestimated. As Dewey (1916/1944) noted, "The educational process has no end beyond itself; it is its own end" (p. 50). He added that the process involves three components: *reorganizing, reconstructing,* and *transforming.* These, then, are the ultimate processes and aims of instrumentalist education. One important aspect of this definition is that it involves an intentional effort to change the environment. A second is that the *processes* of education—reorganization, reconstruction, and transformation of the environment—are also the *ends* of education. However, since the instrumentalist approach did not recognize that education ever ends, Dewey used not *ends* but *aims. Experience,* as it contributes to individual growth, is the aim of education. Experience, as the act of solving a problem by transforming the environment, is also the means of education.

The idea that the aim of education is growth and expanded capacity for growth contains two significant implications. One is that growth is continuous; if growth is continuous, so must be education. Dewey saw education as a lifelong process that both responds to and fosters lifelong growth. The second implication of growth as an educational aim is that it requires that education be concerned with the present. If education has no purpose outside itself, its only concern should be with the present problems that challenge the growth of the learner; these are the stimuli for pragmatic inquiry and experience. As Dewey (1916/1944) wrote, "The future, just as future, lacks urgency and body. To get ready for something, and one knows not what or why, is to throw away the leverage that exists and to seek for motive power in a vague chance" (p. 55).

To Dewey, the aim of education could not be external to the process itself. Dewey listed three criteria for establishing an educational aim. First, it must be an outgrowth of existing conditions. That is, an educational aim should begin with the current situation in which a problem exists and identify a plan of action that will change the situation and resolve the problem. Second, Dewey said, an aim must be flexible, so that it can be adapted to meet changing circumstances as the educational process evolves. "The value of a legitimate aim . . . lies in the fact that we can use it to change conditions," he wrote. "It is a method for dealing with conditions so as to effect desirable alterations in them" (1916/1944, p. 105). Finally, an educational aim must always involve a *freeing* of activities. The idea of an "end in view" must be simply suggestive, the end itself tentative. Activities should develop as the situation changes and as the end in view itself changes. As Dewey wrote, "Strictly speaking, not the target but hitting the target is the end in view" (p. 105). The target itself might well change with experience.

The instrumentalist method is the same as the instrumentalist goal: experience. At its most basic, Dewey's definition of educational method is simple: "Method . . . is but an effective way of employing some materials to some end" (1916/1944, p. 165). But Dewey applied this definition in a unique way. His goal was to strike down the dualism of the classical approach to teaching and replace it with a unity. In the instrumentalist approach, there could be no distinction between ends and means. "The central problem of an education based upon experience is to select the kind of present experiences that live fruitfully and creatively in subsequent experiences" (1938, pp. 16–17). Teaching method, by his definition, involves providing the student with meaningful experiences: "action intelligently directed by ends" (1916/1944, p. 170).

Dewey described two levels of educational method. The first, or general method, was simply the cumulative body of methods for reaching results that are "authorized by past experience and intellectual analysis, which an individual ignores at his peril" (1916/1944, p. 170). The second—and to the instrumentalists the most important—method was the individual method, which was the basic method of pragmatic philosophy. Dewey described its components this way: "They are the features of the reflective situation—problem, collection and analysis of data, projection and elaboration of suggestions or ideas, experimental application and testing; the resulting conclusions or judgments" (p. 173).

In applying the individual method, Dewey advocated a highly individualized approach to education. In fact, he wrote in 1938, "It is not enough that certain materials and methods have proved effective with other individuals at other times. There must be a reason for thinking that they will function in generating an experience that has educative quality with particular individuals at a particular time" (p. 45).

To summarize Dewey's theory thus far, the ultimate *aim* of education is continued capacity for growth, an aim that implies continued expansion of the individual's experiences, since only experience can result in situations in which growth is possible. Experience is also the *means* of education, since the experience of solving problems is how growth is achieved and how new situations for future growth are created. All this implies a highly individualized approach to education.

Just as Dewey did not want to make distinctions between educational aims and educational means, he fought against the separation of educational methods from the subject matter of education. His objection was based on the fundamental assumptions of pragmatism:

> Reflection upon experience gives rise to a distinction of *what* we experience (the experienc*ed*) and the experienc*ing*—the *how*. When we give names to this distinction we have subject matter and method as our terms. . . . This distinction is so natural for certain purposes that we are only too apt to regard it as a separation in existence and not as a distinction of thought. Then we make a division between a self and the environment or world. This separation is the root of the dualism of method and subject matter. [1916/1944, pp. 166–167]

The big danger of this kind of false distinction is that subject matter becomes "something to be learned" and overcomes what, to Dewey, is the real aim of education. Educational method is reduced to a mechanical routine, and the concrete situations of experience— the highly subjective problems that give rise to inquiry and discovery—are lost.

However, this is not to say that subject matter has no place in Dewey's educational scheme of things. The difference between the instrumentalist approach and that of the rationalists is not the *use* of subject matter, but its *place* and *treatment*. In the traditional curriculum, the subject matter lies outside of the immediate experience of the students. It is selected by adults for use by students sometime in the distant future. In the instrumentalist approach, subject matter is seen as a resource available to help the student solve problems of immediate concern. The knowledge of the past becomes a means for understanding the present and for creating the future. Dewey (1938) put the point this way:

> The sound principle that the objectives of learning are in the future and its immediate materials are in present experience can be carried into effect only in the degree that present experience is stretched, as it were, backward. It can expand into the future only as it is also enlarged to take in the past. [p. 93]

The key element, however, is that the subject matter provides an experience that leads the student into previously unfamiliar territory—into a new situation, with a new set of problems and challenges. Unless the student strikes out into new territory, no new problems will arise, and problems are the stimulus to thinking and growth.

It is important to keep in mind that, while the instrumentalist curriculum is individualized, the goal remains, ultimately, a social goal. Dewey (1938) wrote that "the only freedom that is of enduring importance is freedom of intelligence, that is to say, freedom of observation and of judgment exercised in behalf of purposes that are intrinsically worthwhile" (p. 69). With Dewey, as with Peirce before him, individual freedom is not necessarily an end in itself. "Everything then depends, so far as education is concerned, upon what is done with this liberty." "What end does it serve? What consequences flow from it?" (p. 70). The goal is not simply experience, but *meaningful* experience. This social aim is also reflected in a social means: "The principle that development of experience comes about through interaction means that education is essentially a social process. This quality is realized in the degree in which the individuals form a community group" (p. 65).

Dewey's educational philosophy, then, is one in which education is seen as a continuous process of growth with no end other than continued capacity for growth. It is a philosophy that defines growth as action directed toward a goal. It uses knowledge as a resource for helping students understand the present in the process of moving themselves into a future whose goals they already have in mind. It is a curriculum whose primary method is experience in the form of problem solving, a curriculum that balances a concern for the individual with a goal of establishing a working community that can solve what are, ultimately, problems of social importance vital to the continued growth of a democratic society.

Progressive Education

Dewey outlined his instrumentalist philosophy in two major works separated by more than 20 years. The first, *Democracy and Education* (Dewey, 1916/1944), appeared in 1916 at the height of the progressive movement. Dewey moved on to other areas of philosophy, but this early work helped stimulate progressive education, which grew rapidly in the 1920s and 1930s. The second book, *Experience and Education*, was published in 1938. It was, in large measure,

Dewey's response to the paths progressive education had taken in the intervening years.

Those years saw a tension between two elements of instrumentalism that Dewey had never seen as separable. At issue was the relationship between the role of education in serving the needs of the individual student and its role in fostering social change. To Dewey, these could not even be seen as two faces of the same coin; they *were* the coin. However, as progressive education developed in the hands of a younger generation of Dewey's colleagues at Columbia, a debate over a child-centered versus a social reconstructionist curriculum grew louder. The pendulum would swing to both extremes before the outbreak of World War II.

There were several reasons for this divergence in thinking during the 1920s and 1930s. Certainly part of the problem was Dewey's convoluted and often obscure style. Dewey tended to load new meaning onto relatively common terms such as *experience, purpose,* and *democracy* and then to assume that his readers shared that new meaning. Unfortunately, that was not always the case, and the pragmatism that provided the basic assumptions for Dewey's educational work was often lost to his readers. Lacking a full understanding of Dewey's subtleties of meaning, his followers began to apply their own interpretations to his general statements, with the result that progressive education moved in directions quite the opposite of what Dewey had intended. By 1938, he had emerged as one of the most lucid critics of progressive education in practice, while remaining a vocal advocate for progressive education in concept (Hofstadter, 1962).

The movement toward a child-centered curriculum, however, cannot be explained entirely as a misinterpretation of Dewey's awkward prose style. It was one result of many different and sometimes opposing forces that converged on American society after World War I. One factor was the "return to normalcy" that pervaded postwar American society, a deep desire for the quiet life that was epitomized by President Calvin Coolidge. One of its manifestations was a conservative backlash that rejected—and perhaps feared—the social agenda of the progressive movement.

But the chief cause was the development of a competing educational paradigm which, like instrumentalism, looked to science for its basic assumptions. However, where Dewey used the scientific method of inquiry as a way of approaching the problems of life and of transforming the environment, the other group, headed by Edward L. Thorndike, looked to science to provide "laws" by which to measure educational effectiveness. Richard Hofstadter (1962) contrasted the two schools succinctly: "John Dewey was the master of those for whom educational democracy was the central issue; Edward Lee Thorndike of those for whom it was the application to education of 'what science has to tell us'" (p. 335).

Thorndike and his followers believed in the existence of natural laws of education based on laws of psychology. Their educational programs were responses to or applications of psychological observations. Their research focused on identifying and proving the validity of laws that they would then use to create curriculum policies.

Contributing to this overall movement was the development of student aptitude and intelligence testing during and after World War I. It was simultaneously one of the most controversial and one of the most irresistibly inviting issues in education during the 1920s. While Dewey traced his intellectual ancestry to experimental psychology and to Charles Eliot's interest in making the curriculum responsive to the interests of individual students, the measurement movement could be traced to G. Stanley Hall's child studies, to the research ethos that underpinned Thorndike's science of education, and to a Freudian vision in which an individual's activities were controlled by underlying laws of behavior.

The measurement movement was born in France during the years 1905 to 1908, when Alfred Benet and Theodore Simon conceived the idea of an intelligence scale. In America, the idea of measuring intelligence fit well into a research environment that equated intellectual rigor with numbers (Gould, 1981). This, in turn, fed the development of a "science of pedagogy" that had a voracious appetite for a precision that would set the professional apart from the layperson (Cremin, 1961). It also contributed to the development of the student personnel movement.

The movement blossomed during World War I, when Robert Yerkes, then head of the American Psychological Association, offered the organization's resources for developing group intelligence tests for new Army recruits. This offered the psychological community an opportunity to test theories of intelligence measurement on a large scale.

The movement also reflected the new conservatism that Americans had embraced after the war. For instance, while the prewar progressives had worked to help the waves of immigrants that had come to America, and had built a schooling system to Americanize them, statistics from the Army tests were used to support the mistaken contention that the intelligence of European immigrants could be "graded" by their country of origin and to reinforce the myth of black inferiority (Gould, 1981). This sped the drive to close immigration, which is what happened in 1924. In this sense, the measurement movement was associated with an antidemocratic environment that was diametrically opposed to Dewey's ideas.

At the same time, intelligence and achievement tests offered a potentially huge benefit to those educators who were interested in the effective education of the individual student. If individual achievement and intelligence could be measured, then educational programs could be constructed to suit the specific needs and talents of each individual student. This was a two-edged sword for the instrumentalists. Dewey noted that, to the extent that tests helped individuals achieve their potential, they could serve the goal of progress. However, tests could also be used to reduce the individual to a set of statistics; in this case, IQ and achievement tests could be a tool of antidemocratic forces. The IQ, said Dewey, "is an indication of risks and probabilities. Its practical value lies in the stimulus it gives to more intimate and intensive inquiry into individualized abilities and disabilities" (quoted in Cremin, 1961, p. 190). Dewey as much as anyone saw both the benefits and the dangers of measurement statistics.

The effects of educational scientism and the child-centered approach on progressive education were enormous. The chief advocate of the child-centered approach among the progressive educators was William Heard Kilpatrick. Like both Dewey and Thorndike, Kilpatrick was part of a group of educational theorists who found themselves at Teachers College of Columbia University in the 1920s and 1930s. He was best known as a teacher; in his years at Columbia, he is said to have taught more than 35,000 students. His influence was at the grassroots (Cremin, 1961).

Kilpatrick was influenced by both Dewey and Thorndike. From Dewey he inherited the basic ideals of individual inquiry and an overriding concern with the present and with direct experience. But he did not share the instrumentalist assumptions that underlay Dewey's educational philosophy. Many of the basic assumptions behind his approach to the curriculum were instead those of Thorndike. Kilpatrick firmly believed in the existence of "laws of learning" that held the key to educational improvement. To him, these laws were objectively true, quantifiable facts. He wrote (1926), "A law of learning is like any law of nature. Newton didn't *make* the law of gravity; he *discovered* it. . . . A law of nature is nothing but a statement of observed regularity" (p. 20). Building on Thorndike's educational psychology, Kilpatrick described all behavior in terms of stimulus-response mechanisms and psychological bonds. He defined learning as "acquiring new bonds or changing old ones" (p. 29).

The educational psychologists built their theories on the same stimulus-response bond theory. To them, the goal of education was psychological development—in Thorndike's words, the "adjustment of an organism in determining (1) what bonds shall act and (2) which results shall satisfy" (Kilpatrick, 1926, p. 52). The "wider problem of method," wrote Kilpatrick, is how to manage all of the variables (the teacher, the school room, the children, and so forth) "so that the children shall grow most and best from it all" (p. 100).

The differences between Dewey and Kilpatrick are most obvious in their choice of method. Dewey's was the problem-solving method, based on the pragmatic idea that all thinking begins with a problem—a doubt, a confusion, an unsatisfactory environment—and that the goal of reflective experience was to solve the problem by transforming the environment. The method of education, then, was to give the student experience in solving problems. There is in this method an intrinsically *social* purpose; the aim of education is reorganization, reconstruction, and transformation of the environment that uses an outward-looking, future-oriented method.

Kilpatrick's method—the *project method*—retained Dewey's emphasis on the student's direct experience with the environment, but it lacked the social orientation; the goal was not to solve problems or transform the environment, but to involve the student in direct experience as the best way of stimulating individual growth. Kilpatrick (1926) described the project method as "the purposeful way of treating children in order to stir the best in them and then to trust them to themselves as much as possible" (p. 346). A project, he said, was "an instance of purposeful activity—it is the pursuit of a purpose" (p. 347). Kilpatrick identified four types of projects: the producer's project, in which the purpose is to produce something; the consumer's project, in which the purpose is to use and enjoy something; the problem project, in which the purpose is to solve a problem; and the drill project or specific learning project, in which the purpose is to acquire a skill or knowledge (Kilpatrick, 1926).

The key word in these descriptions is "purpose." It was the purposeful nature of an activity, even more than the specific knowledge gained from that activity, that made it educationally valuable to Kilpatrick. In fact, Kilpatrick was very much opposed to instruction that centered around fixed subject matter. As he put it, "Anyone who advocates extrinsic subject matter is likely to leave purpose out of his project definition" (1926, p. 349). This attack on extrinsic subject matter was, in the final analysis, an attack on any educational objective that lay outside the child; this opposition was fundamental to the child-centered approach as he conceived it. The child was an end unto himself to Kilpatrick, just as education was an end unto itself for Dewey (Childs, 1956).

Despite these differences, Kilpatrick continued to share Dewey's concern with the relationships between the individual and society and with the instrumental role of direct experience in transforming the individual, even though his interpretation and application of these ideas were shaped by his psychological approach. For instance, while his educational method clearly began and ended with the child, Kilpatrick saw it in a social context. He accepted the proposition that education was essential to a democracy; however, he defined the purpose of democracy in terms of individual growth. He believed that democracy has no good but the good of the individual; that institutions are means to individual growth; and that only the growth of the whole child could be acceptable as an aim for the democratic school (Childs, 1956).

The child-centered approach was especially well suited to the social climate of the 1920s, a decade that celebrated individualism over social problems and that was fascinated by psychology. However, with the Great Depression, the collapse of the world economy, and the international growth of fascism and communism, the educational pendulum began to swing back toward a society-centered curriculum. The domestic economic situation led many to think that a major social change was under way. The rise of fascism in Europe engendered a sense of crisis that pervaded American society. People again sought answers to the broad social questions that had been set aside in the 1920s. The social consciousness that had been the hallmark of the progressive period prior to and immediately after World War I now reasserted itself, both in society generally and in education specifically. The social orientation of Dewey's pragmatism, which had lain dormant for a decade, came to play an important role in progressive education during the Depression years, at the same time that the Roosevelt administration promised a "New Deal" for American society.

It was a radical environment that found its voice among a few professional educators centered at Teachers College. The most outspoken of the group was George S. Counts (Ravitch, 1983). Counts, who completed his doctorate in 1916, the year Dewey's *Democracy and Education* was published (Dennis & Eaton, 1980), was known more as a social critic than as an educator. Unlike Dewey and Kilpatrick, he did not propose a specific method of study. Instead, he contributed a new awareness of the school's responsibility in society.

Counts was a sociologist and anthropologist. He approached education as a social institution: "Education is always an expression of a particular society and culture at a particular time in history, unless it is imposed by force from without" (Dennis & Eaton, 1980, p. 9). The first task was to understand the social order in which education functions; only with that understanding in place could a meaningful education be created. As Harold Taylor noted, what Counts saw in the late 1920s and early 1930s was

> a time of extremes: the tensions of rich versus poor, autocratic versus democratic, and softhearted idealism versus hard-headed realism seemed to place everything else in juxtaposition and to create a bipolar world. . . . What was required, thought Counts, was a different social structure, one not entirely new, but one already grounded in the roots of the past: the United States Constitution, the basic governmental organization, and the traditions of freedom would be sufficient. [quoted in Dennis & Eaton, 1980, p. 9]

Counts believed in the notion that the national character was shaped by the geography of the nation. In his analysis, democracy, experimentation, and acceptance of change were elements vital to the American national character.

> Closely linked with the democratic heritage is the experimental temper of the American people. . . . Having broken with the past originally to cross the Atlantic and having broken with it again and again in the settlement and conquest of the continent, they tend to be impatient of the authority of tradition. . . . In a word, the American people do not fear change. [Dennis & Eaton, 1980, p. 32]

In fact, he believed that Americans "possess an outlook that welcomes change, that expects improvement from change, . . . that looks with hope to the future" (p. 32). These characteristics, important to American society, are also important characteristics of a democratic education. If this sounds like Dewey's instrumentalism, it is because Counts also believed that "in the domain of practical affairs, where results can be checked, the average American is an instrumentalist by long experience" (p. 33).

Counts did not look just to the past, however, to define the social place of education. He believed that the world was experiencing a major and rapid change in the basic *structure* of civilization: a shift from an agrarian to an industrial society.

> A new civilization is rising in America and throughout the world, a civilization that is coming to be called industrial. . . . We in America are very closely identified with the rise of this new civilization. . . . We have one foot in a civilization that is passing away, the other in a civilization that is only beginning to take form. [Dennis & Eaton, 1980, pp. 74–75]

Counts's chief complaint was that progressive education had not come to grips with the emergence of this industrial civilization (Cremin, 1961). The major reason for this was, in his view, the heavy emphasis that progressive education had come to place on the individual student. He maintained that the individualism that had dominated the agrarian society was being replaced by a more collective group identity. Counts sounded this theme in the first edition of *The Social Frontier*, a journal that he and others of the Columbia group (including Dewey) introduced in 1934. In the first editorial, Counts wrote, "For the American people, the age of individualism in economy is closing and an age of collectivism is opening" (Ravitch, 1983, p. 86). The issue was not the growth of the whole child, but the creation of a new social order. Education, wrote Counts, should "be concerned primarily not with the promotion of individual success, but with the fullest utilization of the human resources of the country for the advancement of the general welfare" (Dennis & Eaton, 1980, p. 52).

While a society-centered curriculum was generally in line with Dewey's instrumentalism, Counts introduced a new element. Dewey had emphasized the quality of inquiry, the idea of setting an end in view that could always change with experience; hence, his goal was to set the student out into a future that only the student could create. Counts, however, had in mind a specific future: a collective, classless society. The purpose of education in the 1930s, he said, "is to prepare the younger generation for labor and sacrifice in building a democratic civilization and culture on the foundations of a collective economy" (Dennis & Eaton, 1980, pp. 50–51).

The movement to reinstate a social orientation to progressive education became known as the "frontier" (referring to the editorial viewpoint of *The Social Frontier*) or "social reconstructionist" movement (Ravitch, 1983). It fell to John Childs, a member of the second generation of progressive educators at Columbia and a younger contemporary of Counts and Kilpatrick, to bring to this movement the essential qualities of Dewey's instrumentalism and to construct a curriculum methodology upon it.

The social reconstructionist viewpoint was stated in a landmark book on progressive education, *The Educational Frontier*, which appeared in 1933. Edited by Kilpatrick, the book included statements by many of the leading progressive educators of the day. It surveyed the range of thinking that had collected under the umbrella of progressive education. The social reconstructionist approach was represented in two chapters conceived by Childs and Dewey and written primarily by Dewey. In these chapters, Childs and Dewey reviewed the instrumentalist position in light of the directions that progressive education had taken in the 1920s. Their main goal was to reintroduce a social purpose to the child-centered approach and, at the same time, avoid the social dogmatism that was becoming associated with the social reconstructionist position.

They defined education as "the process of realization of integrated individualities" (Kilpatrick, 1933, p. 287). They emphasized that "integration can occur only in and through a medium of association" (p. 291) and went on to note that some associations contribute to "the realization of a full personality" (p. 291) while others interfere with it. The result is that education "must promote some forms of association and community life and must work against others" (p. 291).

Having made this connection between individual and social education, Childs and Dewey restated the essential instrumentalist position that education must be tied to a democratic way of life:

> The democratic faith is individual in that it asserts the claim of every individual to the opportunity for realization of potentialities unhampered by birth, family status, unequal legal restrictions, and external authority. By the same token it has been social in character. It has been recognized that the end for individuals cannot be attained except through a particular type of political and legal institutions. [Kilpatrick, 1933, p. 292]

Childs and Dewey proposed a new methodology for the 1930s—*experimentalism*—as a way of reconciling the differences between the child-centered and social reconstructionist positions. Experimentalism was a more specific, more scientifically oriented version of Dewey's original inquiry or problem-solving method. They argued that this method was "the only one compatible with the democratic way of life as we understand it" (Kilpatrick, 1933, p. 317). The last phrase is the key; the social reconstructionists understood democracy to mean a classless and, to one degree or another, a collectivist society. As Dewey and Childs stated the problem, "The experimental method cannot be made an effective reality in its full adequacy except in a certain kind of society. A society which includes warring class interests will always fight against its application" (Kilpatrick, 1933, p. 326). In short, an education in which individuals are experimenting with their environment and which assumes *change* as a natural result of this education, requires a society in which all individuals are equally free to experiment. This was the limit to which progressive education should, in Dewey's and Childs's view, work toward a specific social order.

With this argument, Childs and Dewey attempted to reinstate the instrumentalist vision of education, in reaction to the directions that progressive education had taken. Their advice to the Thorndike camp was that "adequate educational psychology must be a *social* psychology" (p. 293). Childs would continue to advocate this position throughout the 1930s and into the 1950s, placing increasing emphasis on experimentalism as a means of developing values and morals.

Whatever their differences, the progressive educators held in common several key principles and assumptions that together defined progressive education and that would become central to the general education paradigm. The most basic assumption was that democracy and education were inseparably intertwined. Education, as the progressives defined it, could flourish only in a democratic society, and democracy could truly flourish only with an educated populace. All the other major principles of progressive education, and ultimately general education, flowed from this central proposition.

For instance, the progressives believed that educational methods must be matched to educational aims. The argument was that education *for* democracy must be education *by* democracy, that one cannot achieve a democratic end through nondemocratic means. This was perhaps the most obvious break with traditional educational practice. The instrumentalist unity of ends and means was part of the bedrock on which the progressive educational method stood.

The method stressed the relationship of individuals to their society. To be sure, there were vast differences among the progressives on this point, but the battles over these differences were all fought in an arena defined by certain basic considerations. If progressive education were to be by and for democracy, it had to be concerned with the role of the individual in that society, since that relationship defines a democracy. Some put greater emphasis on the individual, saying, as Kilpatrick did, that the sole purpose of a democracy was individual welfare. Others stressed social needs, especially the transformation of America from an agrarian to an industrial society and the challenges that this transformation presented to individuals who would shape the future of the country as a whole. But all were dealing with the same basic principle: The individual and her or his relationship with the environment—with society—were both the ends and the means of progressive education.

The same principles led to a concern with experience as the primary tool of education. Whether it was Dewey's problem-solving approach, the "purposeful activity" of Kilpatrick's project method, or Childs's experimentalism, the progressives were uniformly interested in the educational value of experience. This in turn led to two other, closely related principles. One was a concern with immediate, contemporary issues. The other was a consistent orientation to the future. The premise was that an education designed to help individuals become capable citizens of a democratic community must involve them in direct experience with issues of immediate interest. The corollary was that such an education is inescapably concerned with individual and social transformation—with change.

Most of the core group of progressive educators addressed themselves to public schooling; however, their work had a distinct effect on higher education. The next chapter will examine how the progressive vision, in all its various hues, was applied in three different institutions that contributed to the development of general education.

CHAPTER 5

Instrumentalist Approaches to General Education: Three Case Histories

The instrumentalist philosophy of education was not easily communicated. It relied heavily on a shared sense of underlying meaning or interpretation of many key terms and concepts, ranging from broad concepts such as democracy to more specific educational concepts of method, content, and individualization. These subtleties are one source of confusion about the meaning of general education. Thus, it becomes especially important to see the instrumentalist approach to general education in action, to see how the ideas were translated into specific programs. This chapter will review three curricula from the 1930s that were based explicitly in instrumentalist concepts of general education. The purpose in reviewing these curricula is not to evaluate them as programs per se but to use them as illustrations. The three cases—Bennington College, Sarah Lawrence College, and the University of Minnesota General College—show how varying interpretations of the instrumentalist philosophy influenced how ideas were translated into educational practice, a variety of experience that is important to our understanding of general education today.

Bennington College

When Bennington College in Bennington, Vermont, opened its doors in 1932, it already had a reputation as an educational pioneer. It was the first college to put into place a general education program based on the methods and assumptions of progressive education.

The idea that a new college in Bennington should be a pioneer was introduced at an exploratory meeting in 1923. William A. Neilson, president of Smith College, made a statement that set the pace for the early development of Bennington College:

The next great college should be organized around . . . art, music, literature, the social sciences, and the consideration of problems arising out of the industrial conditions of the modern world. . . . If Bennington College could pioneer and blaze a new path in higher education, it would render a great service to the women of America. [quoted in Brockway, 1981, pp. 4–5]

A planning committee, headed by Old Bennington resident Mrs. Hall Park McCullough, was formed to test the waters. Mrs. McCullough, a novice in higher education curriculum, was given a list of educators by the New York Commissioner of Education; the list included some of the Columbia group. Both John Dewey and William Heard Kilpatrick took an early interest in the college. Kilpatrick, then at the height of his fame as a "new" educator, agreed to be the keynote speaker at a New York fundraising meeting. His speech outlined the basic philosophy on which the Bennington College curriculum would eventually develop. He called for a "New Deal in women's education" that would take advantage of the new methods of progressive education, methods Kilpatrick thought were especially applicable to the educational problems of women. The fact that women in the 1920s did not face the same career pressures as their male counterparts made a women's college a particularly good place to experiment. Kilpatrick challenged Bennington to become the first to apply progressive education at the college level (Brockway, 1981). Not surprisingly, his proposal was a mix of Dewey's instrumentalism and Thorndike's educational psychology. He proposed that the college "consider education as life and not a mere preparation for life" (quoted in Brockway, 1981, p. 8) and that intelligence tests be used to insure the most appropriate student body. Finally, he recommended that members of the board of trustees have fixed terms, with two members retiring each year, with the hope that the regular appearance of fresh faces would help maintain an atmosphere of experimentation and change.

Kilpatrick's speech was not well received by some of the college presidents who attended the meeting. It impressed the planning committee, however, who gave him charge of an executive committee to develop Bennington College and elected him to a six-year term on the board of trustees. His day-to-day influence on the college gradually became greater than that of Dewey. From 1924 until the appointment of a president for the college, Kilpatrick was a highly visible spokesperson for Bennington College and a leader among trustees who wanted Bennington to become a model progressive college. He consistently encouraged a progressive, student-centered curriculum, along with the strong student personnel function needed to support that kind of curriculum.

Kilpatrick also argued against the traditional curriculum of fixed courses in predetermined subject areas, just as he opposed a subject-matter-dominated curriculum in basic education. The choice of subjects, he argued, should be determined through an analysis of the students' interests. One result of this approach was skepticism on the part of some trustees who had expected a curriculum more specifically in line with Dewey. The trustees, wary of this vagueness, gave Amy Kelly, who had earlier made some curriculum proposals to the trustees, a grant to visit other colleges noted for innovation and to report back her recommendations. Kelly's tour took her to Columbia, Wisconsin, and Chicago. Some of her recommendations, which emphasized individual work and the early declaration of a major, eventually found a place in the Bennington curriculum (Brockway, 1981).

In 1928, Robert Devore Leigh became president of Bennington College. Because of funding, the first day of classes was still four years away, but already Bennington had become identified with a student-centered, progressive curriculum. Leigh was an instrumentalist who had studied with Dewey while at Columbia and who had spent three years at Reed College, one of the early innovators in the curriculum reform movement. He enthusiastically supported the progressive ideas Dewey and Kilpatrick had begun to put into place (Brockway, 1981). He was convinced that only a new college could successfully experiment with new methods. He told the Bennington trustees that existing institutions were paralyzed by "tradition, prejudices, vested interests, and administrative machinery" (quoted in Brockway, 1981, p. 29). He immediately set about to add his own ideas to the foundation Dewey and Kilpatrick had built.

In 1929, Leigh wrote "The Educational Plan for Bennington College." In it and other articles during the year, he called for a curriculum that would emphasize "individuality, direct experience, serious interest, creative and independent work, and self-dependence as educational aims" (quoted in Schilpp, 1930, pp. 359–360). He also added some specifics to the proposed curriculum, including a two-year sequence of introductory courses in each of four major fields, plus a trial major "conference" in one field. All courses would be "individually prescribed by deliberate conference" (Brockway, 1981, p. 36). The goal during the first two years would be to discover the individual student's real interests and talents.

To respond to the interests of the students and to build on Kilpatrick's intense distaste for prescribed subject matter, the *content* of the lower-division courses would not be predetermined. The only caveat was that they focus not on the subject matter of the field, but on the *methods* of the field. The curriculum would allow for problem solving, projects, and experiments as appropriate to the subject area. As Leigh noted,

> In the sciences, this will mean the laboratory method; . . . in the fine arts, creation or expression as well as appreciation; in literature the comprehensive, active, understanding of great masterpieces rather than detailed or superficial literary history; in the social studies the careful, intensive, realistic, impartial analysis of contemporary problems. [quoted in Schilpp, 1930, p. 366]

The trial major conference, said Leigh, would "carry the student as rapidly as feasible into the more individual and more informal method characteristic of the last two college years" (quoted in Schilpp, 1930, p. 367). The goal of an early declaration of a major was to focus as much instruction as possible on the student's primary area of interest and to position the student for more individualized work.

If, at the end of two years, the student had demonstrated "clear evidence of distinct ability" in one of the four major fields, she could move on to the senior division, which would function much like an honors program (Brockway, 1981). At the senior level, most work would be built around projects, with the students spending much of their time in the laboratory, the library, or the field, under the supervision of their major faculty advisor and with their work checked through informal group conferences. Kilpatrick's project method here emerged as a central part of the Bennington curriculum. Leigh felt that regular classes would interfere with the development of individual and group arrangements for project work, and so the plan (never fully implemented) was to have *no* classes at the upper division. His claim was that "this is the medium in which self-dependence and initiative in intellectual or artistic work can best be promoted. These qualities are fundamental rather than incidental to the aims of the college" (quoted in Schilpp, 1930, p. 359).

Kilpatrick had placed a good deal of emphasis on student personnel work as part of a total educational plan. For his part, Leigh believed that "the Bennington curriculum, admissions system, and scholarship depend organically upon one another" (quoted in Schilpp, 1930, p. 365). One of Bennington's goals was to offer a place where graduates of progressive elementary and secondary schools could continue their work:

> The newer school program can proceed in a thoroughgoing fashion only up to the point where the college reaches down with its formal admissions requirements; from that point on the progressive schools have had to modify their own chosen programs in the interests of their students' immediate future. . . . There is needed at least one college . . . which by the nature of its entrance requirements will leave the schools free to teach what they think best. [quoted in Schilpp, 1930, p. 359]

Leigh's admissions goal was to attract young women of "serious interest and real promise in at least one of the fields of human achievement in which we offer instruction" (p. 360). Selective admissions would be accompanied by a rigorous counseling program aimed at identifying interests and needs.

Leigh also devised a community living plan which he hoped would create the perfect environment for reaching the instrumentalist ideal of education as a microcosm of society. Each student house was to have its own dining hall and be largely self-governing. Some faculty would have apartments within each student house, and other faculty would have an association of some sort with at least one house. Students would be responsible for budgeting, household management, hygiene, and other practical aspects of group living (Brockway, 1981).

This ideal was never fully realized, but the notion that community life should be an integral part of the total educational program, built on the same principles and objectives as the curriculum, was to have lasting influence. The College's administrative organization, its process for making and enforcing laws, and its organization of student activities all contributed to a general education objective that Barbara Jones (1946) summarized as "training in responsible citizenship, in accordance with the values of social and political democracy" (p. 125). Training in political democracy included learning how to elect intelligently, learning how to settle disputes, collecting facts and making decisions based on evidence, recognizing the proper role of government, and understanding the subtle relationships between the individual and the community. The training in social democracy involved teaching young women to manage their lives as adults, including taking responsibility as members of a social group, developing tolerance for people from other backgrounds, and so forth (Jones, 1946).

One of the more innovative ways in which Leigh reduced the differences between the curriculum and the extracurriculum, thus avoiding the dualism between schooling and work, was a midwinter break that evolved into the Winter Field and Reading Period. It was originally designed in part to help students and staff avoid the harsh Vermont winters and to offset the relative isolation of the college. But more than that, Leigh proposed that the period would give "students and faculty opportunity for travel, field work, and the educational advantages of metropolitan life at its most active season" (Jones, 1946, p. 205). Originally scheduled from Christmas to February 22, the winter period grew steadily in importance throughout the 1930s and, in the early 1940s, was transformed into a "nonresident winter term" (Jones, 1946, p. 212).

In many ways, the winter period came to embody two essential qualities of progressivism at Bennington. First, it was an opportunity for the student to learn through direct participation in actual life experiences. The period was not simply a break or a reading period; each student planned specific activities with her counselor. Activities included observation and practical work in courts, settlement houses, schools, and hospitals, as well as travel and research in major libraries, museums, and art galleries. The goal was not just that the student would learn "about" something or have experience in a new field or environment. Beyond the more traditional objectives, the winter period sought to give the student a gradual introduction into the daily responsibilities of adult life and work. In social studies, especially, faculty encouraged nonacademic experiences that would contribute to general education (Jones, 1946).

The other contribution of the winter period was its project orientation. Most assignments focused on some kind of project, ranging from field research to a job in a professional area. In all cases, the student was on her own, totally responsible for a concentrated, long-term effort on a single project. The reported benefits went beyond the "subject" of the project. As Barbara Jones (1946) noted, students had to learn to work without supervision and to integrate their work with family and social obligations. The objectives of self-dependence and learning to integrate professional and personal goals were important to the total general education program at Bennington.

The winter period was one of the most highly regarded innovations of the Leigh years. While early periods were criticized for the
indefinite nature of projects, a 1935 report noted that "an enormous
variety of individual projects and jobs, if carefully and conscien-
tiously executed, can contribute values to a young woman's college
education which she could perhaps acquire in no other way" (quoted
in Jones, 1946, p. 207). A later evaluation by Alvin Eurich, based on
appraisals of both counselors and the employers for whom the students worked, reported that "the winter period can be regarded as
highly successful in providing direct and concrete experiences outside of those usually offered by colleges" (quoted in Jones, 1946,
p. 210).

Bennington had its first opportunity to test its approach to
general education in the fall of 1932, when the first group of 90
students arrived. Before the first registration, faculty were advised
against announcing the subject matter of their courses. The idea was
that the title and content of courses would evolve in light of the
students' aptitudes, interests, and needs (Brockway, 1981). The radical approach of not announcing any course content did not survive.
Students, reported Brockway, "soon insisted that their interest
should be taken for granted, and lists of courses began to circulate
clandestinely, then openly, and finally appeared in the catalogue
under Leigh's successor" (p. 37). Despite the resistance of both faculty and students to the idea in its most radical form, the goal of a
curriculum that would respond to student interests rather than to a
preordained list of knowledge objectives continued to develop.

The project method also succeeded in practice. In the early days
of the college, most classes met once a week for 1½ to 2 hours,
leaving large blocks of free time for projects and for the writing of
papers (Brockway, 1981). Survey and orientation courses generally
were avoided, and textbooks were used rarely. Most courses involved the intensive study of a few works in a subject area; no
attempt was made to cover every topic in a subject. The goal was
Dewey's; it was, as Jones (1946) put it, "to distinguish between
learning something and merely learning *about* it" (pp. 23–24).

The faculty were organized into divisions rather than into the
narrower academic departments common by that time at almost all
institutions. In the beginning, some divisions consisted of only two or
three faculty who covered a lot of territory at the lower level. As the
faculty grew, individual faculty continued to act, in Jones's phrase, as
"general practitioners" (1946, p. 46) with the younger students.

The divisional structure had a decided effect on general education at Bennington. Unlike the academic departments at larger institutions, the divisions did not ignore general education; if anything, they took too much responsibility for it individually. As Jones (1946) reported, "The divisions became something like separate schools each offering rival *schemes* of general education" (p. 67). Each division tried to deal with general education in its own way, usually focusing on the general education of its own majors and adapting Kilpatrick's methods to the division's particular situation.

The visual arts faculty, for instance, had no difficulty in accepting the progressive maxim that one learns by doing. Faculty found an artistic counterpart to progressive education in the Bauhaus movement, which declared that the key to modern art and the experience of art was not the history of art, but the immediacy of exploration and discovery (Brockway, 1981, p. 116). These two elements—exploration and discovery—*became* general education for the visual arts student; the quality of the individual student's general education relied greatly on the student's own purposes and decisions about what to explore and where to seek (Brockway, 1981).

The idea of direct experience and participation carried over into drama and music, where the border between the curriculum and extracurriculum disappeared almost entirely. In Bennington's announcement for its third year, Leigh defined the major aim of music as the development of "musical taste and understanding not through mere listening and reading, but through a rich experience of participation and study" (quoted in Brockway, 1981, p. 157).

These programs defined general education entirely outside the context of subject matter. General education, in this division at least, was not concerned with knowledge per se, but with providing the students with experiences and helping them develop attitudes that grow out of experience. Brockway (1981) recounts the story of one student who "discovered the depth of her ignorance when she married a Harvard man who seemed to know everything. But she acknowledged, 'I had gotten something out of my education that was totally lacking in his: a sense of experiencing the thing we were doing with our bodies and souls as well as our brains' " (p. 139).

Subjects in the social sciences division ranged from child development to philosophy. Its approach to general education was to offer a series of small one-semester courses for both majors and nonmajors, while respecting the underlying rule of student interest. The result was a collection of small discussion groups on topics chosen by the students. The project method remained integral to the courses, with one group choosing as a project the formulation of a new code of postwar and mid-Depression values that they could accept. As with the arts, this approach caused some problems in terms of measurement. Nonmajors tended to do poorly in tests on economics and history but excelled in tests on contemporary affairs (Brockway, 1981).

Other divisions, though, took much different paths. Leigh's original idea for the introductory course in science was a course on scientific method. That course did not last the first two weeks of the semester; faculty went their own way, teaching separate introductions to their disciplines in a fairly traditional format. Within the major, however, the project method took firm root, starting with an introductory course for majors called "Science Workshop," which acquainted the student with experimental method. By 1937, the division was to rule that promotion to the senior level would depend on successful completion of a project that demonstrated the student's "interest and ability in sustained individual work" and that graduation would require completion of "a project in original investigation" (Brockway, 1981, p. 169). The successful participation in individual experiments and investigations became the goal of general education in this division.

The early catalogs said that introductory courses in literature would emphasize contemporary poetry and prose, "with stress on the reflection of present life and society" (Brockway, 1981, p. 173). By 1937, however, the literature faculty backed a proposal for "the prescription of certain literary landmarks in the introductory courses, against which to compare the modern authors" (p. 174), while the next catalog stated that students would be introduced to literature through "a few classics of English and foreign literature" (p. 174). These courses became a model for a major overhaul of the curriculum in the 1940s.

Leigh had hoped to create an institution that would allow progressive secondary schools to teach as they saw fit, without having to prepare students to pass entrance tests. In 1939, however, he found Bennington facing the same problem when it was denied accreditation because it could not prove to the satisfaction of the accrediting agency that its graduates were adequately prepared for further schooling (Brockway, 1981).

Nevertheless, Bennington students had done exceptionally well on standardized tests. During the 1930s, every Bennington sophomore class ranked in the top 25 percent of college sophomores who took the Co-operative General Culture Test. They scored particularly high in contemporary affairs, foreign literature, and fine arts. They were at the national median in science, English usage, and spelling, and were well above average in mathematics, English, history, social studies, public affairs, and vocabulary. As seniors, they continued to get high scores in foreign literature, fine arts, and contemporary affairs, and ranked slightly above the national average in science and mathematics (Jones, 1946).

Despite the fears of the accrediting agency, 61 percent of Bennington graduates from the 1930s went on to graduate studies and were able to compete successfully, even though their undergraduate preparation was, in the words of Alvin Eurich, "not along traditional pre-graduate lines" (quoted in Brockway, 1981, p. 223).

What the standardized tests were not able to measure were the *additional* benefits that accrued to Bennington students as a result of the total experience of living in the Bennington College community. Bennington's educational objectives were simply not based on traditional, testable areas of objective knowledge or skills, but on the aim of "developing people capable of continuing their own education throughout the years of adult life" (Jones, 1946, p. xiii).

This became obvious with a 1941 evaluation conducted by Alvin Eurich, who tried to apply statistical survey methods to the Bennington program. While he found that Bennington was successful on the basis of its own objectives, he complained that the objectives were not structured to elicit "measurable outcomes" and went on to make recommendations based not on Bennington's stated goals, but on a more traditional—and more measurable—educational paradigm. He criticized student appraisal as being too subjective; he suggested that the curriculum do more to promote an understanding of the past; he suggested courses in "home and family living and vocational adjustment"; and he worried that the students did not get enough physical exercise (Brockway, 1981). Some of these recommendations were at odds with the goals and methods of the college; to implement them would have meant a drastic change in philosophy.

Still, major changes were soon to be made. Leigh resigned in 1941 and was replaced by Lewis Jones, who had been a member of the original Bennington faculty and who was sympathetic to the college's aims. However, he gave a different interpretation to Bennington's mission, for at least two reasons. First, unlike Leigh, whose background was in educational psychology, Jones was a sociologist; hence he saw the mission in more social terms. Second, in 1941, Bennington was operating in a different world—a world that was once again locked in total war.

The major change was the introduction of a Basic Studies program. Its goals were announced in the 1942–1943 catalog:

> to make available to all students, in the most effective way, the fundamental language of each of the important fields of human achievement which together make up the western cultural heritage and the relation within it of specialized fields of the whole; and to bring up for serious common consideration the main lines of philosophical conflict which divide us, as well as those traditional values which unite us, as members of American civilization. [Jones, 1946, p. 86]

The Basic Studies program was to be concerned, as Barbara Jones (1946) wrote, "with education for citizenship in its fullest sense" (p. 86). In the midst of World War II, the emphasis shifted away from the individual and toward "a greater stress on common values and the kind of general education which relates the individual to the cultural tradition" (p. 86). Other elements of the Bennington program continued, such as the winter recess and the emphasis on the total college experience (the curriculum, extracurricular activities, and student governance) as a unified educational method. The emphasis on experience, however, was tied more than ever to a collective, social goal. In effect, what Lewis Jones did was to move Bennington away from Kilpatrick's brand of progressive education and more toward the instrumental approach developed by Dewey and Childs. The idea that education is "part of life" rather than "preparation for life" continued to frame general education at Bennington, but with "life" defined in a more social context.

Sarah Lawrence College

In 1939, *Newsweek* dubbed Sarah Lawrence College and Bennington College "Sisters in Progressivism":

> If any two women's colleges could be called sisters, they are Sarah Lawrence and Bennington. . . . Both are daughters of the doctrine called progressive education; both believe that the students profit the most by studying what interests them most—studying it not from textbooks but at firsthand. The two colleges scorn such academic institutions as examinations, rigid courses, marks, and formal lectures. Their girls can stay out at night as late as they think proper. ["Sisters in Progressivism," 1939, p. 34]

If Sarah Lawrence College had a lot in common with Bennington College, it also had a different set of circumstances and a slightly different orientation within the progressive movement—factors that had a decided effect on the Sarah Lawrence curriculum.

Sarah Lawrence opened its doors in 1928, the dream of a retired drug manufacturer who had decided to found a progressive women's college in memory of his wife. His endowment included a 12-acre estate in fashionable Bronxville, New York, which became the college campus. At first, Sarah Lawrence College was a two-year institution that attracted young women who lacked either the ambition or the ability to go on to a four-year degree. Its mission, according to one faculty member (Doerschuk, 1933), was based on the hope "that with greater freedom, more emphasis on independence and initiative, and greater consideration for individual differences, such students could accomplish far more in this junior college than in the freshman and sophomore years in the usual college" (p. 110). In 1931, the college, under the leadership of President Constance Warren, expanded to a four-year curriculum.

From the beginning, Sarah Lawrence celebrated individualism in much the same way that Robert Devore Leigh and his faculty did at Bennington. The two colleges shared a common philosophy that Constance Warren (1940) described this way:

> Its emphasis is on the individual and what happens to him or her in the process we call education. Each student, we believe, has within herself the seeds of what she is capable of becoming. The purpose of her college education is to enable the student to develop those innate powers to their utmost and grow into a mature individual, emotionally and intellectually capable of coming to terms with whatever life may have in store for her. [pp. 3–4]

The essence of a Sarah Lawrence education, said Warren, was

> individualized education, adapted to the different capacities, interests, and objectives of individual students, to the best of the faculty's ability to understand, recognize, and satisfy such differing needs. The curriculum must be flexible to serve individual ends, and cannot be considered as an end in itself or a straitjacket to fit all alike. [p. 5]

It also shared with Bennington an emphasis on the arts, a light course load to allow students time for more individualized study, and, equally important, a concern that the extracurriculum should be structured as part of the student's total educational experience.

From the college chorus to the bookstore, individual faculty were put in charge of the extracurricular institutions of the college community and encouraged to make educational use of them (Doerschuk, 1933). "All of this is the stuff of modern education," wrote Warren (1940), adding, "None of it is extra-curricular" (p. 7). In all of this, Sarah Lawrence shared with Bennington an instrumentalist philosophy that was flavored by Kilpatrick's student-centered approach. Like Bennington, Sarah Lawrence placed great store in student interests. Students and their parents were expected to complete detailed questionnaires as part of the admissions procedure, in part to gauge the nature of the student's personal interests and aptitudes.

But at the same time, Sarah Lawrence was moving in new directions, toward a curriculum more in line with the social reconstructionist view. Speaking at a conference in 1933, faculty member Beatrice Doerschuk noted the direction in which the college had begun to move:

> We have come to accept what is happening to the student as the sole criterion of the college; we have become more and more concerned with the question of what the enterprise is fundamentally about. We have come to a new idea of what progressive education is. As our philosophy has been tested out in practice, we have come to believe that what constitutes the progressive college is the degree to which it succeeds in continuously adapting itself to the changing needs inherent in the changing student body, and in the changing society in which the college is a factor. [pp. 111–112]

Certainly one thing that led Sarah Lawrence in new directions was its location. Its Bronxville campus was a short half-hour ride from New York City. While Bennington had to build a special field program into its curriculum—the Winter Field and Reading Period—students at Sarah Lawrence College had daily access to a community "laboratory." The problems of New York and its immediate suburbs became the testing grounds for the students' ideas. Students not only studied and observed the city, they took jobs in it and developed projects that involved them directly in the issues facing the community. In the process, the curriculum became more and more oriented not only to the individual student's interests but also to the relationship of the student to her community. Warren (1940) wrote, "The challenge we throw down to the student is: 'Look around you; what kind of a world do you live in?' The transcendent purpose is to help the student discover herself in relation to her environment—an adventure in self-discovery which may lead through time or space or both" (p. 73).

Students who enrolled in a psychology course called "Observation of Personality and Behavior," for instance, found this assignment awaiting them in 1933:

> Walk along 125th Street from the New York Central Station to Amsterdam Avenue. Turn down Amsterdam to Columbia University, then walk east to Morningside Drive. Take the bus to Fifth Avenue and 86th Street and walk four or five blocks along Fifth Avenue. Stop in drugstores as you go along to take notes. Write brief characterizations of ten people from different settings, using adjectives that seem to describe the essential qualities of each person. If you have your camera, take pictures to illustrate your observations. On returning to College, write full descriptions of four people who seem to illustrate significant or interesting types of personality produced by modern civilization. What aspects are most revealing? [Warren, 1940, p. 25]

In one case cited by Warren (1940), a student told her advisor that stories of Depression-era poverty were, in her opinion, much exaggerated. Her advisor arranged for her to work a day in a relief bureau. She noted several case histories and, over the next few months, returned to the community to verify them. The project was, in effect, an informal experiment in which the student stated a hypothesis, collected data, and tested the hypothesis against the data.

The formal curriculum was adjusted to give students more time for field work throughout the year. Classes were small, and there were no formal lectures or recitations, no textbooks, no examinations, and no grades. The college shared Kilpatrick's suspicion of fixed subject matter. The students were assumed to be adults, "with minds and ideas of their own" (Warren, 1940, pp. 12–13). The curriculum was to be flexible, in order to meet changing needs. That flexibility, noted Doerschuk (1933), "is defeated by a fixed curriculum of neatly defined courses which represent stated fragments of the field of knowledge" (p. 113).

Instead, the classroom aspect of the college's general education program centered around a collection of "exploratory" courses. All first-year students were required to take exploratory courses, but no specific courses were required. Instead, students were advised to take courses which they and their advisors felt best matched the student's interests and the individual faculty member's own personality, teaching methods, and viewpoints (Warren, 1940). All academic areas of the college offered exploratory courses. Their common mission, according to Warren, was

> the particular purpose of discovering as fully as possible and as soon as possible something about the students taking them, in what direction and perhaps to what degree they are educable, and how best to guide their future program. But they are equally important to the student in helping her to find herself, adjust to the College environment, and gain maturity of viewpoint. [p. 10]

In addition to their focus on individual student interests, the courses were structured around other instrumentalist concepts: discussions of contemporary issues, projects and work experiences, problem solving, and experiments. "Literature and Society," an exploratory course in literature, examined problems such as "women and the conventions of society" and "culture of social minority groups." Another used readings in contemporary novels to illustrate economic issues. An exploratory course in biology centered around the reproductive process and emphasized the use of the laboratory and scientific method. An art course focused on the artist's experience with a variety of materials and structures.

Classes consisted of no more than 10 to 12 students and met informally in weekly two-hour discussion sessions. In addition, each student in a course had a weekly individual conference with the instructor. The instructor rarely lectured but instead encouraged students to develop and defend their own ideas about specific topics. As there were no textbooks, students were encouraged to use the library, the community, and their own backgrounds to prepare for discussion.

As part of each course, students were required to develop individual projects on topics independent of their regular course work and to present and defend them to their classmates. One student, for instance, had taken the position that the Reorganization Bill then proposed by the Roosevelt Administration would seriously harm Congress. To test the validity of her conviction, she was guided to newspaper and magazine articles, wrote to Washington for a copy of the bill, followed its progress through Congress, and then wrote a 37-page analysis.

These individual projects, structured as they were within exploratory courses, had the element of purposeful activity that was basic to Kilpatrick's project method at Bennington College. But they were also highly structured and designed less to allow students to discover their own interests than to make the student confront her environment and begin to understand her relationship to it. The projects—and the exploratory courses in general—really centered around problem solving of the type integral to Dewey's instrumentalist philosophy of education. They focused on problems, especially social issues or individual attitudes or opinions, that served as hypotheses that the students then tested through library work and direct experience with the issue in the "laboratory" of New York City. At the end, the student would evaluate the original hypothesis against the lessons of direct experience and set a new hypothesis. The method of Sarah Lawrence thus tended to be experimental.

This kind of curriculum required faculty to take on new responsibilities. They not only had to be well equipped in their particular academic areas but also had to guide the individual development of their students and had to evaluate them not simply on their performance in a course, but on the quality of their total educational experience. The job required attention to the student both as an individual and as a member of the community of scholars. The instructor, noted Warren (1940), was a "strategic leader" for his students: "It is distinctly part of the job of the regular instructor to see that his group consolidates the gains from every such experience as it goes along. Without strategic leadership, too many of the values of free interchange would be dissipated" (p. 59).

Faculty member Doerschuk (1933) described the responsibilities of the faculty this way:

> They will be growing, developing persons themselves, if they are to understand and enhance the growth and development of students. . . . They will know that a student learns best where there is readiness to learn, and will adjust their materials and methods accordingly. They will recognize emotional hindrances to the full use of capacity, and seek to resolve them; they will help the student to recognize her own needs. In regard to method, these faculty members will be aware that education must be self-education—that the student herself must do the learning, and that the learning is the important end, rather than the teaching. They will . . . employ group discussion, individual conference, written report, informal lecture, observation, practical experience, library research, as suited to recognized needs. [p. 113]

Faculty also played an important role in student counseling and evaluation. Almost all faculty served as "dons" or advisors to a small group of students each year. The advising relationship was seen as "the core of individualized education" (Warren, 1940, p. 32). The don helped the student shape the first two years of her education at Sarah Lawrence. Initially, the don was an authority figure, but the goal was to shift the responsibility of her education to the student's own shoulders—the development of the student's self-discipline for continued learning. Here, again, the Sarah Lawrence curriculum was very close to Dewey's instrumentalism, which held that the educational process was one of continual growth, whose only goal was continued growth (Dewey, 1916/1944).

Sarah Lawrence College had avoided formal tests and examinations from the beginning; however, the faculty still had a central role in student evaluation. It included a checklist-type report for each student in a course; a central running record, in which instructors had the freedom to make informal, confidential comments; and written reports on student work, potential, and progress. The evaluation was not limited to "class" assignments but covered the overall experience of the faculty with the individual student (Warren, 1940). One goal of the evaluation system was to avoid competition for approval among students, or, in Warren's words, "to substitute the love of work for its own sake in competition only with oneself" (1930, p. 55).

The emphasis on the individual student's direct experience with and involvement in community issues was at the heart of general education as it evolved at Sarah Lawrence. Doerschuk (1933) described the Sarah Lawrence view this way:

> In accepting the student as the unit and point of reference in an educational enterprise, the progressive college recognizes that each person is fundamentally group-formed, a group member, and individual within a *community*, and is, therefore, concerned that the conditions of the community shall be such as will be conducive to the development of good individuals. [p. 114]

In fact, Sarah Lawrence consciously moved toward an increasingly society-centered approach to general education throughout the 1930s. Louis Benezet reviewed a series of statements made by Sarah Lawrence officials during the 1930s to illustrate how this trend developed. Here are a few examples:

> The liberal arts, today, are those studies that lead . . . to higher reaches of the imaginative impulse, to a more generous attitude toward society. (1930–31)

> A college situation of this sort . . . is no ivory tower where a student may retreat from "real life." It is rather a sector of real life where a student may secure the most adequate preparation for subsequent participation in and adjustment to a changing world. (1932–33)

> The common aim is for the development of social responsibility; a synthesis of work, recreation, social life; a sense of comparative values in the use of time. Freedom of choice is essential for the development of such responsibility. (1936–37)

> Colleges must be concerned today with educating young people for social responsibility. By which I mean educating them not only to an awareness of community responsibility but also to be active participants in the mainstream of democracy itself. (1940) [Benezet, 1943, p. 55]

This last statement was by Constance Warren, who also stated, "We must develop students who are in turn ready to think through and support their own convictions while respecting the views of others. This is the method of democracy. . . . It is the only method of developing the 'spirit of emancipated inquiry' without which there can be neither liberal education nor democracy" (Warren, 1940, p. 182).

The experience of Sarah Lawrence College represents a continuous effort to develop a general education curriculum rooted solidly in the instrumentalist philosophy, one based on the assumption that education for democracy must also be willing to use democratic methods. It was built on the basic instrumentalist idea of inquiry and experience as both the goals and method of education. Warren summarized these ideas in 1938: "One of the principles of which we are most convinced is that learning, if effective, must be desired by the student and must start from her own experience" (p. 72). Ultimately, she noted, "We think of education in terms of all the experiences which come to the student while at college" (p. 73).

Instrumentalist ideas also pervaded the administrative approach of the college. Warren (1940) wrote that "this college is seriously trying to find out how to educate and it has been willing to face all the changes necessary in the traditional pattern in order to do so" (p. 208). Under Warren, the school itself became a small laboratory for studying problems such as the effects of authority on young people, the effects of competition and failure, the question of what interests young people of college age, and, ultimately, "What educates on the college level?" (Warren, 1938, p. 74). The college functioned as a dual laboratory, on the one hand directing students to use the college community and the larger community as a laboratory and on the other hand using the college community itself as a laboratory for studying education.

Sarah Lawrence was able to institutionalize its approach to general education, so that its program survived beyond the experimental environment of the 1930s. Like Bennington, the social orientation was strengthened during World War II (although without the dramatic change that occurred at Bennington). In 1950, Warren's successor, Harold Taylor, wrote:

> The function of a college is to act as the creative agent of cultural and social progress. . . . The ideal college must be the model for a democracy. . . . It has the obligations of intellectual leadership when questions are raised. . . . [Its chief duty] is to help the student to understand his world and to take an active part in the conduct of its affairs. [pp. 17–18]

Sarah Lawrence College illustrates the key concepts that underlie the instrumentalist approach to general education: a curriculum that starts with the interests and experiences of the individual student; that helps the student to identify problems and goals and then to experiment with ways of reaching those goals; that is concerned with the future rather than with the past; and that has as its ultimate goal the student's continued education and her ability to change her community environment.

The General College, University of Minnesota

Most of the better-known experiments with the instrumentalist approach to general education developed at elite private schools in the east. Bennington and Sarah Lawrence were also new institutions, so they did not have to fight so much against the academic traditions to which the general education movement was opposed. Moreover, they were schools for women, which in the 1920s and 1930s implied a certain amount of freedom from the vocational orientation that already dominated most colleges and universities for men. Bennington and Sarah Lawrence were the kind of institution that the public had come to identify with experiments in progressive general education at the college level.

A major exception was the University of Minnesota, which opened its experimental General College only a month after Bennington College welcomed its first students in 1932. The University of Minnesota was a land grant institution. Like the University of Wisconsin, where Alexander Meiklejohn's Experimental College had just closed, it was committed to the land grant ideal of a university in service to society. The General College at the University of Minnesota shared many of the assumptions about general education that Bennington and Sarah Lawrence had drawn from Dewey, Kilpatrick, and others. But, not surprisingly, it applied the instrumentalist philosophy to its own situation, interpreting it to fit the land grant orientation, the research ethos that predominated in the large state universities, and the characteristics of the students that the university tended to attract and that the General College was designed specifically to serve.

Land grant institutions had been agencies of democratic social change since their inception in the 1850s. The founders of the General College brought to Dewey's instrumentalist vision an already well-established sense of the relationship between education and democracy—one that reflected the social egalitarianism of the state university movement (Cremin, 1961). This new perspective would stand out as a significant contribution to the general education paradigm.

University of Minnesota President Louis D. Coffman was the prime architect of the General College. Coffman was an outspoken advocate of educational equality during the 1920s and 1930s. He had a special interest in the waves of less-talented students who had come to higher education in the wake of the tremendous success of public schooling in the first few decades of the century. To Coffman, this issue was especially important to the state universities, which, he said, had been designed from their beginning to "provide freedom of opportunity" (Cremin, 1961, p. 314). As he told a group of educators in 1928.

> Long ago they learned that genius and talent do not belong to any class because of wealth or social position. . . . But they are not willing to condemn those of less talent merely because they have less talent. They propose for them just what they propose for the more talented—that each shall be permitted to progress as rapidly as his abilities will permit to the approximate limit of his attainment. The student of few talents will not be denied his opportunity while the student of many talents is given his. [quoted in Cremin, 1961, p. 314]

The problem was how to fill the need for a nonvocational general education within the environment of a utilitarian university.

Coffman formed a Committee of Seven to make recommendations on how the University of Minnesota should deal with this issue. Each dean involved in the committee brought to the concept his own ideas of the purpose of general education. One, a historian, wanted the program to focus less on the needs of individuals than on the need for society to have a commonwealth of citizens who understand social processes and how to assume responsibility for society. The dean of the law school saw general education as a "synthesis of learning" that would give lawyers-in-training a stronger background for their professional work, while the medical school dean was concerned that the specialization of medical training left students blind to the social consequences of their work (MacLean, 1951).

In June 1931, the Committee of Seven recommended that a new unit be created within the university. They proposed (unsuccessfully) that it be called the "Institute of Social Intelligence" (MacLean, 1951, p. 31). For awhile it was called the Junior College, but eventually it was renamed the General College since its work was so different from that of most junior colleges of its time (Cremin, 1961). President Coffman charged the new college with two goals:

> One, to provide for the study of individual abilities, interests, and potentialities of a very considerable number of young people whose needs were not being met elsewhere in the University; and, second, to experiment with a new program of instruction, a program which involves the revamping, reorganizing, and re-evaluation of materials of instruction with a view to familiarizing students more with the world in which they are to live and which uses techniques of instruction which have not been regarded as pedagogically respectable in many colleges and universities; . . . an educational program which will serve students who desire to come face to face with problems upon which they must exercise judgment later on. [MacLean, 1951, p. 32]

Malcolm S. MacLean was named Dean of the College. To him, the need to serve this special group of students was not simply a matter of fairness and egalitarianism; it was a major social issue. MacLean looked not only at the increasing rate of high-school graduation but also at the improvements in health care that had lowered the infant mortality rate, as well as at changes in technology that were beginning to affect the world of work. He saw in all of this the distinct possibility of intergenerational struggle in the future: "We can foresee . . . a time in the not distant future when the adult-youth conflict will become so sharp that the elders will have to refuse all employment to the younger generation until the age of twenty-five" (MacLean, 1934, p. 442).

He saw only three possible responses to the situation. One was another world war that would wipe out a quarter of the population. The second was a "sinister youth movement such as has led to certain intolerable phases of Nazism in Germany" (MacLean, 1934, p. 442). And third was "more education at higher levels for a larger portion of youth than has ever before dreamed of carrying study into early manhood and womanhood" (p. 442). He argued that this should be combined with more emphasis on civil and public works projects for youth who did not or could not go further. In short, general education was part of a broad new social mission for higher education. In the past, college dropouts were, in MacLean's words, "the waste products of higher education" (p. 443), but one purpose of the General College would be to determine if they might be better viewed as "raw materials" that could become "valuable by-products" (1934, p. 443). MacLean called his curriculum "*socialized* general education," the goal of which was "to fill a present social need, to keep pace with social change, and perhaps, if our jobs be done well enough, to help breed and accelerate change for the better" (p. 449).

Another, more immediate goal would be to counter what MacLean saw as the overspecialization of education. Setting aside the traditional departmental structure, he set up a package of 24 experimental courses designed to "give a sound, broad layman's view of a field of human knowledge and human activity, integrated in itself, and demonstrating its inter-relations with other fields" (1934, p. 444). The goals were twofold: first, to keep the courses *general* and second, to keep them *experimental*, so that individual courses could be dropped or merged if they failed to work. "All courses must meet one test. If they awaken interest and stimulate the students in the course to self-propelled exploration and study, they are standard courses" (p. 444).

In addition to its experimental quality and interdisciplinary approach, this initial curriculum had other traits that marked it clearly as instrumentalist. The courses were to be tailored to student interests, with the students having free election of these courses as well as access to the more specialized university courses, so they could follow through on interests. They also were very much oriented to the present and future. Wrote MacLean (1934), "We are experimenting to see if opening each course on the present will not so increase desire, strengthen motivation to learn, that a student will, in his self-propulsion, work his way back to the past" (p. 445).

The key to the curriculum was a set of comprehensive examinations—one for each of the four areas of concentration. A typical comprehensive examination would include five sections, the first three of which tested the students' grasp of the basic vocabulary, facts, and principles of an area of knowledge. The fourth section was "made up of situations to be analyzed, problems to be solved which the students have never met before; . . . for this the problems or situations newly confronting society from day to day offer valid sources" (MacLean, 1934, p. 446). The final section tested attitude rather than understanding and was used not to evaluate the students but the course itself. The program was continuously analyzed and evaluated.

Finally, the curriculum relied heavily on student counseling. It was not limited to the immediate concerns of academic work or career choices. The goal was to come to a better understanding of the student's overall personal and social goals and abilities, to help structure a program that was, indeed, based on student needs (MacLean, 1934).

For the 1932–1933 academic year, 625 students enrolled in the General College; by the end of the decade, the student population had grown to 1,114. All were subjected to intense testing in order to learn more about their home life, special aptitudes, recreational interests, social outlook, and personal goals, in addition to their academic work. Eckert (1943) reported the profile that emerged: "Most of these young people possess neither the types of abstract intelligence, the special scholastic aptitudes, nor the patterns of interests to permit them to embark successfully on the usual liberal arts program" (p. 64). More than half of the students who entered the college in a given year did not return the following year. Only a quarter of all students enrolled during the first eight years of the college transferred to another division of the university for upper-division work, and less than 1 percent requested that their transcripts be sent to other institutions (Eckert, 1943). For most of its students, the General College was the end of formal education.

This research gave MacLean and his staff a new perspective on what it was these students really wanted. The result was a major reorganization in 1938. The most significant change was the creation of four core courses dealing with basic life relationships: vocational orientation, individual orientation, family-life orientation, and socio-civic orientation. Students were able to choose up to three areas per year and two or three courses in each area. The goal was to acquaint the student with major problems in different areas of life

(Eckert, 1943). Typical students would take two orientation courses in the first year and, if they returned, a third in their second year (Thornton, 1940).

These new orientation courses reflected a new interpretation of the basic *social* role of instrumentalist education, a movement toward individual student *adaptation* to society, rather than the transformation of society as the driving force. For example, the "Individual Orientation" program consisted of three two-hour courses in Minnesota's quarter system: "The Basis of Self-Understanding," "Sociability and Recreation," and "Philosophy of Life." The purpose was "to provide students with opportunity to develop a realistic understanding of themselves in relation to other people and to the world in which they live, to the end that they may function more effectively and happily in those relationships" (Thornton, 1940, p. 236). The first two courses were fairly straightforward and factual, but the third-quarter course—"Philosophy of Life"—centered around a series of philosophic problems, with specific situations presented to the class for discussion. Personal counseling activities accompanied the courses; these included interviews related to term papers, diaries of individual students' "participation and enjoyment" in extracurricular activities, and a variety of individual activities (Hahn, 1940).

The "Vocational Orientation" core program consisted of two courses and a lab. In the first quarter, "The Choice of an Occupation" looked at the overall problem of vocational choice; one of its major goals was to increase the student's awareness of the need for advice and help from "competent sources" in selecting a career (Hahn, 1940). The second course, "The World at Work," classified the range of work activities according to the different talents needed for success and emphasized the interrelatedness of all areas of work. The "Vocational Laboratory" in the third quarter had no lecture sessions. Instead, students discovered job-getting techniques by actually applying for jobs and then analyzing their experiences (Wilson & Ylvisakas, 1940).

The "Socio-Civic Orientation" area consisted of two courses, along with a number of "contributing" courses that students could use to explore specialized areas of interest. The two core courses replaced 16 separate social studies courses in the original curriculum and attempted to emphasize the "fundamentally associational nature of modern society" (Wilson & Ylvisakas, 1940, p. 295). In addition, both courses stressed social dynamics, used problem-solving techniques, and used contemporary issues as the frame of reference.

The first course, "Contemporary Society," ran for two quarters.

In the first quarter, the course analyzed significant economic and social factors at work in contemporary society, with the focal point being American business. The second quarter focused more on the political aspects of modern society, interweaving politics, economics, and social problems. The emphasis in both quarters was to "relate larger problems of society not only to experiences and interests of students, but to their community manifestations as well" (Wilson & Ylvisakas, 1940, p. 297).

The second course, "Current History," ran for three quarters and attracted as many as 300 students per quarter. While the section size required more reliance on the lecture, the course tried to keep an instrumentalist approach. It used current news headlines as a "point of departure for interpreting and understanding past events and future developments" (Spafford, 1940, p. 299). The only required text was a weekly news magazine.

The final orientation course, "Home-Life Orientation," was based directly on data that emerged from student counseling. According to that data, many students felt that their problems in life centered in their family-relationship situations (Spafford, 1940, p. 301). There were three components to this program. In the first quarter, a course called "The Home in Present Society" dealt with topics such as "values which people most want out of life," "the effect of changing social conditions on the home," and "society's stake in home life." The course was required for the comprehensive examination, as was either one of the remaining two courses. The second course, "Maintenance Aspects of Home Life," looked at issues of family spending, setting goals, and so forth. The third course, "Human Relationships and Family Life," dealt with the individual's relationships with family and friends and with marriage and child rearing. In all three courses, the primary instructional method was class discussion, although there was also a project in which the student identified a person whom he or she knew well and then studied that person's family relationships (Cremin, 1961).

Even subject matter courses in the General College were designed to appeal distinctly to student interests and immediate needs. In psychology, for instance, course titles included "Practical Applications of Psychology," "How to Study," "Straight and Crooked Thinking," and "Biography," while social science courses included "American Citizen and His Government" and "Functions of Government" (MacLean, 1951).

As dean, MacLean wanted to create the sense of community that was essential to the instrumentalist view of general education;

however, he had to work under the limitations of a college within the larger university. The General College drew faculty from other academic departments of the university, and many students took "regular" courses along with their General College courses. There was a distinct danger of repeating the mistake of Meiklejohn at the University of Wisconsin. Since MacLean had little control over the extracurriculum or the general institutional environment, creating a sense of community had to be done through the curriculum, that is, through the instructional design of individual courses. The Minnesota curriculum emphasized the egalitarianism of the land grant university and its unique interpretation of the role of education in democracy. MacLean hearkened back to William James's concept that each individual is a "multitude of folk" and to the Shakespearean idea that one plays many roles in life (Cremin, 1961). As the descriptions of the courses illustrate, the goal became to integrate individual students with their communities, to help students play the various roles that society demanded of them.

By 1943, the General College had collected a massive amount of data on its students and on the new curriculum. Student evaluations ranged from enthusiastic to antagonistic. As Eckert (1943) noted, however, "When former students were asked whether or not they had gained greater understanding or skill in each of the four basic areas of out-of-school living as a result of their General College residence, they attached most value to the help they had obtained on socio-civic problems and on those relating to personal adjustment" (p. 154). At the same time, it was difficult to show student change as a result of the courses. Eckert noted, for instance, that "a year's residence in the General College effected no essential modification of social and economics views" (p. 156) and that, at the end of the freshman year, the students' tastes and social patterns were very similar to what they were at the beginning of the year. Since most students stayed only one year, it is safe to say that the impact was not significant, at least in the socio-civic area.

However, it is also safe to say that the long-term significance of the General College's contribution to the general education paradigm rested less on its success with individual students than with how it shaped what other educators meant when they used the term *general education*. As Frederick Rudolph (1962) observed, "It represented the state university's obligation to society at large; it underwrote the American commitment to the idea that in democratic America there were no failures" (pp. 478–479). In some ways, this was a natural extension of Dewey's instrumentalist vision; however, the college's goals could also be seen as a distortion of instrumentalism. The college was designed to help students adapt to society, while Dewey hoped to develop adults who could make society adapt to their needs. The college was designed to be an end to formal education for its students, while Dewey saw continued, lifelong education as an end in itself. Nevertheless, the General College model was widely imitated, especially by junior and community colleges. It became part of the public perception of general education.

CHAPTER 6

The General Education Paradigm on the Eve of World War II

The instrumentalist and humanist experiments in general education resulted in a wide variety of programs. There were fundamental differences between the humanists and instrumentalists, just as there were differences within the instrumentalist and humanist camps. While their philosophical roots differed—and, indeed, conflicted on some important points—their educational practices shared several key assumptions that were organized to achieve similar ends. These commonly held assumptions and the shared organization of ideas into practice are what, by the end of the 1930s, became widely accepted and understood as the basic paradigm of general education.

The most fundamental assumption of the new general education paradigm was that there is a direct relationship between education and democracy. *General education is concerned with developing the relationship of the individual to the community in contemporary democratic society.* There were many shadings to this essential concept among both the humanists and the instrumentalists, but both built their educational philosophies and practices around this fundamental relationship. Taken by itself, it can be interpreted very broadly. Robert Maynard Hutchins did just that when he tried to use the same broad relationship to justify the social relevance of his classical Great Books program. The statement, by itself, does little to distinguish general education from classical humanism or from any other form of education that is not obviously *against* democracy. What makes this assumption significant is the specific meaning that advocates of general education have associated with it and what they have done because of it.

The proponents of general education made a second fundamental assumption that helped define their response to the first assumption and which itself grew from the idea that education and democracy are inextricably related. This assumption was that *the needs of both education and a democratic society require a unity between educational aims and educational methods.* This was more than just a statement of educational policy; it was, to the general educationists, a fundamental philosophical statement. The philosophical issue was clear to them: You cannot achieve democratic ends by undemocratic means. The educational implication is that education *for* democracy must be education *by* democracy. It was the logic of this idea, paired with the basic assumption about the social purpose of education, that led to a new educational paradigm. In the process, a clear separation evolved between general education and the dualistic tradition of classical humanism.

These two fundamental assumptions about general education led to a number of other premises that together defined the paradigm by the end of the 1930s. One is that *general education is concerned with a specific society at a specific time and place.* This characteristic flows directly from the two basic assumptions stated above. It builds on the idea that general education should have a direct relationship to American society. It also is a logical extension of the idea of a unity between educational aims and means. If the aim of education is the further development of the democratic ideal of progress and social change, education must deal with the specific, immediate issues facing society. This concept is evident in all of the examples seen in the last few chapters, from Columbia's emphasis on contemporary civilization to Meiklejohn's (1932) concern with "The American mind at work upon the situation in the midst of which he is to live" (p. 14), to the use of New York City as a laboratory at Sarah Lawrence and the life-orientation courses at the University of Minnesota.

Building on the preceding premise leads us to another: *General education has a fundamental commitment to education through direct experience.* This was most evident in the project method and experimentalism of the instrumentalists, but Meiklejohn shared Dewey's use of problem solving as a methodology and, like the instrumentalists, tied that approach to an emphasis on, in his words, "local and contemporary and specific issues" (1932, p. 74). It is a specific response to the overall social purpose of general education.

Further, *general education is concerned with the present and the future rather than with the past.* Unlike the classical humanists, the advocates of general education were not concerned with preserving the best of the past but with making the future. This went hand in hand with the emphasis that general education programs of the period placed on specific, contemporary issues, direct experience, and problem solving. It was a natural extension of instrumentalism, but for the humanists, it presented a philosophical paradox that limited their ability to be consistent throughout their programs.

The experimenters in general education brought to all of these assumptions a particular definition of *democracy* that must be kept in mind if the paradigm of general education is to be understood and interpreted properly. To them, democracy was not defined by the institutions or the economic or international policies of a government. Rather, the only cherished tradition of democracy was the capacity of individual citizens to shape the future of society. With this in mind, their definition of democracy hinged on the relationship of the individual to society. They had a particular society in mind, one that (1) protected individual freedom, including the individual's ability to transform society as a way of establishing a more satisfying life, and (2) required the individual's willingness and ability to function in a community where certain values and assumptions are shared. The individual's ability to achieve social change is, in this view, limited unless she or he is able to work within a community of people who share the same values and goals. The precarious balance between the individual and the community had a special importance in the general education paradigm.

Both the humanists and the instrumentalists agreed that *general education begins with the individual and her or his needs and interests.* General education was not looked at as something that could exist apart from the individual, especially since democratic society itself was defined most fundamentally by the rights and needs of the individual. At the same time, they believed that *general education must have a direct relationship to the community,* whether it be the community of scholars or society at large. This is the unifying factor underlying the constant emphasis on the educational value of the extracurriculum at Bennington, the community laboratory concept at Sarah Lawrence, the involvement of students in governance at Columbia, and the "adaptation" approach at Minnesota. Alexander Meiklejohn's failure to make effective use of the total student environment at Wisconsin points to the importance of both of these concepts. The two assumptions cannot be separated.

The definition of the general education paradigm also involves a particular view of *knowledge*. Knowledge is not, in itself, an educational end; rather, it is a tool that, properly used, can contribute to educational ends. An education that (1) is dedicated to furthering a democratic society by developing citizens willing and able to transform both themselves and that society, (2) is committed to a unity of educational ends and means, and (3) is organized around individual student needs and education by direct experience could not separate subject matter from the other aspects of the process. William Heard

Kilpatrick was the most outspoken of the experimenters on this subject; when he fought against the use of "subject matter fixed in advance" he was not simply protecting student options, he was trying to establish a new approach to the use of subject matter that fit into the developing paradigm. The issue was not lost on the humanists—it was Meiklejohn who called subject matter "the permanent problem of a liberal education"—but they lacked the philosophical base on which to build a program that was not self-contradictory in this respect. As a result, the humanists never quite abandoned the classical dualism, and even the instrumentalists had a constant struggle to avoid it in practice.

Several closely related characteristics grew out of how general education responded to the issue of "subject matter fixed in advance." One is that general education, by its nature, tends to be interdisciplinary. The divisional structure at Bennington, Sarah Lawrence, and Minnesota, and the elimination of departmental requirements in the wake of Columbia's Contemporary Civilization programs all had as a goal the breaking down of the rigid departmental structure of academic life. The controversy over the interdisciplinarity required of Meiklejohn's staff at the University of Wisconsin illustrates the significance of this characteristic. Many educators came to see general education primarily in these terms; to them, it was an academic reform movement. However, the interdisciplinarity of general education is best seen within the context of the total paradigm.

Ultimately, the product of general education was not objective knowledge, at least not of the kind that would result from a "permanent studies" program like that of Hutchins. Instead, the goal was a set of attitudes and values, an orientation to the community—in Meiklejohn's phrase, a "scheme of reference"—that enables people to develop and test hypotheses, to experiment with their environment, to solve problems, to make the future by changing society.

Finally, *general education is characterized by the fact that it does not have an end outside itself.* This is not to say that it is a "subject" studied for its own sake. It means that general education is not preparation in the usual, curricular sense of the word; it is neither preparation for more specialized academic study nor for a particular vocation. The general education paradigm assumes, rather, that both the processes and benefits of an education must continue for life if that education is to be considered successful. Thus, *general education is an ongoing, lifelong education.* The process is meant to be self-sustaining beyond the formal college or university experience.

By the end of the 1930s, the experimenting had ended. The general education paradigm—its philosophical and practical characteristics—had become established. The question, after World War II, would be whether and how general education would be institutionalized in the postwar world.

CHAPTER 7

General Education for Democracy

The national mobilization for World War II brought an abrupt end to the experimental phase in the development of the general education paradigm. In the aftermath of the war, general education ceased to be an issue solely for educational philosophers; the debate over general education moved into the public arena. The general education paradigm was essentially in place. The new challenge in the postwar and Cold War society was how to institutionalize these concepts to meet what were perceived as crucial social needs. In the 1940s and 1950s, the practice—and to some degree the perception— of general education would be shaped largely by external pressures on higher education. General education would become a matter of social policy.

A Mobilized Society

If the American experience after World War II proved anything, it was that history does not always repeat itself. In the years following World War I, most Americans had wanted only to return to "normalcy," a state epitomized by the presidency of Calvin Coolidge. But prewar "normalcy" was not the goal after World War II. Instead, the society remained mobilized, in a state of ongoing preparedness for crises such as economic depression or renewed war, which many feared could break out at any time and undermine American society. This continued mobilization had a direct effect on how Americans perceived the need for general education and how colleges and universities responded.

Why were Americans not tempted to return to "normalcy" after World War II? Many, including the men and women who had fought in the war and worked in the defense factories for four years, had grown up through a decade of economic chaos. To them, "normalcy" meant a return to the Great Depression. They feared that the coun-

try would fall into another depression after the war, and their fear
was shared by most politicians, business leaders, and labor leaders.
Simply put, to this generation, there was nothing to go back to
(Robertson, 1980).

The experiences of the Depression and the world war set the
direction in which the postwar generation would take the country.
This was the first generation of Americans to grow up in a mobilized
society. The New Deal had introduced an unprecedented level of
federal involvement in society, and even that level had been dwarfed
by the total mobilization for war during the 1940s. The Depression
and the war had enhanced the power and influence of the presidency
and the federal bureaucracy. To the postwar generation, federal
intervention was nothing new (Grantham, 1976). They easily accepted acts of peacetime mobilization such as the G.I. Bill and the
Employment Act of 1946, the latter of which proclaimed "the continuing policy and responsibility of the Federal Government to use all
practicable means . . . to promote maximum employment, production, and purchasing power" (quoted in Grantham, 1976, p. 5).

Another reason for peacetime mobilization was the international picture. The United States and the Soviet Union emerged
from World War II as competing world powers. They came to see
themselves as defenders of their respective ways of life and each
other as the primary threat to that way of life. The United States
took on the role of protecting the *idea* of democracy throughout the
world. This new self-image and the foreign policy strategies that
accompanied it contributed to a new internationalism in American
thought, punctuated by America's role in the creation of the United
Nations on one hand and by the creation of the Central Intelligence
Agency on the other (Grantham, 1976).

The new internationalism also brought with it a more fundamental change. As historian Eric Goldman (1966) noted, the notion
that "the business of America is America" had long been a bedrock
assumption of American culture. Historically, Americans had
wanted to get on with this business with neither assistance nor
interference from other nations. In an international crisis, the American goal was to deal with the problem quickly and totally so that the
country could get back to its own affairs. This notion had been part
and parcel of the return to normalcy—and the defeat of the League
of Nations—after World War I. In the atomic age, however, quick
"surgical" action in international affairs followed by a return to quiet
isolationism was a potentially disastrous policy. The Truman Administration took a radically new approach. It responded to the "Soviet

menace" after World War II by putting into place a policy of containment. Instead of swift action, this policy proposed a series of complicated, subtle steps designed to contain the spread of communism and to protect America and its allies over the decades (Goldman, 1966).

The strategy of containment and coexistence—the Cold War—required ongoing preparedness, a continual mobilization symbolized by the transfiguration of the War Department into the Defense Department (Robertson, 1980). The defense policy was not simply the protection of the nation's borders, but the vigilant protection and expansion of an idea. International democracy became synonymous with the American way of life. The worldwide defense of this idea took on the proportions of a crusade. James Oliver Robertson (1980) put the situation this way:

> Instead of normalcy, what Americans have sought for themselves individually, and for the nation, is stability and security in a world they no longer believe to be fundamentally stable or secure. Consciously and unconsciously, they have sought and created an economic and moral equivalent of war. [p. 335]

This fundamental change in American values was accompanied by a rapid, radical change in the American demographic profile during the postwar years. One of the most significant changes for education was the "baby boom." After the war, the marrying age for both men and women dropped and the birth rate began a steady, 10-year increase. At the same time, the death rate decreased. While the total population doubled between 1900 and 1970, the older population quadrupled. Postwar prosperity made Americans more mobile, and this, along with the increasing demands for more freedom on the part of women, had an effect on the role of the family in American society (Grantham, 1976). At the same time, the boom in advertising, supported by television, democratized Americans' expectations, simultaneously giving the average American access to experiences and information previously reserved for the wealthy few, while reducing the value of firsthand experience (Boorstin, 1974). This situation resulted in sometimes unrealistic expectations of "the good life."

While middle-class America was striving to attain new, media-generated vistas and enjoying the vast new opportunities presented by the postwar prosperity, black Americans were beginning to demand their share of the American dream. The first student sit-ins took place as early as 1941 in Chicago (Raines, 1977). In the 1950s, black activism grew steadily. In 1954, the Supreme Court handed down the landmark *Brown* v. *Board of Education* integration decision. The following year, the 381-day Montgomery, Alabama bus boycott attracted national attention for the civil rights movement. By the 1960s, the movement would become a rallying point for a new generation of college students.

The decade and a half following World War II was a time of many contradictions. The general affluence of American life was accompanied by an equally generalized anxiety, brought on perhaps by the fear of atomic war or by the knowledge that the "good old days" were truly gone forever. The new opportunities and mobility of American life came hand-in-hand with ever-increasing change and a lack of stability in daily life. The new internationalism brought constant suspicion and fear of war; the Marshall Plan to rebuild Europe was followed in less than a decade by McCarthyism and loyalty tests.

Impact on Higher Education

These rapid and far-reaching changes in American life were not lost on American higher education. Colleges and universities became even more sensitive to external conditions after World War II. In the mobilized postwar society, many saw education as a tool of social policy. This perception transformed education to a degree that had not been seen since the Morrill Act and the emergence of state universities in the nineteenth century.

The central issue was one of access, and the catalyst was the G.I. Bill. This legislation had been passed before the end of the war with two ideas in mind: first, to assist veterans in their readjustment and, second, to reduce the risk of postwar unemployment. By the fall of 1945, 88,000 veterans were enrolled in colleges with federal support. That year, Congress widened the eligibility and increased the subsidy; by the next fall, well over 1 million veterans were enrolled in colleges and universities through a federal subsidy. Total American college enrollment at that time was 57 percent higher than in 1939. Veterans represented 57 percent of the total full-time enrollment; in the larger universities, former G.I.s represented 78 percent of the male student count. Many veterans did not come alone; they brought their wives and children, and in the process they changed the tempo and tenor of college life for many years to come (Lee,

1970). By the mid-1950s, over 2.2 million veterans had attended institutions of higher education (Ravitch, 1983).

The veterans cared little for freshman beanies and even less for dull, arcane faculty. To them, college was not a social interlude, it was a ticket to a good job (Ravitch, 1983), a job that would protect them from the "normalcy" of recession. In the June graduation of 1949, the average male senior was 24 years old; 70 percent of the males were veterans, and 30 percent were married. It was this graduating class that, in the words of Calvin Lee, "established the gray flannel mentality that was to dominate the fifties" (1970, p. 85). College became the ultimate economic opportunity for people of every economic group (Lee, 1970). The G.I. Bill, through largely nonselective subsidies, had broken the historic link between income and educational opportunity (Lee, 1970; Ravitch, 1983); it marked a permanent change in the role of higher education that would greatly affect the curriculum in years to come. The immediate questions for educators and social policymakers alike became, Who gets access to this opportunity? How long should students be supported? Should public funds be available only to public institutions? With these questions came another: What will these students be taught?

The example of Japanese higher education under the American occupation government provided one intimation of what was to come in American higher education. As one not particularly sympathetic observer put it, "General eduation at the college level, seen as an essential requirement of education for democracy, was foisted on the Japanese system by the United States occupation authority headed by General MacArthur" (Ben-David, 1972). While the U.S. Constitution prevented such direct federal involvement in American college life, federal funding—through postwar and Cold War programs such as the G.I. Bill and, later, the National Defense Education Act—had an enormous effect on how colleges saw themselves in relation to the larger society.

The General Education Movement in Postwar Society

The years following World War II were not good years for progressive education. Cremin (1961) points out three reasons for its decline. The first is that the followers of progressive education kept the reformist enthusiasm but lost track of the intellectual and philosophical roots of the movement, leaving its practices open to distortion and attack. Second, the tendency of progressive practices to move toward what came to be called the "life adjustment" curriculum—as illustrated by the General College curriculum at the University of Minnesota—came under sharp criticism from the postwar intelligentsia and provided a focal point for a generalized attack on progressive education. Third, progressive ideas and practices ran counter to both the solidly anticommunist postwar conservatives as well as a general public that was "ready for educational reform of a nonprogressive variety" (p. 343). As the Cold War took root, progressives were also accused of being soft on communism. The socialist sympathies of Dewey, Counts, and others (who had denounced Soviet socialism even before the war) were brought out as evidence. In general, the progressives' orientation toward social change did not sit well with the new postwar view of democracy. The progressive movement collapsed. In 1955, the Progressive Education Association closed, having lost much of its membership (Ravitch, 1983).

The same was not true of the general education movement. Joseph Ben-David called the postwar period the "hey-day of general education" (Ben-David, 1972, p. 72). However, given the changes that were under way in postwar society, it was not always clear what, exactly, one meant by the term *general education*. H. T. Morse noted that one reason for the continued interest in general education was its potential for democratizing higher education (Henry, 1952). However, Morse saw this advantage as a two-edged sword:

> The question of preservation of democracy with its attendant problem of the most effective way of preparing young people for their civic responsibility brings into sharp focus one of the most controversial issues in general education. This is a question of the extent to which a general education program should encourage reflective thought primarily or whether it should also concern itself with the specifics of social action. [quoted in Henry, 1952, p. 349]

It was an issue that came to affect all of higher education when Senator Joseph McCarthy's hunt for communists extended to academia. As Calvin Lee (1970) recounts,

> A pall was cast on the campuses, creating doubt as to how far scholars and students should go in discussing controversial issues. An atmosphere of general mistrust existed. One student of the period recalls that in his course in Contemporary Civilization, the professor ruefully pointed to the syllabus reading list, which contained the *Communist*

Manifesto. With a grim smile he said, "Go home, pull down the blinds, and read it." [p. 93]

The questioning, inquiry, and experimentation—not to mention the explicit goal of social change—that were at the heart of the instrumentalist approach to general education in the 1930s became dangerous ideas during the Red Scare period. The unity of goals and methods that marked the general education paradigm had grown out of the idea that a democratic education—that is, an education committed to progressive social change—must be accomplished by democratic means. This put the individual student in a position to control the direction of change. However, in the postwar and Cold War years, people began to define democracy differently. Democracy was no longer seen as a *process* that encouraged change; it was a political ideal that was to be *preserved* in the face of the communist threat. The focus was not on the individual's right to change society but on the individual's *responsibility* as a citizen to protect democracy, which was now identified with the *status quo*.

One of the most dramatic examples of this shift is Alexander Meiklejohn's *Education Between Two Worlds* (1965). Written during World War II, only a decade after his Wisconsin experiment with an education to "make culture," the book asserted that the needs of the state must have precedence over the needs of the individual and that concepts of freedom that in the past had been seen as *rights* of the individual should instead be seen as *responsibilities* of individuals in a democratic society. A state committed to human dignity and freedom, Meiklejohn wrote, "rests upon a social agreement that life shall be made reasonable. But such reasonableness can be created only by individuals who act for the state rather than for themselves" (p. 271). The goal of education should be the achievement of a common loyalty, "a fellowship of civilizing intelligence into which every human being, so far as he is capable of it, must be initiated" (p. 283).

Meiklejohn's was a radical position, taken in reaction to the horrors of fascism in the midst of a world war. After the war, however, other philosophers of the general education movement also recognized that a shift had taken place. They tried to reconceive general education within this new context. The result was a tendency to emphasize the role of general education in developing individual values and attitudes important to democratic society. This was not a new element in the general education paradigm, but it reflected a stronger emphasis on teaching values that supported the social conditions and needs under which education was to take place. The roots of this position were embedded in Dewey's instrumentalism. Near the turn of the century Meiklejohn had written, "The moral responsibility of the school, and of those who conduct it, is to society. The school is fundamentally an institution erected by society to do a specific work—to exercise a certain specific function in maintaining the life and advancing the welfare of society" (1920, p. 7).

The social reconstructionists tied this idea to the instrumentalist vision of a democratic society and of the individual. The most active advocate was experimentalist John Childs, who now called for a focus on individual values and morals as objectives of general education. In doing so, he argued against the monolithic view of postwar democracy:

> Democracy is a movement of plural moral meanings. We believe that the deepest of these is its regard for the worth of human personality. According to the democratic conception, individual human beings constitute the realm of ends, and all social and political institutions, including the state, pertain to the realm of means. One of the distinguishing characteristics of a democratic society is that . . . it has no moral purpose, other than the enrichment of the lives of individual human beings. [1950, p. 178]

Thus, while the moral responsibility of the schools is to society, society's responsibility is to the individual, whose enrichment is the ultimate end of both education and society. Childs warned against the growing authoritarianism of postwar education. Democratic society, he said, must not only be organized but *open*, by which he meant "a society that deliberately seeks its own improvement, not the mere perpetuation of the status quo" (p. 180). It is this openness, he argued, that distinguishes democratic societies from totalitarian ones and that also distinguishes democratic education from authoritarian education. To Childs, the postwar call for education to instill in young people predetermined values of specific institutions—business, the church, the government—negated basic democratic principles:

> It violates the conception that each person shall be treated as an end in himself; it also violates the principle that a democratic society is a free society, open to continuous change from within, not a finished, closed, authoritarian system, determined to maintain the *status quo* regardless of changes in life conditions. [p. 185]

Childs put these ideas into a practical context by referring back to Dewey's basic idea of a community of faith: "There should be no uncertainty about the moral right of a democratic society to use its schools to cultivate its characteristic patterns of conduct and thought in the lives of the young" (1950, p. 238). The key, to him, was the recognition that individual freedom is a *function* of a democratic community. Further, he argued, morality should not be taught as an abstract but as an integral part of life:

> We need a morality today that is actively concerned with the organization and the control of our industrialized ways of making a living, with the development of more just conditions for minority racial and religious groups, and with the modification of the role of the nation-state in an interdependent world equipped with scientific means of mass-destruction. [p. 266]

Childs translated the basic elements of the general education paradigm to meet the new circumstances of postwar and Cold War America. In practice, however, the new concern with values and morals would contribute to a growing confusion between general and liberal education; many would readily accept the goals of moral education, but apply to it their own assumptions and methods. Values, in the form of the Western heritage, had long been the province of liberal education. Looking only at the generalized goal of moral education, it would not prove difficult for some people to see liberal education and general education as being much the same thing.

Similarly, the emphasis on morals and values as a goal, when taken out of context of Childs's overall thesis and applied to the absolute values of classical humanism, would tend to move the focus away from the student and back to the authority figure of the instructor. Robert Crosen made this point in 1952 in a paper entitled "Contributions of General Education Toward Strengthening the Moral and Spiritual Foundations of Modern Society":

> The impact of the personality of the instructor on the student cannot be overlooked nor should it be. This emphasizes the importance of instructional personnel who have convictions, who believe that values can and must be brought into the thinking of the students. There should be reinforcement of values from instructor to instructor and from field to field. [p. 126]

The postwar period also saw a new spokesperson for general education. In the immediate postwar period, Earl J. McGrath was dean of the College of Liberal Arts at the State University of Iowa. He later served as the U.S. Commissioner of Education. From this position, he was able to have a great deal of influence over the directions that general education would take in the 1950s. McGrath, more than anyone in the period, was able to identify and articulate the common ground that united prewar and postwar ideas about general education. He recognized that, in postwar society, the challenges facing education were of a completely new character. As he wrote in 1952,

> The most critical problems with which contemporary education must deal are social, rather than physical, in character. They are rooted in the relations existing among men and societies, rather than in man's relation to his natural environment. Of transcendent importance is the problem of achieving a lasting peace with justice in a world torn between conflicting idealogies, one based upon the freedom and dignity of the individual, and the other dedicated to the supremacy of the state. Closely entwined with the urgent international challenge is the need to strengthen our political and economic institutions within a framework of democratic values, so that the United States can fulfill its moral and material responsibilities as leader of the free world. . . . The concerns which cause social tensions—widespread ignorance, poverty, economic inequality, disease, political oppression, and racial intolerance—must become the objects of concerned assault. [quoted in Johnson, 1952, p. vii]

The function of general education, then, was to train citizens for their individual responsibilities. As McGrath put it, "General education seeks to instill attitudes and understandings which form the essence of good citizenship" (McGrath, other names, 1949, p. 9). The emphasis was still on the individual, but within the context of social goals. McGrath differed from Childs in that, for him, the social goal was not necessarily always identical with the individual goal. General education, in McGrath's view, seeks

> to make possible the maximum development of the individual consistent with the general good, it encourages respect for inventive genius and tolerance for variations in opinion, while at the same time it rests on the principle that deviations in thought or in act must be based upon understanding rather than ignorance of the purposes, standards, and values of society. [p. 9]

McGrath saw the reality of a mobilized society. He found an institutional role for general education that maintained the basic elements of the paradigm within the context of the relationship between education and democracy as it was defined in the postwar world. This reconception would guide general education well beyond the 1950s.

The President's Commission on Higher Education

Access to education became an overwhelming concern just as American society was coming to grips with another issue: civil rights. The importance of both of these issues can be seen in two commissions that were created in the Truman years. The first was the Commission for Civil Rights, which made its report in 1947. This commission, noted Diane Ravitch (1983), marked the first time that the issue of civil rights was declared to be "not a Negro problem or a Jewish problem, but a national problem, a problem of bringing America's practice into congruence with its ideals" (p. 21). The second was the Commission on Higher Education. Its report, one of the most prophetic and influential of the century, at once illustrated the new role of the federal government in higher education and set goals for how higher education could be shaped to meet better the social agenda of the United States in the postwar period.

The President's Commission on Higher Education was one product of the postwar spirit of a new start in American life. It was appointed by President Truman in July 1946. His charge to the commission reflects the changing view of education that was emerging in the postwar years as millions of veterans crowded U.S. campuses and as people looked to education to play an important role in a mobilized, peacetime America. Truman wrote, "We should now re-examine our system of higher education in terms of its objectives, methods, and facilities; and in the light of the social role it has to play" (quoted in Kennedy, 1952, p. vi.). The commission, for its part, took the charge seriously. The six-volume report, published between December 1947 and February 1948, was titled *Higher Education for American Democracy*. As the title suggests, the report defined the purpose of higher education in social terms and then made sweeping recommendations for how America's colleges and universities could meet the new social challenge.

The commission tackled the access issue head on. It listed access as the primary issue and set increased access as a major social policy goal, viewing it as a projection of the existing commitment to public schooling. For instance, the commission recommended that

> by 1960 a minimum of 4,600,000 young people should be enrolled in nonprofit institutions for education beyond the traditional twelfth grade. Of this total number, 2,500,000 should be in the thirteenth and fourteenth grades (junior college level); 1,500,000 in the fifteenth and sixteenth grades (senior college level); and 600,000 in graduate and professional schools beyond the first degree. [quoted in Kennedy, 1952, p. 18]

The commission called upon colleges and universities to "become the means by which every citizen, youth, and adult is enabled and encouraged to carry his education, formal and informal, as far as his native capacities permit" and to "prepare Americans to contribute their utmost to the achievement of world order and peace among men" (quoted in Kennedy, 1952, pp. 34–35). To absorb the mass of new students, the commission encouraged the expansion of the community college as a "center for learning for the entire community" (p. 33).

The commission pointed to four reasons why mass access to higher education was "an increasingly critical need." First, noted the report, science and invention had transformed interpersonal relationships in work, in personal life, and in citizenship. Thus, "the increasing complexity that technological progress has brought to our society has made a broader understanding of social processes and problems essential for effective living" (quoted in Kennedy, 1952, p. 2). Second, the commission recognized that the ethnic diversity of the nation called for "a dynamic unity, . . . a democratic reconciliation, so as to make of the national life one continuous process of interpersonal, intervocational, and intercultural cooperation" (p. 2). This new domestic vision matched the new internationalism of postwar America. International peace, wrote the commission, required "a knowledge of other peoples" (p. 2). As its third and fourth reasons for mass access, the commission pointed to the uncertainties that accompanied America's entry into the atomic age. This brought with it two new responsibilities for higher education. One was for anticipating and preparing students for the social and economic changes that would accompany peacetime uses of atomic power. The other was for fulfilling "the need for education and research for the self-protection of our democracy, for demonstrating the merits of our way of life to other people" (p. 3).

In short, the commission called for higher education to "come decisively to grips with the worldwide crises of mankind" (quoted in Kennedy, 1952, p. 5) and for many more Americans to be educated specifically to deal with these crises. The commission set three goals for higher education:

1. Education for a fuller realization of democracy in every phase of living.
2. Education directly and explicitly for international understanding and cooperation.
3. Education for the application of creative imagination and trained intelligence to the solution of social problems and to the administration of public affairs. [quoted in Kennedy, 1952, p. 5]

It was a social reconstructionist vision that placed *general* education at the heart of the educational enterprise. Stated the report, "The crucial task of higher education today . . . is to provide a unified general education for American youth. . . . General education should give to the student the values, attitudes, knowledge, and skills that will equip him to live rightly and well in a free society" (quoted in Kennedy, 1952, p. 24).

Building on this social role, the commission established 11 objectives for general education:

1. To develop for the regulation of one's personal and civic life a code of behavior based on ethical principles consistent with democratic ideals.
2. To participate actively as an informed and responsible citizen in solving the social, economic, and political problems of one's community, State, and Nation.
3. To recognize interdependence of the different peoples of the world and one's personal responsibility for fostering international understanding and peace.
4. To understand the common phenomena in one's physical environment, to apply habits of scientific thought to both personal and civic problems, and to appreciate the implications of scientific discoveries for human welfare.
5. To understand the ideas of others and to express one's own effectively.
6. To attain a satisfactory emotional and social adjustment.
7. To maintain and improve [one's] own health and to cooperate actively and intelligently in solving community health problems.
8. To understand and enjoy literature, art, music, and other cultural activities as expressions of personal and social experience, and to participate to some extent in some form of creative activity.

9. To acquire the knowledge and attitudes basic to a satisfying family life.
10. To choose a socially useful and personally satisfying vocation that will permit one to use to the full [one's] particular interests and abilities.
11. To acquire and use the skills and habits involved in critical and constructive thinking. [quoted in Kennedy, 1952, pp. 25–30]

The objectives read like a catalog of social reconstructionist goals. As one might expect from such a commission, the objectives seem to reflect compromise among the various forces within the general education movement. They include a fair share of "adaptation" objectives, such as family life, vocational choice, emotional and social adjustment, and health. There are objectives that speak to the problem-solving emphasis that marked Dewey's thinking, as well as to the instrumentalists' concerns with scientific method and critical thinking. But there are also objectives that speak to the naturalistic humanists' goals and even some that could satisfy the more traditional classical humanist. What brings them together is that they all contribute to the *social* goals of higher education in postwar society: the "fuller realization of democracy in every phase of living" (quoted in Kennedy, 1952, p. 5).

While the commission's vision of general education includes much that builds on the prewar general education paradigm, there is also a significant difference. The general education writers of the 1920s and 1930s were writing from within the educational community; thus, the paradigm that emerged was an *educational* philosophy. The Truman Commission was recommending *social policy*. The two are not necessarily incompatible; the general education paradigm assumes a direct relationship between education and social planning. In this case, however, the distinction between educational philosophy and social policy is that the commission focused on the social *goals* of general education but paid little attention to the union of ends and means that was so essential to the educational philosophy behind the paradigm. While they saw general education as a means to a social policy end, the commission generally did not deal with instructional method. The one major exception is this statement regarding the objective of international understanding: "If the college were conducted as a community rather than as a hotel, it would afford much greater opportunity for students to acquire the practical experience so essential to the life of democracy outside the college" (quoted in

Kennedy, 1952, p. 26). In general, however, the commission's main concerns were with access to education and with outcomes of education, not with how students got from the first point to the second. The commission's position was that educational unity must come from "a consistency of aim that will infuse and harmonize all teaching and all campus activities" (p. 24).

The treatment of educational goals in isolation from educational means further opened the door to confusion about the meaning of general education. The commission itself contributed to the confusion with this comparison of general education and liberal education:

> Thus conceived, general education is not sharply distinguished from liberal education; the two differ mainly in degree, not in kind. General education undertakes to redefine liberal education in terms of life's problems as men face them, to give it human orientation and social direction, to invest it with content that is directly relevant to the demands of contemporary society. General education is liberal education with its matter and method shifted from its original aristocratic intent to the service of democracy. General education seeks to extend to all men the benefits of an education that liberates. [quoted in Kennedy, 1952, p. 24]

The debate over the commission's report was vocal. Robert Maynard Hutchins argued that the commission had not considered the social desirability of doubling the college population. The real need, he maintained, was not for increased access, but for "a moral, intellectual, and spiritual revolution" led by higher education (quoted in Kennedy, 1952, p. 89). This, in fact, is what came about, but not through the means that Hutchins wanted. James Bryant Conant of Harvard University saw the possibility of a return to a Jeffersonian vision of freedom of the mind combined with equality of opportunity (Kennedy, 1952), while Robert S. Lynd of Columbia University worried about who would define "democracy," given "the dilemma of American education, caught . . . ever more firmly in the vise of big-business power" (p. 60). Others debated the commission's prediction of a doubling of college enrollments, and Seymour Harris of Harvard argued that, by the 1960s, there would be "far more graduates than jobs" (p. 69).

But the general public's response was positive. *Life* magazine printed a full-page editorial that argued that access to higher education should be "a civic birthright" (quoted in Ravitch, 1983, p. 17). A 1949 Roper survey showed that 56 percent of the population be-

lieved that the federal government should finance a college education for worthy students of limited means (Kennedy, 1952). This
new egalitarian perception of higher education would have important ramifications for general education.

General Education and the Community College

The community college played a central role in the commission's
vision of an educational system equally accessible to all Americans.
The commission encouraged the growth of community colleges as a
national policy and called for careful planning on a statewide basis.
The community college was to be the expansion point that would
help higher education absorb the huge numbers of students who,
predicted the commission, would demand access to postsecondary
education.

The commission also encouraged community colleges to be comprehensive, to offer complete, self-contained curricula rather than
simply duplicate the first two years of a four-year curriculum
(Henderson & Henderson, 1974). These colleges should offer two-
year terminal degrees that would provide occupational training in
technology and the service industries, laced with general education
"for personal and social development" (quoted in Kennedy, 1952,
p. 33). The commission envisioned the community college as "a center for learning for the entire community, with or without the
restrictions that surround formal course work in traditional institutions of higher education" (p. 33). It would be, by definition, responsive to the needs of the local community, offering the specific educational experiences that its community required.

The community college movement had already begun to gather
steam when the commission issued its report. The first community
college had opened in 1901 (Henderson & Henderson, 1974), and, by
the outbreak of World War II, more than 200 were in operation
(Jencks & Riesman, 1968). Growth continued through the 1950s;
during the 1960s, when masses of youth, true to the commission's
predictions, were ready to descend upon college campuses, the
number grew rapidly.

For the most part, community colleges shared the commission's
vision of their egalitarian role. Jencks and Riesman (1968) defined it
this way: "A community college . . . is local, and it is proud of it.
Equally important, a community college is inclusive rather than
exclusive, seeking unity and solidarity rather than hierarchy and

exclusion, serving the whole population, not a select minority" (p. 481).

Its relationship to the community, its comprehensive nature, its purely instructional mission, and its commitment to lifelong education and to both formal and informal programs made the community college especially sympathetic to the general education paradigm. In the 1950s, community colleges in several states worked to develop an approach to general education that responded to this unique mission.

California took the commission's recommendations to heart and conducted an institutional study that became a model for other states. The California Study of General Education in the Junior College was suggested in the year that the President's Commission made its report, and the study was conducted in 1950. It was significant not only because California's community colleges at that time enrolled 53.8 percent of all public junior college students in the nation, but also because it dealt less with the theory of general education than with its practice in the community college. Its stimulus and its recommendations, therefore, were institutional.

The way California's community college system was organized had a great effect on how individual colleges viewed general education. The colleges—at that time called junior colleges—were extensions of the state's public school system; they were tax-supported and tuition free. The student population ranged in age from 15 to 80 years. Some were full-time students, while others were working adults attending school part time. They came from all economic backgrounds and from many cultural backgrounds; some were newly arrived immigrants. Most students saw junior college as the last stop in their formal schooling (Johnson, 1952). The study's director, B. Lamar Johnson, described the system this way: "In this state the junior college has more nearly become the people's college, the community college, than in any other section of the nation or of the world" (1952, p. vii). The purpose of the study, then, was not to redefine the institution or its mission. Rather, the reasons were (1) to report on what California's community colleges were doing in the area of general education, (2) to identify problems with the general education programs in the community colleges, (3) to encourage solutions to the problems, and (4) to recommend ways to strengthen the system's general education program (Johnson, 1952).

The study acknowledged the confusion that had begun to surround the term *general education*. It tried to find a working definition through conducting a general education workshop. Fearing that the workshop would become "fouled up in hairsplitting arguments over definition" (Johnson, 1952, p. 19), workshop participants agreed to limit the definition to a statement of goals and objectives of general education. They also agreed on six assumptions on which these goals would be based:

1. General education must be based on the characteristics of students and of society.
2. All areas of experience, at home and in the community, as well as in the college, interact to affect the student's growth.
3. The junior college will not complete the student's general education; rather it will aim to equip and encourage him to pursue the goals of general education throughout his life.
4. Students in California junior colleges differ greatly in experiences, needs, capacities, interests, and aspirations.
5. The general education program must promote the growth and development of each individual student on the basis of his particular abilities, interests, and other characteristics.
6. The final test of a program of general education is changed student behavior, motivated by the student's desire to improve himself and society. [Johnson, 1952, pp. 20–21]

With this set of assumptions in mind, the workshop members drafted the following statement of goals by which the system's general education program was to be studied:

Students in California Public Junior Colleges differ greatly in experiences, needs, capacities, aspirations, and interests. The general education program aims to help each student increase his competence in:

1. Exercising the privileges and responsibilities of democratic citizenship.
2. Developing a set of sound moral and spiritual values by which he guides his life.
3. Expressing his thoughts clearly in speaking and writing and in reading and listening with understanding.
4. Using the basic mathematical and mechanical skills necessary in everyday life.
5. Using methods of critical thinking for the solution of problems and for the discrimination among values.
6. Understanding his cultural heritage so that he may gain a perspective of his time and place in the world.
7. Understanding his interaction with his biological and physical environment so that he may better adjust to and improve that environment.

8. Maintaining good mental and physical health for himself, his family, and his community.
9. Developing a balanced personal and social adjustment.
10. Sharing in the development of a satisfactory home and family life.
11. Achieving a satisfactory vocational adjustment.
12. Taking part in some form of satisfying creative activity and in appreciating the creative activities of others. [Johnson, 1952, pp. 21–22]

These assumptions and goals were, for the most part, consistent with the general education paradigm as it had come to be known. Unlike the President's Commission on Higher Education, the study did not ignore the fundamental assumption of a unity of ends and means. The statements of assumptions and goals include several that deal specifically with (1) the value, to the student's growth, of all levels of experience; (2) the idea of individual student abilities and interests being the starting point for education; and (3) the use of problem solving. Moreover, the study emphasized that "these goals must always be interpreted in terms of behavior and of performance rather than simply in terms of mastering any given body of knowledge" (Johnson, 1952, p. 22).

The question now became, How were California's junior colleges—a diverse set of institutions serving an even more diverse student population—meeting the goals of general education? Not unexpectedly, the study found diversity in practice. It also found a number of structural factors that shaped how individual junior colleges responded to general education. For instance, California law required that students take courses in physical education, health education, English, American institutions, and the American Constitution. This affected the organization of the curriculum by mandating that colleges prescribe study in these topics, leaving other areas as electives. As a result, the study discovered, some general education goals were given limited recognition, while a few were totally ignored (Johnson, 1952).

The study recommended, first, that California's junior colleges adopt a distribution system to insure that all students would receive a balanced general education program. It also recommended that the curriculum cover eight subject areas. Three of these—communication skills, citizenship, and health—were already mandated by state law. The remaining five—personal adjustment, vocational orientation, family-life orientation, literature and the creative arts, and natural sciences—were to be supportive of the study's 12 goals, just listed. Finally, it recommended that individual college programs in general education include five characteristics: they should be designed to educate the *total personality*; they should be planned for *all* students; they should permeate the *total* college curriculum; they should take a *functional* approach in which individual courses and programs would build on the needs of the students and society; and they should include both required and recommended courses, along with other experiences, so that the total program would address both *community* needs and the *individuality* of students (Johnson, 1952).

The California study is noteworthy for the comprehensive role it advocates for the community college and thus for its curriculum; this made it possible for community college leaders to develop a new, comprehensive curriculum that was unique to the mission of the community college, thus opening the door to innovations. As a result, the eight proposed content goals bear little resemblance to the standard undergraduate disciplines in a four-year college; instead, they reflect the *functional* mission of the college to serve both the community and the individual student.

In Iowa, junior colleges also attempted to tackle the issue of institutionalizing general education on a statewide level. However, the situation facing junior colleges in Iowa was much different from that in California. Iowa's public junior colleges had been established by local authorities rather than as a state system. Their original purpose had been to allow local students to remain at home while beginning work toward a four-year college or university degree. As a result, the curricula at the junior colleges were dominated by the larger, four-year institutions; the content and method of courses tended to be carbon copies of those at the four-year institutions (Starrak & Hughes, 1954). There were few vocational or occupational courses, with the exception of some courses in business and commercial subjects and certification programs for elementary school teachers. Only the larger junior colleges offered any academic majors, and only one offered instruction for adults (Starrak & Hughes, 1954). Some Iowans felt a change was in order. As Starrak and Hughes wrote in their 1954 report,

> It is apparent that Iowa's junior colleges are not now serving the educational needs of those young people who wish preparation for entrance into certain occupations, directly following one or two years of post-high school preparation, or who are already engaged in some occupation and wish part-time training in it. . . . The administrators of our junior colleges would be among the first to admit that their institu-

tions do not serve adequately the current educational needs of all the residents of respective communities. The existing junior colleges can be made to do so only by expanding their curricula and service areas. [p. 8]

General education would be reconsidered as part of an overall plan to reorganize Iowa's junior colleges into community colleges sensitive to the occupational and vocational needs of local community residents.

The plan that Starrak and Hughes developed included specific recommendations for the curriculum as part of the overall organization of a community college system. They believed that the new community colleges should serve three primary groups: those who intend to go on to a four-year program, those who want a terminal degree in a vocational-technical subject, and those "who wish to increase their general cultural and social-civic competence" (1954, p. 102). The community colleges would offer four types of programs to serve these students:

1. The first two years of a four-year curriculum.
2. A terminal degree of "general cultural and social-civic education."
3. Vocational-technical instruction.
4. Adult education, both general and vocational. [p. 102]

General education was defined broadly as "instruction in citizenship, cultural appreciation and understanding, and healthful living" (Starrak & Hughes, 1954, p. 66). Beyond that, a few specific guidelines were given. Starrak and Hughes recommended that what they called the "principle of generality"—instruction in "citizenship, cultural appreciation and understanding, and healthful living" (p. 66)—should apply to vocational and other programs, as well as to the terminal degree in cultural and social-civic understanding. They also asked that the curriculum be flexible to meet local community needs and the needs of students. They called for the development of short, intensive courses as well as more traditional, semester-length courses and suggested that courses begin and end at times most convenient to the people who wanted to take them. They also recommended that the curricula accommodate both full-time and part-time students, and that cooperative work experience be built into courses where possible. Equally important for general education, they recommended that the traditional college entrance standards be abandoned and that the only entrance standard be "maximum service to all persons in the community by equipping them to solve their everyday economic, occupational and social problems" (p. 102).

These guidelines were formalized in legislation drafted to create the community college system. The bill stated that there would be no uniform, statewide curriculum prescribed by law. Instead, each college was to develop a curriculum designed to serve the educational needs of its residents. The curriculum was to be determined by comprehensive surveys of the four groups that were to be served by the colleges and adjusted to meet their needs and interests (Starrak & Hughes, 1954).

As the California and Iowa cases suggest, the community college response to the equal access issue brought about a new perspective on general education. There was an implicit relationship between the assumptions behind the mission of the community college (equal access and service to the needs of the entire community) and the assumptions of general education that made it possible for the general education paradigm to be realized in ways that the experimenters at Bennington and Sarah Lawrence could not have imagined. The significant change was that the community college mission blurred the distinction between the "student" and the "community." In California and Iowa, the student *was* the community. The requirement in Iowa that a community college survey its community and remain responsive to its needs is not significantly different from Kilpatrick's goal of starting with student interests rather than with fixed subject matter. It simply puts that component of general education into a closer relationship with the use of the community as a laboratory. This opened up the possibility that the student-centered curriculum and the community laboratory could be brought together in a new kind of unity.

These innovations moved community colleges onto the cutting edge of general education development. As the colleges continued to respond to local community needs in subsequent years—reaching out to adult part-time students, for instance—their contributions to community-based, individual-oriented general education would continue.

General Education at Harvard

The community colleges were not alone in trying to put to work the social reconstructionist goals of general education in the postwar years. As Joseph Ben-David (1972) says of that era, "The utopian idea that it was possible to create a synthesis of Western culture and impart it through a course in general education to all college students was widely acclaimed and accepted" (pp. 71–72). Like the community colleges, the four-year institutions were coming to grips with masses of new students; however, unlike the community colleges, they had to contend with their own history. A half-century after the research movement took firm root, colleges and universities were still trying to deal with two by-products of the research ethos: overspecialization and the professionalization of the curriculum. These longstanding issues would dictate the speed—and to a great extent the direction—of general education's development among four-year institutions.

However, the larger social issues defined the *purpose* of general education among the four-year institutions. In this sense, general education during the 1940s and 1950s was an institutional response to the problems of a specific culture at a specific time. Harry Carman, dean of Columbia College, saw the principle task of the College as "the training of youth for citizenship and leadership in a democratic society in a new world" (McGrath, 1976, p. 24).

Carman sounded a major theme in postwar general education at the University level: "To me, general education is that kind of education which provides a common core of knowledge and which stresses behavior in a free society in terms of motives and attitudes" (McGrath, 1976, p. 26). Florida State University, after an institutional study of its own, picked up the adaptation approach to general education that had been developed at Minnesota, but its description of general education carried Carman's themes to the state university arena. General education, said a Florida State report, was "that part of the total educational program which seeks primarily to develop in the student those skills, understandings, and attitudes, and that set of values which will equip him for effective personal and family living and for responsible citizenship in a democratic society" (Stickler, Stoakes, & Shores, 1950, p. v). Similarly, Harvard's James Bryant Conant wrote, "General education, as education for an informed, responsible life in our society, has chiefly to do with . . . the question of common standards and common purposes" (Committee on the Objectives, 1945, p. 4).

As these few quotations suggest, the social reconstructionist ideas about the *aims* of general education had begun to take hold at the university level. However, they also imply a change in the overall objective that was, in part, a response to the external pressures from a mobilized society and, in part, a concession to the older, more elitist, liberal education curriculum of the universities. The emphasis is not on the creation of citizens able to shape a democracy, but on citizens who recognize their *responsibilities*. The concern is less with personal values than with *common standards*. The balance between the individual and the community had always been a delicate one in general education; now the balance had definitely shifted toward community standards.

Ultimately, the social and philosophical issue of goals would be overshadowed by internal debates over method and structure. The real challenge facing the universities would be how to institutionalize general education concepts without endangering another delicate balance—that between research and instruction, which had helped stimulate specialization. At the university level, higher education had become highly specialized and departmentalized. Specialization and departmentalization had isolated the faculty from one another and encouraged students even in the liberal arts to focus on specialized, professional goals rather than on more general educational goals. These problems had been with the universities for years, but they took on crisis proportions with the rising tide of postwar students. For many university faculty and administrators, the real value of general education was less in its intrinsic philosophical and methodological unity than in its potential as a response to the problems of fragmentation and overspecialization.

Nowhere were these issues more dramatically presented—and the response more widely noted and imitated—than at Harvard University, where in 1943 President Conant appointed a committee to study general education. Harvard's concern for general education was a reaction to all of the forces, internal and external, that would play on higher education after World War II. The Committee on the Objectives of a General Education in a Free Society (1945) gave three reasons why the time had come for Harvard to look at general education. One was social: the ever-increasing complexity of modern society. But the other two reasons were more internal to education: "the staggering expansion of knowledge produced largely by specialism and certainly conducing to it; the concurrent and hardly less staggering growth of our educational system" (p. 5).

Specialization and the rapid growth of knowledge had made a marked impression on the Harvard curriculum. In 1940–1941, Harvard offered 400 undergraduate courses, none of them required. The committee described it as follows:

> This is, then, the present state of educational prescription at Harvard: one prescribed course in English composition for freshmen who cannot

demonstrate their proficiency; a reading knowledge in one of ten languages, ancient or modern; a freshman curriculum which limits, though not finally, the choice to about forty-six courses; a choice of concentration among thirty-two fields, many of them further subdivided; a prescription of general distribution so wide as to include in most of its sections the entire curricula of several departments. [Committee on the Objectives, 1945, p. 188]

This diversity was a natural outgrowth of the professional, research orientation of faculty at Harvard. By the 1940s, however, it had overpowered Harvard's elective system, which was based on the assumption that students would have free choice, but from among a relatively limited number of options. A student could choose whatever course she or he wanted and still, at the end, arrive at an education that contained in it basic elements common to all students. That, obviously, could not be the case if students had to choose from among 400 courses which were specialized in subject matter and professional in approach.

The issue of curriculum structure had taken on as much, if not more, weight as the social goals of general education. As the committee wrote, "We are faced with a diversity of education which, if it has many virtues, nevertheless works against the good of society by helping to destroy the common ground of training and outlook on which any society depends" (Committee on the Objectives, 1945, p. 43). The committee came to see some kind of general education as a way of achieving structural unity in the curriculum and of insuring that the curriculum would serve the "good of society." The internal issues were those of diversity versus unity, election versus prescription, and specialization versus a nonspecialized "general" education. As the committee grappled with these long-standing and by now quite basic issues of curriculum structure, traditional liberal education goals came to the fore.

The philosophical issue centered around Harvard's definition of *common ground*. The committee defined general education as "education for an informed and responsible life in our society [that] has chiefly to do with . . . the question of common standards and common purposes" (Committee on the Objectives, 1945, p. 4). This definition has some things in common with the instrumentalist approach. The major departure is that the Harvard definition focuses less on the individual's role as a maker of society than on common standards which an individual must learn and demonstrate in order to be a part of a community. The emphasis had shifted from the transformation of the individual to the protection of a basic democratic institution—the community of shared values.

This suggests a larger problem with Harvard's approach to general education. The committee looked at American society and saw two major themes: *heritage* and *change*. These themes were also associated with the two competing educational paradigms of liberal and general education. The general education program at Harvard was an attempt to reconcile these two conflicting ideals. The committee saw the problem as being "how to reconcile this necessity for common belief with the equally obvious necessity for new and independent insights leading to change" (Committee on the Objectives, 1945, p. 46). It resolved the dilemma by attempting to marry the "questioning, innovating, experimental attitude of pragmatism" (p. 46) with the traditional liberal education concern with Western heritage. "Belief in the dignity and mutual obligation of men," the committee wrote, "is the common ground between these contrasting but mutually necessary forces in our culture" (p. 50).

Harvard's definition of general education reflected an extremely delicate balance based on the belief that

> education can therefore be wholly devoted neither to tradition nor to experiment, neither to the belief that the ideal in itself is enough nor to the view that means are valuable apart from the ideal. It must uphold at the same time tradition and experiment, the idea and the means, subserving, like our culture itself, change within commitment. [Committee on the Objectives, 1945, p. 51]

While its discussion of *goals* showed a concern for balance between liberal and general education, the subject matter and methodology that the committee recommended demonstrate that Harvard had called, in effect, for a return to a liberal education that, in substance, was in direct conflict with the methods of general education. The committee summarized its view of the issues as follows:

> We must distinguish between liberalism in education and education in liberalism. The former, based as it is on the doctrine of individualism, expresses the view that the student should be free in his choice of courses. But education in liberalism is an altogether different matter; it is education which has a pattern of its own, namely the pattern associated with the liberal outlook. In this view there are truths which no one can be free to ignore, if one is to have that wisdom through which life can become useful. [p. 57]

The committee supported this authoritarian goal with an authoritarian structure: a much more prescriptive curriculum that undercut the original goals of free election.

The committee's approach to the issues of general versus liberal versus specialized education led to several conclusions. One was that the emphasis on individual freedom which marked both the elective system and the general education movement would be replaced at Harvard by an emphasis on the teaching of "liberal" values. Similarly, the attempt to unify "heritage" and "change" as equal curriculum goals would require not only that the curriculum be prescribed, but that the specific content and treatment of individual courses be carefully monitored. In short, "heritage" overpowered "change" when it came time to consider the content and methods of the curriculum.

Because the objectives of the program—the development of liberal values—were settled, the committee focused a good deal of attention on the structure of the program, which was proposed to be an elaboration of the distribution formula. The committee proposed that 6 of the 16 courses required for an undergraduate degree should be general education courses. Of these, all students would be required to take 1 course each in the humanities, social sciences, and sciences. And of these, a particular humanities course and a particular social sciences course were prescribed for all students.

The required humanities course illustrates how the committee's basic assumptions about liberal education versus specialized education shaped the approach to individual courses. The course was entitled "Great Texts of Literature"; however, unlike a traditional survey course it had a very narrow reading list. The method was "knowledge *through* literature, rather than knowledge *of* literature" (Committee on the Objectives, 1945, p. 205). It also illustrates how different the authoritarian method was from the student-centered method associated with general education. The emphasis was not on the student's freedom to pursue an interest, but on the central role of the instructor to become the "means by which the authors teach the course" (p. 207).

The committee also recommended a number of general electives in the humanities. These were not to be survey courses but innovative and, ideally, interdisciplinary approaches to the humanities. For instance, the committee called for a general education course in philosophy to be taken late in the college career of students "who have attained some mastery of another field of learning but who are beginners in philosophy" (Committee on the Objectives, 1945, p. 210).

Another of the required courses would follow a pattern associated with the general education paradigm. "Western Thought and Institutions," a course in social sciences, would be largely historical and theoretical and would follow the model of the Contemporary Civilization Program at Columbia (Committee on the Objectives, 1945, p. 217). For general education electives, the committee suggested comprehensive courses on "American Democracy" and "Human Relations."

The recommended science courses illustrate how specialization and professionalization had become part of basic liberal education assumptions associated with the traditional disciplines. The courses would be designed (1) to introduce students to basic concepts and skills in science and mathematics and (2) to provide more advanced students with science material related to their areas of specialization. The courses would combine lecture, laboratory work, and conferences and would focus on realistic problems facing scientists in one of two fields—physics or biology. The broad social goals are nowhere to be found.

The Harvard program was an attempt to strike a balance among three sets of forces. It attempted to reconcile the paradigms of general and liberal education by treating them as the educational counterparts to two aspects of democratic society: tradition and change. At the same time, it tried to offset academic specialization by encouraging interdisciplinary study, by distinguishing liberal education goals from the goals of professional education, and by presenting general education as the context for specialized study. Structurally, it attempted to guarantee that all students would receive an education in liberal values by introducing an element of prescription into an otherwise loose system of elective distribution.

The result was a series of paradoxes and contradictions that bear little resemblance to the general education paradigm. In trying to arrive at a compromise between social goals and academic preferences, the committee did its best to avoid a commitment to either instrumentalism or classical humanism and missed the spirit of both. The focus came to rest on the curriculum itself, rather than on its goals. It also set the stage for a running battle with the forces of specialization. By 1959, a faculty committee would weaken the science objectives so that any two natural science courses would meet the general education requirement. In 1964, there was an attempt to change the social studies requirement and reorganize the curriculum.

By 1971 any two *departmental* courses could replace a general education course (McGrath, 1976). In short, specialization reasserted itself, leaving in place few, if any, of the original assumptions.

Harvard's attempt to institutionalize general education illustrates the problems that many of the more elitist, four-year institutions had in trying to introduce general education concepts into an institutional setting that had developed around an entirely different set of assumptions. It reflects the dilemma facing the traditionally elitist institutions as they tried to respond to the democratization of education and to the new relationship between education and society that developed in the postwar years. While the Harvard program attracted widespread attention, it tended to accelerate the growing confusion between liberal and general education rather than to clarify the distinctions between them.

However, the Harvard program also reinforced several key elements of general education and redefined them in terms of the dominant curriculum structures of postwar higher education. Like Columbia, it allied the concept of general education with that of interdisciplinary study, providing a mechanism that would allow basic general education concepts eventually to be articulated within the departmental structure of the larger colleges and universities. It also made the case for four-year institutions that California and Iowa made for the community colleges: that general education should not be limited to the first two years of study but should permeate the entire curriculum, serving as a context in which other kinds of study took place.

The Harvard report was widely read and its recommendations widely imitated. Harvard's program was popularly identified as general education by many academics. Despite the confusion, the report had one lasting benefit: it gave the goals of general education a home, however tenuous, in the research-oriented institutions. This contribution would make it possible for general education to become diffused throughout higher education in the 1960s as social upheaval and a spirit of innovation prompted new experiments in general education.

Summary and Conclusions

The directions that general education took in the 1940s and 1950s reflected a change in how people defined democracy in the postwar years. The founders of the general education movement had seen democracy as a *process*, a way in which individuals in a community solve problems and create their culture. In the postwar years, however, not only educators, but others—including the public officials who would have an increasing voice in American higher education—came to see democracy as an *institution*, an almost tangible idea synonymous with the American way of life. Preservation of this institution became the goal of education.

This change in perspective had an enormous effect on general education. Many of the assumptions around which the general education paradigm was structured had grown out of the image of democracy as a process. To the instrumentalist mind, the processes of a democratic society had important implications for the substance or goals of that society; both process and substance were essential to an open society. A similar formula had been applied to general education. The process of the curriculum—the methods and procedures of instruction—had implications for the substance or content of the curriculum; and the two—process and substance—provided the central unity of the curriculum. The concept of the unity of ends and means—the idea that an education for democracy should be education by democracy—was both a philosophical and a practical result of a process-oriented vision of democracy.

The postwar vision of democracy as an institution, on the other hand, did not inspire as much concern for educational method. In fact, the institutional vision of democracy encouraged an authoritarian approach that was in direct conflict with the goals. While educators accepted the goals of the general education paradigm, they did not accept the means; they neglected the notion that the means themselves—the procedures of the curriculum—can have substantive implications.

The new community colleges recognized a connection between the institution and the process of democracy and developed a community-centered curriculum that made it possible to balance the interests of the individual and the community. Theirs was perhaps the major innovation in general education during the period.

Older, established institutions, on the other hand, tended to respond to the postwar issues within the framework of their own histories and their own institutional images. As schools such as Harvard tried to deal with the contradictory assumptions of general education goals and liberal education methods and subject matter, confusion between general education and liberal education developed. These programs became more concerned with the past than with the present and future; they began to place greater emphasis on tradition and heritage as ends unto themselves than on the use of the past to develop individual values and to solve problems; they looked more to the individual's responsibility to the community than to the individual's ability to shape the community; and they relied more on external authority than on the student's direct experiences to verify educational truths.

The confusion over general education was reinforced by other factors within institutions of higher education. The rapid growth in student enrollments throughout the period was a cause of constant concern to the established, more elitist colleges and universities. Some faculty began to equate the process-oriented goals of general education with the democratizing forces of mass education. At the same time, colleges were trying to deal with internal fragmentation caused by overspecialization; general education came to be seen by some as a countervailing force to specialized or vocational education. Others saw in general education a way of reforming liberal education, which had itself become professionalized over the years.

The structure of the curriculum also shaped the perception and practice of general education. Most four-year schools had, like Harvard, developed some system based on the distribution of elective and required courses. Just as general education came to be seen as a tool of mass education, it began to be associated with some degree of prescription, a means of insuring that everyone would get the *same* education.

What, then, had general education become? Clearly, it had become many things to many people. In many cases, however, it was being defined negatively, that is, in terms of what it was meant to replace rather than its own inherent qualities. In the final analysis, no clear, positive vision of general education emerged from the 1940s and 1950s. While there had been a retreat from some of the methods that had marked general education in the 1930s, no new ideas emerged to replace the general education paradigm.

Robert Belknap and Richard Kuhns (1977) look back on this period as a series of aimless responses to crisis. The 1940s and 1950s are best seen as a period when general education was a kind of safety valve that colleges and universities used to respond to a plethora of crises that preoccupied postwar society: the crisis of international communism, the democratization of higher education in America, the boom in American mobility, and the general crisis of a society facing a new world in which change did not always mean progress.

If the preoccupation with crises and the political constraints of the time did not permit the total concept of general education to be put into place, the times did allow some new emphases in general education to emerge. There was, for instance, a swing of the pendulum away from the individual and toward the community and a much greater awareness of the relationships among individuals, the community, and the college. The period saw a more sophisticated idea of the role of values as a goal of general education.

With all of the confusion, the basic *goals* of the general education paradigm found their way into the fabric of higher education, to the point where general education was no longer seen as a "movement" separate from the mainstream of higher education. What remained to be seen was if the higher education mainstream would ever adopt the means to those goals.

CHAPTER 8

General Education for Diversity

The postwar and Cold War periods were times of mixed blessings for general education. The sense of ongoing crisis that pervaded society in the 1950s stimulated interest in general education as an issue, but it also turned the curriculum away from the goal of individual and social change. The goals of the curriculum came to be the preservation of basic institutions rather than innovation, experimentation, and transformation of the individual and his/her environment. This change in basic assumptions and attitudes about democracy contributed to the growing confusion over the term *general education*.

Beginning in the 1960s and continuing into the 1970s, the pendulum swung in the other direction. Increasingly, undergraduate education came to focus on the interests of individual students and their responsibility for dealing with social problems, for changing the social environment. General education, as a self-conscious reform movement, was at a low ebb as the 1960s began. However, the new interest in the individual, combined with the diversity that accompanied higher education's response to educating the baby-boom generation, opened new doors. In the midst of rapid growth and diversification, the basic assumptions underlying the general education movement found their way into the mainstream of education. New approaches to the curriculum were built on key aspects of the general education paradigm and on instrumentalist concepts, but they were applied to the radically different institutional environment in which higher education operated in the new, postindustrial society. The image of general education as a national movement tended to be replaced by a diversity of specific programs that often had little in common.

Postindustrial Higher Education

By the 1960s, it had become obvious to some that the experience of the postwar and Cold War periods had wrought a change in higher education that was much farther reaching than even the President's Commission on Higher Education had predicted. The general shift in the relationship between higher education and society would help shape the direction of general education in the 1960s and 1970s. The key was that the line between higher education and society had become increasingly blurred; in some areas it had disappeared entirely. Clark Kerr argued that the American university in the 1960s was undergoing its second major transformation, the first being the result of the Jacksonian and industrial revolutions which had fostered the land grant movement. Kerr (1982) wrote, "Today, more than ever, education is inextricably involved in the quality of a nation. . . . The university has become a prime instrument of national purpose" (p. 87).

Kerr's view was widely shared. This new awareness of the role that higher education played in the broader society led to an interesting phenomenon: Academic researchers began to see higher education as an object of study in its own right. The 1960s saw a period of self-examination spurred by the blurring of lines between society and the college. With self-examination came an attempt by educators to gain—or regain—control of the institution, at the same time that other elements in society, including the students themselves, were also vying for control. The result was a self-conscious concern with curriculum that had seldom been seen since the professional educators lost control of the general education movement in the 1940s. General education again became a central issue within higher education.

Social Factors

In 1960, Adolf A. Berle, a professor of law at Columbia University, listed the issues that he felt would be preeminent in the coming decade. He predicted "an American moral crisis" and described it this way:

> Included in it will be a demand that Americans generally stop their self-indulgence, develop a far higher degree of personal conscientiousness,

accept great engagements toward common effort looking towards a
better civilization both here and in other parts of the earth. There will
be insistence on a new era of intense personal responsibility, resting on
every man, woman and child, in every expression of life. [p. 4]

The moral crisis would gather around issues that reflected the
changes society had undergone in the postwar and Cold War eras:
the civil rights movement for blacks and other minorities, protests
against the war in Vietnam, renewed demands for women's rights, a
new movement to protect the environment from industrial pollution
and misuse, citizen action against the use of nuclear power and
nuclear armaments, and public debate over a wide variety of social
and technological issues, from abortion to the institutionalization of
mentally handicapped citizens to prayer in the schools.

Many of these were not, essentially, broad ideological issues.
They were practical issues that affected local communities, neigh-
borhoods, and families. They called for individuals to face highly
personal, ethical dilemmas and to make decisions rooted in their
individual values. These issues generated a renewed concern with
the relationship between individual rights and community responsibility that reflected a growing frustration with the mobilized Cold
War society of the 1950s. With the abuses of the McCarthy period
still fresh in the national psyche, the nation became wary of big
government and protective of individual freedoms.

This dual concern with individual freedoms and social problems
arose at a time when the nation was entering a period of rapid
technological and social change that would challenge some of the
basic assumptions about social organization. Knowledge, as Clark
Kerr noted, had become the knowledge industry (1982). Computers,
the furnaces of the knowledge industry, began to play an increasingly visible role in our personal lives. In the 1960s, long before
anyone had imagined a "personal" computer, the fear of technology
was largely a fear that technology would take away personal freedoms. The tension between America's traditional individualism and
the latest product of America's traditional fascination with machines
was epitomized in the 1960s slogan, "Do not fold, staple, or muti-
late."

Colleges and universities played an uncertain role in this most
recent change. Traditionally, higher education institutions had been,
in Berle's phrase, "guardians of our intellectual dynamo" whose
mission was "to give definition, form, and intellectual leadership in

developing the new social concepts and the new measures we obviously need" (1960, p. 7). On the other hand, education had become, in Kerr's view, the engine of the knowledge industry, and the professor had become an entrepreneur (1982). Boyer and Kaplan (1977) captured the essence of the issue for the curriculum: "The college curriculum, no less than the individual, had to rediscover its identity in this wondrous and terrible new world" (p. 34).

Educators who tried to meet the challenges of a postindustrial education would find themselves working in an environment quite different from the higher education community of the 1930s. The university, for instance, had moved more and more toward an industrial or research and development model. It was, as Kerr (1982) noted, "a producer, wholesaler, and retailer of knowledge" (p. 114). Much of the research was being funded by the federal government, which meant that external factors were increasingly influential in selecting research topics and defining the speed and direction of specialization.

If the university had become a "multiversity"—Kerr's "city of infinite variety" (1982, p. 40)—it was also part of a much broader, more diverse learning society. Higher education had become "postsecondary education," an umbrella term under which gathered a growing variety of institutions, from vocational training institutes to community colleges, to public and private liberal arts colleges and, increasingly, corporation-based universities.

Similarly, the clientele of higher education had grown both in numbers and in the variety of people coming into postsecondary education. The baby-boom generation, the children of the veterans who had crowded college campuses thanks to the G.I. Bill, themselves reached college age in the 1960s, fulfilling the predictions of the President's Commission on Higher Education (Ravitch, 1983). Increasing numbers of women were attending college, and adult students were coming to college, either to get the education they missed as youngsters or to retrain for a new career. As the social reforms of the 1960s progressed, minorities and disadvantaged students began to arrive on campus in larger numbers, supported by federal funds. Each of these new populations put new demands on the curriculum.

At the same time that institutions were diversifying to reach new student populations, the curriculum itself was diversifying to provide the expertise needed to run the technological society. New degree programs were developed, including a vast number of associate degrees in technical and vocational areas; and new majors evolved to meet the need for increasingly specialized professionals to staff new social service professions.

Combined, these factors have contributed to an ever-widening diversity in higher education since the 1960s. For the most part, increased diversity has worked against the interests of general education by increasing specialization, further fragmenting the curriculum, and making it difficult to identify the commonalities that held together narrow areas of knowledge or the different "clients" that constituted the academic community. However, in some respects, these same forces created a new demand for general education. The knowledge explosion made it impossible to limit teaching to "facts"; the new need was for a contextual education with which students could assimilate and learn to apply newly generated knowledge to their daily lives as individuals, as citizens, or as workers. The speed of social change brought about an interest in educating people to control the *process* of change. Diversity itself provided a nonthreatening environment in which some elements of the general education paradigm could enter the mainstream.

Students and General Education

Many of these new opportunities were not evident as the 1960s got under way. A Carnegie Corporation study from the period reported that general education was in a state of disarray. Nevitt Sanford (1968) noted that "specialization has even deeper implications for the student; it contributes toward the fragmentation of *him*" (p. 199). Indeed, the students were increasingly disaffected with college life, despite the fact that, by 1970, one of every three college-age youths was enrolled in some type of college or university. For these students, higher education was no longer a privilege of the elite or a path to higher social standing. It was mass education, a necessity for many white-collar occupations and, for many students, simply another obstacle on the way to adulthood (Ravitch, 1983). It also became, for some, a symbol of bureaucratic authority and of the military-industrial complex (Kerr, 1982). The curriculum played a key role in student disaffection. The explosion of specialized majors, combined with the expansion of enrollment by the baby boomers, made it difficult to achieve a sense of community on a college campus. The increased student population also meant large classrooms, less contact with faculty, and less communication among students in a particular class (Ravitch, 1983). To the students, higher education was increasingly irrelevant to their lives and to the social problems that they saw around them.

Ultimately, a radical group of students took the underlying social goals associated with general education into their own hands as colleges and universities lost control over student life. It was a situation not unlike the creation of fraternities and literary societies as a response to the dry classical curriculum of the early 1800s. However, the students of the 1960s were driven not only by an irrelevant curriculum but by the urgent social problems of their time, issues that ranged from the rights of blacks to the potential for nuclear disaster.

The classic statement of the youth movement was "The Port Huron Statement," written primarily by Tom Hayden at the first convention of Students for a Democratic Society (SDS) in 1962. SDS eventually became identified with the most radical student factions, but this early document states the principal themes of the mainstream student movement. It is remarkable in its pragmatic approach; in many ways, it is a demand for a real general education that would strip away the long-standing institutional constraints. "We are people of this generation," it begins, "bred in at least modest comfort, housed now in universities, looking uncomfortably to the world we inherit" (Students for a Democratic Society, 1962/1972, p. 176). Their discomfort centered around two things: racial bigotry and "the enclosing fact of the Cold War, symbolized by the presence of the Bomb" (p. 176). They saw in society a fear of change and a general apathy that isolated the individual. As SDS put it, "The vital democratic connection between community and leadership . . . has been so wrenched and perverted that disastrous policies go unchallenged time and again" (p. 181).

The language of the Port Huron Statement was reminiscent of John Dewey and George Counts. It called for a commitment to that brand of pragmatism that guided the social reconstructionists and for an education that would be committed to nurturing the "democratic connection between community and leadership." Campus activism, which included both students and faculty, served to create a new sense of community within the universities and, to a great degree, forced higher education to take direct action on undergraduate education in order to integrate the general education concerns of the student activists. In short, extracurricular concerns invaded the curriculum, in the form of teach-ins, student-run free university classes, demonstrations, campus speakers, and demands for student participation in curriculum planning. These confrontations in some cases also led to new experiments to make the curriculum relevant.

A Resurgence of Pragmatism

The students weren't alone in wanting to place more emphasis on the individual's role in dealing with social problems and in fostering social change. There evolved a general shift away from the ideological emphasis of the Cold War and toward a more pragmatic, change-oriented approach. With the end of the McCarthy era and the beginning of the Kennedy and Johnson administrations, the country became more concerned with domestic affairs and especially with social reforms to help minorities and the poor. The resources of government came to be focused on problem solving and experiments in social engineering.

In addition, the rapid growth of technology was introducing new levels of decision making that some felt could not be left to the federal bureaucracy but which needed to be controlled by the citizens. One implication of technological growth was a change in the relationship between knowledge and society. In the past, knowledge, because it was held in the heads of a relatively small elite, had been the means to power. But in the new technological society, knowledge exploded and access to it became widespread. Professional knowledge in some technical fields went out of date every few years; new knowledge was being generated rapidly in all fields. The real test of education became not simply the acquisition of knowledge but the effective application of knowledge to solving problems. A concern with the process by which knowledge is applied became important to all levels of education, including professional schools, and thus moved some general education concepts to the fore in vocational and professional curricula.

Americans searched for something that would give a new context and meaning to the changes that assaulted them every day. Some saw in pragmatism a guiding philosophy for postindustrial society. John Smith pointed to three reasons why pragmatism was important in the 1970s. First, he wrote, the relationships among action, thinking, and knowing had become major issues in society. Second, certain aspects of technological culture raised the question of the relationship between science and human values. Third, pragmatism, as a philosophy of experience, had a direct relationship to

other popular philosophies of the day, including existentialism, phe-
nomenology, and Wittgenstein's demand that we return to experience for a "second look" (Smith, 1978, p. 9).

Pragmatic concepts went right to the heart of the new character
of the universities. Clark Kerr, who popularized the term *multiversity*
in the 1960s, later wrote that he wished he had read William James's
discussion of the "multiverse." James's pragmatic pluralism, which
provides for a degree of individuality and dysfunction within organizations and which sees many different levels and types of relationship among the parts of the whole, said Kerr, "may be taken also as a
good description of the multiversity" (1982, p. 138).

All of these issues and concerns were gathered by Alvin Toffler
(1970) under the general rubric of "future shock," or "what happens
to people when they are overwhelmed by change" (p. 1). Toffler
called for "education in the future tense," a curriculum in which
nothing is required "unless it can be strongly justified in terms of the
future" (p. 409). The times seemed to demand a second look at the
instrumentalist approach to general education.

Harold Taylor, former president of Sarah Lawrence, sounded
the call in 1960, when he argued for a shift away from the institu-
tion-centered, knowledge-based curriculum and back to a more so-
cial-reconstructionist approach. The problem, Taylor argued, was
not ideological but practical:

> The national purpose is to establish a just and peaceful world order in
> which we as the greatest democratic power take the leadership in
> democracy. We therefore need to concentrate our national attention on
> the proposition that a free society in a free world can only be achieved
> when our educational system has not only taught its citizens the skills
> and techniques necessary to run a modern industrial society, but has
> taught them to believe in the generosity of heart, the boldness of
> imagination, and the liberal ideals of a truly democratic philosophy.
> [1960, p. 46]

The following year, Charles Frankel made note of the essentially
student-oriented nature of American higher education: "The differences between John Dewey and his opponents are very slim indeed
when looked at against the background of other systems of education. Almost all American schools from the grade school on up have
tried to provide the individual with a special little microcosm of the
adult world" (1961/1970, p. 119). This is not to suggest that there

were no differences between the assumptions underlying the general education movement and those behind the rationalist approach to curriculum. There are very real differences. The import of Frankel's remark is that, in *practice*, Dewey's instrumentalism had been accepted by many educators, providing a fertile ground in which general education could grow.

Nevitt Sanford (1970) identified education with "the continuing examination of innumerable means-ends relationships, and of the origins and consequences of ends, so that our means may become increasingly effective and our ends ever more intelligently chosen" (p. 141). He suggested that general education be kept broad to meet the needs of the new professions for which colleges and universities were preparing students. As he put it,

> Education to produce good scientists and good men—that is to say, education aimed at developing the individual's potential as fully as possible—is in the best sense *general education*. Developing the generalist approach to inquiry, the synthetic function is closer to the mark; and so is involvement in significant experiences with people and things. But this is by no means all. General education aims at development toward full humanity, and all the resources of a college should be organized to this end. [Sanford, 1968, p. 197]

Sanford's goal was to clear up the common misconception that general education was simply synonymous with the lower division of undergraduate education. This was a widely held view among those who defined general education negatively—as the opposite of specialized education. Sandford aimed to reopen the door to a vision of general education as a comprehensive education.

These renewed calls for general education did not, however, assume a nationwide adoption of the experiments of the 1930s. The higher education scene had changed dramatically since World War II. While some colleges adopted a comprehensive view of general education, other new approaches were being shaped to fit the new diversity in higher education. General education could no longer be seen as a two-year undergraduate program. As McGrath and Meeth (1965) noted, general education in some colleges would focus on the major field and professional specialization and on the creation of new majors. The goal was not to establish highly visible new programs, but to work within the mainstream (Gaff, 1982). Especially during the 1960s and early 1970s, the emphasis was not on reform, but on innovation (Henderson, 1970), which in some cases allowed general education concepts to find a home in the mainstream. But innovation also added to the confusion by providing even more programs to which the general education label was loosely applied.

New Approaches at Columbia

Some of the implications of the new environment for general education were explored in depth at Columbia University, where the concept of general education had first taken root after World War I.

By the 1960s, Columbia's half-century experiment in the humanist approach to general education had come under pressure from the specialized professional disciplines. As early as 1954, Columbia College had abandoned the "maturity credit" system, which had allowed students to take a general undergraduate degree, and replaced it with a required major or concentration in one academic department. In 1959, the college abolished the requirement that all students take a second-year Contemporary Civilization course. It was replaced by a program that gave the student the option of two different terms or one continuous year of study in anthropology, economics, geography, government, sociology, Oriental civilization, or the old Contemporary Civilization course (Bell, 1966). The reasons for the change were many. The old course material was considered by many faculty to be superficial and out of step with new developments in the related disciplines. Few of the departments were willing to commit faculty to teach the courses. Also, the change made it possible for students in the social sciences to begin work in their major area in the second year of study (Bell, 1966). In short, Columbia's general education program was gradually succumbing to the pressures of professionalization and specialization in undergraduate education—the same pressures that had weakened Harvard's attempt at general education.

Sociologist Daniel Bell began the reconsideration of Columbia's general education program in 1966. His book, *The Reforming of General Education* (1966), focused specifically on Columbia's general education program but attempted to put it into a national perspective. He proposed some significant revisions in the general education curriculum based on his assessment of the role that higher education would play in what he called the "new national society" (p. 72).

Bell noted four trends in the national society that, he felt, should shape the university's approach to general education. The first was the evolution of a national economy in which different aspects of society were linked through government rather than through the commercial marketplace. In this national economy, the government was the major funding source for science and research. As a result, science had emerged as a political constituency in its own right and the university-based intelligentsia (the professional and technical talent that fueled the research aspects of the economy) had become a social class unto itself.

The second trend was the *knowledge revolution*, which, said Bell (1966), "can be explored from four angles: the 'exponential growth' of knowledge, the 'branching' of new fields of knowledge, the rise of a new intellectual technology, and the rapid expansion of research and development as an organized activity of government" (p. 74).

Third, Bell saw society becoming simultaneously more future oriented and more planned. This was something that was happening at all levels of society, from a government that was trying to anticipate new social needs and future problems; to corporations that were planning for future diversification and growth; to individuals who, for the first time, had to choose from among a wealth of career options, some of which did not even exist in the previous generation, and plan their personal futures.

Finally, Bell argued that, in the emerging postindustrial society, intellectual achievement would be highly prized, with the highest status accorded to research scientists, mathematicians, and economists.

Bell felt that these broad sociological developments had a direct effect on the university. As he put it,

> [The university] has come to be a quasi-public institution in which the needs of public service, as defined by the research endeavor . . . become paramount in the activities of the university. What is equally new is that the universities, like the economy and the polity, are becoming part of a national system. [1966, p. 88]

At the same time, Bell recognized changes that were occurring within higher education. Faculty increasingly identified themselves with their disciplines rather than with the institution. The emphasis on research gave increased power and prestige to the graduate school, with the effect that young graduate students who, a generation before, would have taught undergraduate courses, were able to "buy-off" teaching time with research money. The effect was that many faculty—and, at places like Columbia, a good number of students—perceived undergraduate education as simply a way station on the route from secondary school to graduate school.

Bell's assessment of the external and internal environments at Columbia suggests two things about the prospects for general education in the 1960s. First, society in general was becoming more hospitable to the underlying assumptions of the general education paradigm, since it was becoming more future oriented and more interested in planning for the future. Second, the strong central government had, in effect, created a national community. These developments were in harmony with the general education paradigm, which itself is future and planning oriented and is concerned with social issues facing the community. Internally, however, the university had become more specialized and more fragmented, with individual faculty less able to see how their particular specialty could contribute to the general education of the student.

The situation required that Columbia take a fresh look at its basic role in society. Bell (1966) summarized the situation this way:

> Each generation . . . seeks to discover its own entelechy and, in doing so, to renew history as the present and to reshape the past, to assimilate the received ideas and to choose those relevant to its concerns. In this regard, the university is in an anomalous position: it is called upon not only to conserve the past and reinterpret the present, but also to test the new. [p. 146]

This new social mission would directly affect general education. Bell believed that, in an era of mass education and narrow specialization, it was no longer enough to give the "prospective specialist" a survey of the humanities, a sampling of the major disciplines, or even more work in philosophy or the classics. The problem, he said, "is not just the lack of cultivation of the person but the increased narrowness of the intellectual tasks themselves. And this is not redeemed by making a man an amateur, a connoisseur, or gentleman in realms outside his subspecialized field" (p. 165). Clearly, Bell felt that the traditional distribution system or discipline-based liberal education curriculum would not meet the need.

Bell argued that the distinction between "general" and "specialized" education was, ultimately, a false distinction. The real need was to move beyond a knowledge-based approach and instead to focus general education on *method* and on meaningful problems and moral choices that students would encounter in their professional lives. He defined general education as "education in the conduct and strategy of inquiry itself" (1966, p. 188). He felt that this emphasis on method—on what he called "the modes of conceptualization, the principles of explanation, and the nature of verification" (p. 165)—rather than on knowledge would give the college a new and positive role in the national educational system:

> The college, standing between the secondary school (concentrating on facts and skills) and the graduate school (with its necessary emphasis on specialization and research), can exercise a singular function—the training in conceptual analysis in the grounds of knowledge, the criteria of theory, and the standards of judgment. . . . The college is the place now where a student legitimately begins his training in a discipline. But it is also the place where, unlike the graduate school with its concentration on narrow problems, it is possible to deal with the interrelationships of disciplines, and to apply these disciplines to general problems. [p. 181]

Bell went on to propose a revision in Columbia's general education curriculum, to allow it to assume this new role. The proposals had two objectives: first, to reorganize the existing general education program to provide a more unified lower-college experience and, second, to integrate the lower-college and upper-college curricula.

Bell's recommendation for the lower-division curriculum focused on a revitalization of the Contemporary Civilization program and a closer relationship between it and the humanities course work. By the 1960s, Contemporary Civilization had become structured around historical periods—the medieval period in the first semester and the Age of Enlightenment in the second semester. This required a great deal of reading, and the program tried to cover many topics in a single year. Meanwhile, the humanities program, structured as a two-semester great books program, concentrated on Greek and Roman classics and provided little historical context.

Bell's solution was to include an interdisciplinary treatment of topics from Greek and Roman culture in the first semester of the Contemporary Civilization program. The remaining two semesters would deal with European history; however, instead of a chronological approach, the courses would be thematic, organized around political, economic, social, intellectual history, with students being able to choose two of the three courses. Thus, *history* would be the theme through which the method of general education would be articulated. The fourth semester would continue to provide for an introductory course in a single discipline.

In the humanities area, Bell (1966) recommended that the readings be reduced in number and related more directly to topics in Contemporary Civilization. One goal of having fewer readings was to reduce the sense of "intellectual tourism" (p. 228) that accompanied the great books approach, but Bell also wanted to redirect the overall instructional objective of the course. He wrote, "The problem for the course is not only to make a student aware of a text, but of the scholarly context in which it arose; not only of his own sensibility, but aware, as well, of the emotions and responses to emotions the work has aroused in others" (p. 231).

The redirecting of the Contemporary Civilization and humanities programs would serve to integrate the lower-division curriculum. Bell felt, however, that general education required "vertical" as well as "horizontal" integration; this meant that general education should also function at the upper division. His most innovative recommendation was the addition of a "third tier" to the curriculum. Its purpose would be twofold:

> [first,] to deal with the methodological and philosophical . . . presuppositions of a field; [and, second,] to show the application of the discipline to general problems, or to issues requiring a multidisciplinary approach, in order to test the operation of the discipline in a wider context. These contexts . . . involve issues of value or of moral choice; and the explication of the value problems involved would be an added purpose of these courses. [1966, p. 257]

Each college division would offer its own third-tier courses, geared to the specific assumptions and problems of the individual field. There would be four kinds of courses: (1) the historical foundations of the disciplines in a particular field, (2) the methods and philosophies of those disciplines, (3) the extension of the disciplines to specific problems, and (4) comparative studies in non-Western civilization as a way of testing the generalizations and assumptions that grow out of the Western tradition.

With the third-tier courses, the nature of Bell's innovation becomes clear. His concern was that Columbia College not react against the directions in which the university was heading but instead find a logical, positive role to play in the new environment. His proposal for an undergraduate curriculum gives adequate room for specialized study but integrates knowledge-based specialization with a method-based general education that functions at all levels of the university. The resulting curriculum plan has four discrete but closely related components:

1. Contemporary Civilization and humanities, to provide a background in the history and traditions of Western civilization
2. An introduction to a discipline in the fourth semester
3. A major or concentration
4. The third tier of general education at the senior level, to help students take the knowledge they have gained through study in the major area and apply it to the problems that they will encounter in their professional fields

Bell's most important contribution to the general education paradigm was to abolish the idea that general and specialized education were inherently different because they had different knowledge bases. Instead, he made the point that the two were inextricably related, since general education dealt with the methods by which specialized knowledge is applied in the world. The effect was to free general education from being limited to the first two years of the undergraduate curriculum and return it to Dewey's concept of a lifelong process.

The activity that followed the appearance of Bell's proposals was cut short by the years of student activism and social protest at Columbia which began in 1968 and continued into the early 1970s. In the mid-1970s, however, the university's Committee on General Education returned to many of Bell's ideas and began to put them into action (Belknap & Kuhns, 1977). In the intervening years, some of the issues that Bell had raised in the 1960s had come into even sharper focus. In their report, Belknap and Kuhns noted the continued isolation of the disciplines and the need for the university to "provide the cross-criticism that can force narrow groups to bring their minds to bear afresh upon problems about which they have become complacent" (p. 34). They described the institutional dilemma facing general education this way:

> If a university abandons the traditional organization of its curriculum into disciplines and its teaching staff into departments, it is likely to lose the fruits of two centuries' division of labor; if it does not, it must devise educational instruments to keep students in touch with the historical, philosophical, sociological, ecological, and other implications of their work in their specialty. Failure to find such instruments can

lead to a generation unfit to deal with the complexities of modern life.
[p. 74]

This issue did not apply just to undergraduates, but to graduate
students, faculty, and administrators as well. Columbia's response
was to replace the undergraduate goal of general education with a
universitywide goal. General education was expanded to the graduate curriculum and to faculty and administrative training. Columbia's primary instrument of general education at the postgraduate
level is the University's Seminars program. Seminars are designed to
insure the continuing general education of scholars. As Belknap and
Kuhns (1977) observed, "Rather than letting our education end
when our training begins, the University Seminars shape the awareness of the teachers in a way that makes them particularly receptive
to the broader implications of their subject matter" (p. 58).

A University Seminar is an invited group of 10 to 30 people. The
group includes Columbia faculty, faculty from other colleges and
universities, and experts from any number of fields, such as politics,
industry, entertainment, and so forth (Belknap & Kuhns, 1977).
Several kinds of seminars are offered. In 1973, the Carnegie Corporation funded a series of Thursday General Education Seminars on
the nature, goals, and techniques of general education. The seminars
were attended by students, faculty, and administrators. In the following year, the seminars looked at particular courses or programs
and their potential for general education (Belknap & Kuhns, 1977).
In the third year, the fall seminar dealt with professionalism and
human values, while the spring semester focused on the teaching of
science and human values (Flexner & Hauser, 1979).

Other seminars in the professional schools also serve a graduate
and postgraduate general education function. In the medical science
area, for instance, a seminar entitled "Health Sciences General Education Seminar on Ethics and Values in Health Care" covers issues in
reproduction, behavior modification, allocation of health care resources, and death and survival (Belknap & Kuhns, 1977, p. 72).

The effect of these seminars is widespread throughout the university. In some cases, for instance, seminar proceedings are used as
texts in classes and in other seminars (Flexner & Hauser, 1979). The
effect is environmental; the interdisciplinary knowledge, attitudes,
and values that are generated among the graduate faculty eventually
affect research activities, graduate teaching, and undergraduate
teaching.

The Columbia experience in the 1970s is very revealing in terms of the potential for general education in contemporary higher education. It demonstrates how the spirit of community that marked Dewey's original instrumentalism can be developed in the complex, often fragmented "city of the intellect" of the "multiversity." It also illustrates a revival of the idea that general education is a lifelong endeavor and a process that, at its best, should pervade the entire institution—curriculum, extracurriculum, and administration.

Columbia is an excellent illustration of how the paradigm of general education has been adapted to fit the needs of a complex urban university. Other institutions, working in different environments with different traditions, took other approaches to general education during the same period. What marked general education in the 1960s and 1970s is diversity. Many programs were developed over the two decades. While they differ greatly, they also share key aspects of the general education paradigm. The remainder of this chapter will look at how general education concepts have been applied in different institutional settings and with a variety of knowledge bases.

Other Innovations

The curriculum innovations of the past 20 years both reflected and stimulated the tendency toward diversification that has marked higher education since the 1960s. In many ways, as we have noted, innovation has contributed to the growing confusion over the meaning of general education; the proliferation of curriculum models has made it difficult to identify common threads from which a common understanding of general education could be woven. Moreover, most curriculum innovations have been hybrids made up of bits and pieces of existing curriculum paradigms; hence, it is not unusual to find notions of liberal education mixed in with those of general education. Such hybrids sometimes have been the result of attempts to innovate without threatening the traditional, specialized, discipline-based mainstream.

Among the innovations, however, are some that attempted more comprehensive change. These innovations broke down distinctions between liberal and vocational education, between undergraduate and graduate education, between the curriculum and the extracurriculum. By breaking down old perceptions about instruction, these innovations made it possible for the general education paradigm to find a new home amid the diversity.

For some observers, there is a much more direct connection between innovation and the general education paradigm. They believe that the social and academic conditions that stimulated innovation are the same conditions that stimulated general education. Flexner (1972), for example, notes striking similarities between proposals for innovation in the 1960s and the instrumentalist approach. Among them are a high priority on the total development of the individual student, a concern with the present social context and the student's ability to function in society, an emphasis on interdisciplinary study as a means of achieving problem-oriented instruction, a desire for extra-institutional experience, a call to restructure the curriculum to provide for greater student input and more faculty-student cooperation, an emphasis on faculty commitment to teaching and student development, and a call for changes in graduate education and training of college teachers. Flexner concludes,

> Curricular and structural reforms and innovations during the preceding two or three decades, and especially in recent years, may be viewed as a continuation and expansion of general education. I suggest that we are witnessing, if not the fullest development of general education— one hopes that further reforms are on the way—then at least a fuller one than before. [p. 56]

Algo Henderson, who served on the President's Commission on Higher Education, is also a spokesperson for this point of view. To him, the thrust toward innovation was directly tied to the need for social change—and especially to the demands of students—as society entered "the first and painful stages in the emergence of postindustrial society" (Henderson, 1970, p. 4). He frames his ideas about innovation with several assumptions that dovetail neatly with the general education paradigm of the 1930s. The most basic of these assumptions is that "social change is a means of achieving the democratic ideal" (p. 4). From this base, Henderson's philosophy of education builds on the now-familiar propositions that (1) higher education in a democracy inevitably concerns the "fulfillment of individual and societal needs" (p. 4), (2) a democratic society has a responsibility to solve problems, and (3) the individual must have an environment that makes it possible "to create a good life for himself" (p. 6). His view of general education attempts to consolidate the pragmatism of the instrumentalist approach, the social orientation of the postwar period, and the values and problem orientation that became increasingly important in the 1960s. He and Jean Henderson defined a general education as one that "attempts to analyze the functions of man in life today and the aspects of knowledge that should facilitate the performance of these functions" (Henderson & Henderson, 1974, p. 83). They list eight basic objectives for general education:

1. To retrieve a unity of knowledge for the student, . . . to assist the student to relate the part to the whole.
2. To enable the student to acquire intellectual competencies, such as skill in critical thinking and in communication.
3. To select the most significant knowledge that has accumulated through men's past experience and thus assist the student in finding his way in the morass of available materials. In part, the objective is also to break away from the use of sequentially oriented introductory courses in specific knowledge areas as the units for a curriculum in general education.
4. To provide a historical perspective of our civilization and of world cultures; to get away from the past tendency of liberal education to confine itself to Western culture.
5. To acquaint a student with and to stimulate his interest in the environment, physical and social, in which he lives; to prepare him for effective living in a complex world, the events of which are increasingly influenced by the advances being made in science and technology.
6. To help the student relate his education to living today, to his occupation, his family life, his community activities, and his endeavors to lead a richer life; to make culture functional in relation to his living rather than leisure-time sophistication.
7. To provide the student with a framework of knowledge into which he can fit his special intellectual and occupational interests; to assist him in achieving a social conscience and a mature philosophy of life.
8. To make general education an essential part of the education of everyone in a democratic society rather than the privilege of a few, so that there may be some common understandings about historical directions and ethical bases for the conduct of individuals and the ordering of society. [pp. 83–84]

Like many of the innovations of the period, these criteria draw upon some aspects of the general education paradigm but ignore others. They represent a change from the postwar President's Commission report (see Kennedy, 1952) in some respects, notably in the greater emphasis on the individual student. However, they also retain some of the commission's basic attitudes. For instance, Henderson and Henderson (1974) deal very little with the means/ends unity that marks the instrumentalist approach. Instead, these objectives seek a unity between knowledge and the *use* of knowledge. Herein lies a fine point, for while Henderson and Henderson list objectives that are oriented to the product of education rather than the process, the product itself is not knowledge but the functional use of knowledge; that is, the product *is* the process. Where Henderson and Henderson differ from Dewey, Childs, and the other instrumentalists is that, unlike the latters' means/ends unity, Henderson and Henderson's product/process unity does not dictate the method of instruction.

Henderson and Henderson's objectives (1974) are a good synthesis of how general education developed through a wide range of innovations since the 1960s. These innovations have taken many forms. Some, such as interdisciplinary study, student-centered curricula, thematic approaches, differently "layered" curricula that combine general and specialized education in new ways, have experimented with the structure and subject matter of the curriculum. Others have focused on the new clientele of postsecondary education or on the use of new technologies. Not all of these innovations have contributed to the development of the general education paradigm; indeed, most could not be seen as general education at all. However, among the innovations of recent years are a good many that draw upon some aspects of the general education paradigm and some that add new perspectives on the paradigm as they adapt it to contemporary needs. The examples that follow in the next sections will serve to illustrate the ways in which basic concepts of general education have found a home in an environment of diversity.

New Instrumentalist Experiments

Among the innovations of the last 20 years has been a new interest in the student-centered curriculum on the models of Bennington and Sarah Lawrence. The newer programs, though, are not simply a revival of Dewey and Kilpatrick. Rather, they are a response to recent research in how students learn and, in particular, the emergence of a *developmental theory* of student learning. However, the principles of developmental theory, as identified by Joseph Katz, have grown out of the work of the instrumentalists. For example, Katz discovered (1) that students learn best if their studies contribute to the achievement of their personal and vocational identity and the creation of a satisfactory lifestyle; (2) that the student should participate in the planning and execution of learning; (3) that learning must be useful to the student and others—that is, the "product" should be more than a grade; and (4) that cognitive learning should be tied to other developmental tasks (Henderson & Henderson, 1974).

Flexner (1972) noted the relevance of developmental theory—especially Erikson's stages of maturation and Marcia's four states of ego identity—to the needs of students who had entered postsecondary education as a result of the postwar growth of community colleges. The majority of these students, he said, came to college with poor academic records. Having failed to succeed in traditional classroom settings, these students needed experiences that responded to their unique strengths and weaknesses. He cited Henry and Renaud's conclusions that most college curricula deal with only one of Marcia's four stages of development.

As President of Antioch College, Algo Henderson had applied developmental theory to an extension of the college's famed work-study program. The goal was to mix general and vocational elements of the curriculum and to relate both to an actual work situation. Under this plan, work and study become mutually supportive; the student's work experience becomes a motivating force for more academic study, and at the same time the results of academic study can be applied directly to "real-world" experience (Henderson, 1970).

The implications of developmental theory for general education are even more clear at Hampshire College. Hampshire's curriculum is based on the idea that "the most important contribution a college can make to its students is to develop in them a capacity to continue their education throughout their lives" (Simmons, 1982). The original goal of Hampshire College was to help students acquire the tools needed to build both personal lives and society. As noted by Franklin Patterson and Charles Longworth, "The most continually experimental thing about Hampshire College will be its constant effort, in collaboration with its students, to discern what these tools are and how best they may come to fit one's hand" (quoted in Simmons, 1982, pp. 5-6).

The Hampshire College curriculum, by the early 1980s, consisted of three divisions: a "basic studies" division for first-year students that included seminars on topics ranging from "Nutrition and Fitness" to "Innovation and Social Change"; an upper-division concentration or major; and a third-tier-type program for which the student is expected to develop a major independent project or thesis based on the student's personal and professional interests (Simmons, 1982). In 1982, the college inaugurated a Coordinated Basic Studies program in which three faculty members and about 50 entering students "form a small, self-contained learning community" that conducts classes, field trips, retreats, and special events organized around a common theme (Simmons, 1983).

The Hampshire curriculum is an excellent example of how the general education paradigm continues to function in the small-college environment.

Thematic and Interdisciplinary Programs

Thematic and interdisciplinary programs have been another approach to innovation in the past two decades. While general education is inherently interdisciplinary, a thematic or interdisciplinary curriculum is not inherently a general education program. The reason is that one's approach to interdisciplinary study can be as focused and specialized as any single-discipline program. Similarly, one can study around any theme and still not deal with the individual and social-change issues that are basic to the general education paradigm. The issue, as always, is not *what* is studied but *how* it is studied and *to what end* it is studied.

In the late 1960s, Newark State College experimented with an Individualized General Education (IGE) program that integrated interdisciplinary study into a student-centered approach to general education. As reported by Flexner and Hauser (1979), the program was distinguished by several characterisics. It was, first, individualized rather than regimented, with each student treated as a unique individual. It was integral and general rather than piecemeal and specialized; study was not broken into a series of unrelated courses but instead involved readings, experiences, and projects that built on individual interests to reveal different aspects of contemporary life. As these characteristics suggest, the IGE program actively involved the students in the creation of their own curriculum. The program was also characterized by its approach to subject matter. It was organized around what Newark faculty called "disciplines of mind and spirit": problem solving, creativity, valuing, and deciding. Students were to learn skills that were functional in life rather than solely academic or verbal (Flexner & Hauser, 1979).

Other institutions have developed institutionwide thematic curricula in which a theme pervades both general and professional instruction. At the University of Wisconsin at Green Bay, for instance, the curriculum is organized around the environment. Four colleges organized around different environmental themes are complemented by a Professional Studies unit that offers vocational programs related to each of the thematic colleges. Thus, the College of Community Sciences focuses on the role of individuals in the social environment and the ways in which individuals modify the environment; the College of Environmental Sciences prepares students to participate in solving environmental quality problems and to manage environmental resources, the College of Creative Communication emphasizes issues of aesthetics and values related to the environment, and the College of Human Biology focuses on the environmental stresses on humans that arise from the needs of society.

Courses in these programs are complemented by a core program of Liberal Education Seminars that continue throughout the undergraduate curriculum. At the freshman level, seminars cover topics such as technology and human values, resource utilization and the American character, and contemporary moral problems. During the sophomore and junior years, seminars become more project oriented and involve cross-cultural comparisons. During the senior year, the seminars are designed to be integrative. Working with students from other concentrations, the student applies more specialized knowledge to themes such as "social consciousness and the scientist" (Quehl, 1977).

Programs such as these illustrate how basic elements of the general education paradigm can be articulated in thematic and interdisciplinary programs. The key is that the programs emphasize the functional importance of the theme or interdisciplinary topic. As these examples show, general education goals are achieved when the theme or interdisciplinary subject is not an end in itself but provides a context for developing personal skills. This process is known by various terms: Bell's "method," Henderson's "life function," or Dewey's "transformation." The common element is the use or application of subject matter that is chosen specifically because it will contribute to the student's ability to solve problems or, as is literally the case at Green Bay, to transform the social environment.

Current Concerns

Despite some notable programs that attempted a comprehensive general education curriculum in the 1960s and 1970s, the general confusion about its nature and meaning has continued to retard the growth of general education. In the 1980s, the confusion has been compounded by a growing vocationalism on the part of undergraduate students. Of late, however, the concern over vocationalism has been one factor contributing to a new and critical look at undergraduate education. With this fresh look has come a new interest in general education. These issues were the focus of three national reports issued in 1984 and 1985. A look at these reports will illustrate the nature of the problems facing general education in the 1980s.

The first report, "Involvement in Learning: Realizing the Potential of American Higher Education" (Mortimer et al., 1984), was conducted under the aegis of the National Institute of Education. The report focuses on what it calls the excessive vocationalism of the undergraduate curriculum and on the weakened ability of the bachelor's degree "to foster the shared values and knowledge that bind us together as a society" (Scully, 1984, p. 1). The report rarely, if ever, uses the term *general education*, favoring instead *liberal education*. However, its recommendations call for what clearly are elements of the general education paradigm to be incorporated into undergraduate education.

The report cites three conditions needed to improve the college curriculum. One is student involvement in the learning process. Among the report's recommendations for achieving this is greater use of "active modes of teaching [that] require that students be inquirers—creators, as well as receivers, of knowledge" (Mortimer et al., 1984, p. 41). Specific methods mentioned by the report include involvement in research projects and field experiments, internships and other kinds of experiential learning, simulations, individual projects, and small-group activities. The report also recommends ongoing guidance and student advisement and the creation of "learning communities, organized around specific intellectual themes or tasks" (Mortimer et al., 1984, p. 41).

A second recommendation is that colleges establish higher expectations for undergraduate education. In this area, the report advocates a reform of liberal education "to insure that (1) curricular content is directly addressed not only to subject matter but also to the development of capacities of analysis, problem solving, communication, and synthesis, and (2) students and faculty integrate knowledge from various disciplines" (Mortimer et al., 1984, p. 43). To reach this goal, the report recommends that each institution review not only the content of the curriculum, but also its delivery and organization.

Third, the report calls for improved assessment and feedback. Assessment, it states, should be "an organic part of learning" (Mortimer et al., 1984, p. 45). Here, the report emphasizes the faculty's role in the total learning environment; it recommends that they be involved in the design and implementation of assessment measures; that they take on the responsibility of insuring that "the instruments and methods used are appropriate"; and that they "participate in the development, adoption, and scoring of the instruments and procedures used in student assessment and, in the process, be trained in the ways of using assessment as a teaching tool" (Mortimer et al., 1984, p. 45).

A second recent national report also calls for a reform of undergraduate education, but takes a much different approach. Entitled "To Reclaim a Legacy," the report was written in 1985 by National Endowment for the Humanities Chairman William J. Bennett, who shortly thereafter became U.S. Secretary of Education. While the NIE report uses the phrase *liberal education* to describe general education themes, Bennett calls for a "general education" that is, in fact, rooted strongly in the knowledge orientation and study of the past that mark traditional liberal education. The objective of Bennett's "general education" is to identify the "landmarks of human achievement" (p. 17) through readings in original texts covering the range of Western civilization. Writes Bennett, "A curriculum is rarely stronger than the syllabi of its courses, the array of texts singled out for careful reading and discussion" (p. 18). Bennett goes on to suggest 33 specific authors, along with a number of other documents ranging from the Bible to the Declaration of Independence. In short, Bennett, like Hutchins a generation before, advocates a great books program under the rubric of general education. Like Hutchins, his view of general education tends to be rather simple; as he describes it, general education is what all educated people hold in common, or the opposite of "specialized education."

Between these two poles comes yet a third national report that takes the middle ground. "Integrity in the College Curriculum: A Report to the Academic Community" was issued in February 1985 by the American Colleges Committee's Project on Redefining the Meaning and Purpose of Baccalaureate Degrees. The project calls for the current attack on "decline and devaluation" (p. 12) to include reforms of both the structure and process of the curriculum. While generally conservative, the project's position embodies some basic elements of general education. Its middle-ground position is summed up as follows:

Our message to administrators and professors alike is that the curriculum requires structure, a framework sturdier than simply a major and

general distribution requirements and more reliable than student interest. We do not believe that concern for coverage and factual knowledge
is where the construction of a curriculum should begin. We propose a
minimum required program of study for all students, consisting of the
intellectual, aesthetic, and philosophic experiences that should enter
into the lives of men and women engaged in baccalaureate education.
We *do not* believe that the road to a coherent undergraduate education
can be constructed from a set of required subjects or academic disciplines. We *do* believe that there are methods and processes, modes of
access to understanding and judgment, that should inform all study.
While learning cannot of course take place devoid of subject matter,
how that subject matter is experienced is what concerns us here. We
are in search of an education that will enable the American people to
live responsibly and joyfully, fulfilling their promise as individual humans and their obligations as democratic citizens. [p. 18]

At first glance the statement is reminiscent of Harvard's postwar report on general education (Committee on the Objectives,
1945); however, the project proposes to avoid the problem inherent
at Harvard. While the project calls for nine specific elements in its
"minimum course of study," it does not call for a prescribed curriculum or for particular distribution requirements or for required mul-
tidisciplinary courses. These "old solutions," states the report, would
be more likely to perpetuate than to remedy the problem: "The
integrity of a college requires more than a curriculum that looks
'right' on paper. The curriculum requires support, an environment in
which the priorities of the college actively encourage the realization
of the learning desired" (American Colleges, 1985, p. 24). The report
is not speaking directly of general education, but of the curriculum
as a whole. Within the larger context of the undergraduate curriculum, however, it calls for the kind of means/end unity that is central
to general education. Its vision of integrity is evocative of the instru-
mentalist-inspired general education curricula at Bennington College and Sarah Lawrence College.

The three reports illustrate the variety of images attached to
general education in the 1980s. Concepts historically associated with
general education are labeled liberal education by one; liberal education is labeled general education by another; and a third applies some
of the basic assumptions of general education to the undergraduate
curriculum as a whole, while ignoring general education as a self-
contained philosophy.

The question remains: Is there, within this confusion, a common
ground on which a stable, workable definition of general education

can be built? Yet another report, the Carnegie Foundation's 1986 study entitled "College: The Undergraduate Experience in America," suggests that a compromise may be emerging, however slowly, as elements of the older curriculum concepts are put into the context of general education. The report states, "Ideally general education . . . is not something to 'get out of the way,' but should extend vertically from freshman to senior year. And in a properly designed baccalaureate program, general education and specialized education will be joined" (p. 19). Carnegie's solution is an "integrated core" that introduces essential knowledge and makes connections, across disciplines and ultimately "to the application of knowledge to life beyond campus" and an "enriched major" that puts "the specialized fields of study in perspective" (p. 19). The outline suggested by Carnegie is a variation on Daniel Bell's proposals at Columbia. In effect, it integrates breadth and depth—the core and the major—through general education, with the major program to include social, economic, ethical, and moral implications of the major as well as the traditional skills.

While the general education experiments of the 1930s and 1950s were, for the most part, "noble experiments" with few imitators, the reports discussed in this section suggest that the social, economic, and educational conditions of the 1980s may be sympathetic to a more broad-based acceptance of general education concepts.

Trends and Opportunities in General Education

The basic paradigm of general education has been in place since the 1930s. The experience of the 1960s and 1970s added some refinements that reflected the needs of the times and the organizational realities within higher education. For the most part, there is agreement on the goals of general education, although some—like Bennett and, before him, Hutchins—use the term without subscribing to the goals. The real issue has centered around the methods of general education and their relationship to the goals and to the structure of the curriculum. It is here that confusion, especially confusion between liberal and general education, inhibits action.

In the final analysis, the major innovations of the period have been organizational, the goal being not to create a new paradigm but to articulate the existing paradigm in ways that would be compatible with the institutional environment. Two major innovations have been, first, the identification of general education with interdisciplinary study as a focal point for organizing the curriculum and, second, a better-articulated relationship between general education and professional or specialized education.

The recent reports illustrate that the confusion has become almost structural. The tension remains between graduate and undergraduate teaching needs, between the research and teaching missions in general, and between the student's interests and the institution's interests. This tension makes it difficult for many colleges and universities to act. Within a given college or university, there is rarely the community of shared vision needed to build a self-conscious general education program. However, outside the institutions some trends are developing which may push higher education toward a more serious consideration of general education. The potential impact of these trends is to move elements of the general education paradigm into the mainstream curriculum. Whether they eventually result in a consistent, self-conscious, comprehensive general education or remain bits and pieces that contribute to the splintering of an already-fragmented curriculum remains to be seen. These trends are in essence the raw materials for general education reform. They fall into three not totally unrelated areas: changes in the need for professional education, the growing importance of adult learners, and the use of technology in instruction.

Changes in Professional Education

One of the more simplistic images of general education defines it simply as the opposite of specialized education. Arthur Levine (1978), for instance, calls general education simply "the breadth component of the undergraduate curriculum" (p. 3). This image has been compounded by programs such as the early Contemporary Civilization curriculum, Meiklejohn's Experimental College, and Minnesota's General College, all of which focused on the first two years of a four-year program. However, from Sarah Lawrence College to Columbia University's reconsideration of general education in the 1970s, there has been a consistent theme within the general education movement that makes a different kind of distinction between general and specialized or professional education. Daniel Bell (1966) stated this position very succinctly when he noted that the difference between general and professional education is not one of content, but one of method; to Bell, general education provides the context for specialized study.

Bell's four-tiered curriculum has not been widely imitated; however, there is some evidence that pressure from the professions themselves may move the curriculum toward this more integrated vision. In *Future Shock*, Alvin Toffler (1970) calls for education to "shift into the future tense" (p. 427), in order to meet the needs of an increasingly "differentiating society" (p. 411) where people and professions will be so interdependent that no one person or profession can be counted on to plan the future. To master the rapid change that he sees as the root of future shock, Toffler says, "we shall therefore need both a clarification of important long-range social goals *and* a democratization of the way in which we arrive at them. . . . We need to initiate, in short, a continuing plebiscite on the future" (pp. 477–478).

More than a decade later, John Naisbitt (1984) saw a similar trend developing as the business world began to come to grips with rapid change caused by the technological revolution. He argues that American business schools have produced a generation of managers whose eyes are on short-term gains rather than long-term growth. Noting widespread criticism of this short-term management within the business community itself, Naisbitt takes the position that, because of a drastically changed situation, the need is now for long-term thinking, in which the process of reconceptualizing the business is a constant process and in which the job of the professional team is "righteously questioning every aspect of an institution's purpose—and the questioning of the purpose itself" (p. 94).

Naisbitt (1984) generalizes this situation to argue for a relationship between a future orientation in business and a future orientation in society. He notes a shift from representative democracy to participative democracy and a similar shift to participatory decision making in corporations: "The guiding principle of this participatory democracy is that people must be part of the process of arriving at decisions that affect their lives" (p. 159). This shift to long-term thinking, predicts Naisbitt, could "transform" education: "If you specialize too much, you may find your specialty becoming obsolete in the long run. As a generalist, committed to lifelong education, you can change with the times" (p. 96).

If one follows Naisbitt's thinking, it is possible to see a process-oriented, future-oriented general education being stimulated not by undergraduate colleges, but by the professional schools as they combine the traditional knowledge base of the specialized field with a general education that deals with the process and contextual issues facing the professions. Some examples of this approach have already begun to appear. One is California Polytechnic State University, which has an "upside-down" curriculum. Students begin to explore vocational interests and to take vocational courses in their first year. The curriculum broadens as students progress (Henderson & Henderson, 1974). The students' professional interests, instead of coming after general study, become the "thematic" base for general education, which is structured to provide a broad social context for the students' professional activity.

Even more dramatic is the curriculum at the National War College, whose students are a highly select group of military officers. It is difficult to imagine a more specialized professional program, and yet general education concepts—both methods and objectives—are integral to the curriculum. The goal of the college is to teach strategy to students whose previous training has been highly specialized. As one journalist described the students, "They come to the War College from a crisp world of finite thinking: they talk, people listen—and obey. Objectives are clear. At the school they learn about ambiguities, and then leave for a world in which a good question is: What's the question?" (Yoffe, 1984, p. 8). The goal, in sum, is to create students who are able to make decisions and solve problems—to shape the future—in a highly sensitive environment where no clear precedents may exist. While the subject matter is not as comprehensive as the world that is usually envisioned in general education, the change-oriented relationship between the individual and that environment is just as critical. The goal is general education, but within a more restricted context.

The curriculum at the National War College also matches the methods to the goals. Much of the instruction is conducted through games and simulations. In one simulation, "Prudent Strike," students work in teams of 12. Each team has a scenario of a world situation. They work together to decide on a course of action, which they submit to a "control team" of faculty and regional experts, who then update the scenario based on the team's actions. Raymond Bell, deputy director of the college's War Gaming and Simulation Center, notes that the objectives are broad strategic issues: "The object might be to familiarize students with the steps government takes to respond to international crises, or to test a new defense theory, or a theory on arms control, or how you deal with terrorism" (quoted in Yoffe, 1984, p. 17). The emphasis on realistic situations and direct action in order to achieve a desired future state, on simulation and experimentation as primary methods, and on group problem solving essentially parallels the methods of general education.

This kind of development raises some new issues for general education. Within the context of professional education, does "general" education mean education that applies to every student, or does the meaning shift, becoming education that prepares a particular student (or a professional in a particular field) to deal with "general" issues? Is it possible for a physician to receive a general education different from that received by a lawyer? In short, is it possible to have a general education program that is not universal?

The answer would appear to be a qualified yes. The positive answer assumes that students in professional programs will have had access earlier to a general education that deals with the broad needs of individuals in society. A second-level general education would provide a context within which individuals could better function as part of their professional communities. While the specific subject matter might differ from profession to profession, such a curriculum would be directed toward similar issues confronting all professionals: the role of the profession in society, individual and professional ethics, problem-solving skills specific to a profession, and how to deal with the social implications of professional activity. Such an approach is well suited to the goals of general education.

The Adult Learner

In the last decade, the tide of demographic, social, and technological change has carried new kinds of students into higher education, causing colleges and universities to rethink some of the assumptions behind the curriculum. Perhaps the most influential group of new students are the adult learners, students beyond the traditional college age, many of whom are already established in adult roles. These students have, in fact, been quietly infiltrating the halls of academe for years, through continuing education and evening courses. In the 1970s, though, they began to move to the forefront; adult participation in education became synonymous with the idea of a "learning society" in which Dewey's goal of truly lifelong education would be realized.

K. Patricia Cross (1981) declared the growth of the learning society to be inevitable and gave three reasons why. The first is demographic. In the 1980s, the baby-boom generation has passed through undergraduate and graduate school; the bulk of the baby boomers are now between their mid-twenties and mid-thirties, traditionally an age of high adult participation in adult education of all kinds. At the same time, colleges are beginning to feel the effects of the "baby bust"—the declining in numbers of citizens of traditional college age. Thus, the middle-aged adult population has grown both in numbers and as a percentage of the total population.

A second influence, according to Cross (1981), is social change. Not only are the baby boomers now adults, but they are living differently than their parents. More women are working; more people are changing careers in mid-life; there is more leisure time; the structure of family life has changed; people are more mobile; and not only do today's adults change their place of residence more often, they also move from career to career. In short, there is greater potential for change in our personal lives. Many people have adopted what Cross calls a "blended" lifestyle in which work, family life, leisure activity, and education are interwoven and interdependent (p. 9). Education has ceased to be a *stage* in life usually confined to one's youth and instead is a continuing *aspect* of daily life, supporting and supported by one's work, enjoyment of leisure, and family and community activity. The blended lifestyle calls for education—formal and informal—to become a central, lifelong function.

The third influence, technological change, is also a major factor contributing to the emergence of a blended lifestyle. The speed at which knowledge is generated and incorporated into the technology with which we work requires that adults of all walks of life continue their education. Cross (1981) notes that most professionals must become self-directed learners, using journals, conferences, and experience to keep up with their professions; but many also turn to more organized education. At the same time, technology is constantly creating new occupations and new specialties within existing occupations, spurring mid-career change and with it the need for re-education as well as continuing education. This is all part of the diversification that Naisbitt described in *Megatrends* (1984).

That the adult learner will have an effect on higher education is obvious; the implications for general education, however, are yet to be seen. How colleges will respond to the growth in adult students presents something of a dilemma for general education. On one hand, the rise of the adult student could foster a new sensitivity to individual and community needs, a sensitivity that could create a more sympathetic environment for general education. Kenneth G. Ryder (1985), President of Northeastern University, put the challenge this way:

> Adult education must be tuned very closely to the marketplace. We must not be too dependent on what is traditional. It is essential, in fact, that we keep very closely in touch with the changing economic and social conditions because if education for adults is to be useful and to respond to needs it must know exactly what is going on in this rapidly changing world. [p. 4]

Ryder's call for a more contemporary, present-oriented, needs-based education could be read as a call for an instrumentalist general education like that developed by California community colleges in the 1950s. Tuning education to the marketplace, however, could just as easily result in an adult education that is even more narrow and more vocational than traditional undergraduate education. If general education is to benefit the increased numbers of adults in higher education, it will have to be the result of a very conscious, purposeful decision by colleges and universities.

Another factor works in favor of general education. The very nature of the adult students and of the planning process for adult education programs suggests that there may be a closer relationship between adult and general education than might appear at first glance. The heart of the issue is the nature of the adult student and the factors that motivate an adult to participate in formal education. Most adult students come to education to meet a specific personal need, whether it be to qualify for a pay raise or to satisfy a long-standing intellectual curiosity. They expect to get immediate satisfaction from education by putting it to work in their daily lives. These two factors, combined with the fact that adult education is generally voluntary, change our assumptions about teaching. Malcolm Knowles recognized this change by introducing a new word—*andragogy*—to distinguish the assumptions of adult education from those of pedagogy, or child education (Godbey, 1978).

The assumptions of andragogy bear a resemblance to the assumptions that underlie Dewey's instrumentalist approach to general education. Andragogy assumes that the adult student is a mature, independent person fully capable of self-direction; that adults bring a vast store of personal experiences that can contribute to the learning process; and that the adult learner is continually evaluating past learning and assessing the need for additional learning as part of the educational process. These assumptions lead naturally to a student-centered approach to the education of adults; in this approach, both the content and process of learning are based on the individual's needs and interests. Since the student's concern is usually with immediate application of learning, adult education tends to center around problem-solving relevant to the student's specific situation and needs rather than concepts treated in the abstract. Finally, the teacher's role becomes to guide rather than control learning; the teacher-student relationship becomes reciprocal and mutually supportive (Godbey, 1978).

Adult students are coming to higher education from all directions. Many are enrolling as part-time credit students: The percentage of part-time students in American colleges increased from 32 percent to 42 percent between 1970 and 1980 and is expected to reach 52 percent by 1990. While the phenomenon is most visible in community colleges, the number of part-time students between the ages of 25 and 34 is growing twice as fast in four-year institutions as it is in community colleges (Cross, 1981). Many other adults are not interested in traditional degree programs; they are demanding noncredit programs, more than a thousand of which were introduced by colleges and universities between 1968 and 1978 (Cross, 1981).

Some educators have begun to consider the opportunities that adult students present to general education. Zwerling (1984), for instance, has suggested a general education program based on the Columbia model as well as a problem-centered curriculum that would allow adult students to meet basic academic content requirements, but in the context of "vital issues in their lives" (p. 3).

Perhaps even greater potential for general education will be reached when concepts of adult education are applied to the new role of general education in vocational and professional training. The goals of general education, the interests of adults, and the changing needs of professional education discussed earlier are so closely related that it is difficult to imagine that the three will not work synergistically as continuing professional education becomes more important to the total curriculum.

It may well be that adult or continuing education has already become the cutting edge of general education. Continuing education programs, by force of economics if nothing else, tend to be student centered, future oriented, and change oriented programs. The methods of adult education are especially sympathetic to the goals of general education. As the percentage of adult students—full time and part time—in the overall student population grows, becoming the majority by 1990 if Cross (1981) is right, and as competition for students continues to mount, these methods will become increasingly important, moving general education concepts into new areas of the curriculum.

The New Technologies

Since the 1960s, general education has been inextricably linked to the issue of technology. Helping students to deal with technological change and to direct the social response to technology has become a goal of general education. Only recently, however, have educators experimented with the use of technology as a tool of general education.

Educators have been experimenting with the use of computers in instruction since the 1960s. Initially, the emphasis was on drill and practice, record keeping, and grading. However, in the early 1970s, applications began to expand as low-cost computers made it possible for greater numbers of students to use computers in more sophisticated ways. Samuel Spero (1973) of Cuyahoga Community College broke the instructional process into four steps—motivation, the learning experience, reinforcement, and evaluation—and described how computers could be used at each step. Spero's recommendations for the application of computers to the first two steps—motivation and the learning experience—had direct implications for general education. He recommended the use of computer *gaming* to motivate the students. Gaming requires that students make knowledgeable decisions in order to win; this not only serves to motivate but adds an element of direct experience to the educational process. Spero saw several ways in which computers could add to the learning experience. For instance, he recommended computer programming as a way of giving students experience with learning a new concept in order to apply it. In addition, he advocated the use of computers to simulate laboratory experiments.

The computer's capabilities for gaming and simulation seem to offer the greatest potential for general education. Computer games and simulations make it possible to compress time so that the effects of individual decisions can be seen over a long term. The classic example of this type of simulation is "Hammurabi," which Carl Sagan (1977) described this way:

This is the ancient kingdom of Sumeria, and you are its venerated ruler. The fate of Sumeria's economy and of your loyal subjects is entirely in your hands. Your minister, Hammurabi, will report to you each year on population and economy. Using his information you must learn to allocate resources for your kingdom wisely. Someone is entering your council chamber. . . . [p. 219]

This kind of simulation gives every student access to a body of information and a set of circumstances with which the student can experiment. Just as the community served as a general education laboratory at Sarah Lawrence, computer simulations can be used as problem-solving tools. In colleges and universities where general education must survive side by side with mass education, this use of technology as a laboratory gives large numbers of students an opportunity to make judgments and see long-term consequences compressed into a short period of time.

Computers can also be a tool in fostering inquiry, that is, encouraging students to do their own thinking and come to their own conclusions. In the mid-1970s, faculty at the University of Washington at Seattle developed an inquiry-based physics course for nonmajors, which used computers to give students "experience" with physical phenomena. The course used computerized demonstrations; by manipulating variables in the demonstrations, students learned physical principles by direct experience (Kiester, 1978).

The potential of computer games, simulations, and demonstrations for general education is in the fact that they allow instruction to focus on processes and principles—on the use, rather than simply the acquisition, of knowledge. Obviously, computers are not the only way of reaching this goal. The potential benefit is in being able to reach more students with a technology that makes it possible for instruction to be individualized and self-paced. This capability could encourage the integration of general education concepts into the curriculum. The technical capability is there. What is needed is a conscious effort to use the technology for general education; the effort would require the development of computer programs and the incorporation of computing into the curriculum so that the limitations of computer-based instruction would be balanced with other experiences.

The use of computers for giving students experience in problem solving, inquiry, and experimentation; the growth in the numbers of adult learners in higher education; and trends in professional education are all forces that could shape the direction of the curriculum in the years ahead. Because they share some elements in common with general education, their influence could help to create an environment more sympathetic to general education. For that to happen, higher education will need to make a self-conscious effort to make the connections between the needs of professional education and the purposes of general education, between the learning styles of adults and the instructional methods associated with general education, and between the capabilities of the new technologies and the goals of general education. Without a unifying vision, these trends will simply add to the current confusion.

Summary and Conclusions

The period from the 1960s through the mid-1980s has been important to general education in both positive and negative ways. The innovations of the 1960s and early 1970s did much to revitalize interest in general education. The 1950s saw a shift in the curriculum away from the student and toward the needs of society, which was overwhelmingly concerned with conserving traditional values and ideas in the face of what was seen as an international threat to democracy. General education, with its emphasis on individual and social change, did not often find a sympathetic ear during the Cold War. The 1960s and 1970s saw a return to a more student-centered, future-looking curriculum and thus to an environment more amenable to the ideas of general education. The experience at Columbia and other trends also exploded the popular myth that general education should be limited to the first two years of undergraduate education, revitalizing Dewey's idea of a lifelong general education. On the negative side, increasing diversity in higher education, the increased importance of mass education as a mission of higher education, and a burgeoning vocationalism contributed to an almost paralyzing confusion over the definition of general education.

The return of the student to a central place in the curriculum was not just a result of the student movement and the emergence of a youth culture brought about by the baby-boom generation. It was also affected by developmental psychology, which put great emphasis on the individual's readiness to learn. Another factor was the nation's new awareness of social problems as it entered the 1960s. John F. Kennedy's inaugural challenge to Americans to "ask not what your country can do for you, ask what you can do for your country," signaled the return of a sense of individual commitment to solving social problems. Many of the innovations of the 1960s responded to the combination of these two interests—individualism and social activism. Although the two could be seen as contradictory, what brought them together in the 1960s and 1970s was an overarching spirit of social change that guided them both.

Since the same interests are at the heart of the general education paradigm, it was natural for curriculum innovations to contain at least some aspects of general education. For instance, innovative curricula that dealt with the interactions among science, technology, and society or that used environmental issues or basic problem-solving skills as thematic contexts for instruction were, in effect, built around contemporary issues that affected the students' ability to solve the problems of their times. This is, in essence, the goal of general education.

The aggregate effect of this type of innovation was the creation of an academic environment in which individual elements of general education were accepted and worked into the mainstream of the curriculum. This environment made it possible for educators to experiment with general education without rocking the boat of the mainstream curriculum. Some of the experiences of the last two decades have served to put general education back into its original perspective as a lifelong need that provides a context for specialized education. Daniel Bell's (1966) proposals and the resulting reform of general education at Columbia are the clearest examples of this development. This approach to curriculum established a relationship between general and professional education which, if not new in theory, was new in practice. It also responded to the complex institutional environment of the 1970s.

The innovations of the last two decades, however, have also served to increase confusion over the entire issue of general education. The piecemeal acceptance of specific elements of general education into the mainstream curriculum has blurred the old distinctions among general education, liberal education, interdisciplinary activity, undergraduate education, and even professional education.

There are some trends in higher education that offer opportunities for general education. These include changes in the needs of various professions, the rise of adults as students, and the use of new technologies. Some think that postindustrial society is especially well suited to the instrumentalist or pragmatist thought that gave birth to general education. What is needed and is apparently thus far lacking is a unifying vision of general education that allows the various trends, innovations, psychological theories, and institution-society relationships to come together in an environment of self-conscious curriculum making that takes into account both goals and methods and applies them to the specific problems of our times. For that to happen, the makers of curricula must dispel the confusion and agree on a common definition of general education.

CHAPTER 9

Conclusions:
The Meaning of General Education

General education has been with us for a long time, both in concept and in practice. Confusion about general education has been with us almost as long. The confusion over general education stems from many sources: the development of social goals for the curriculum without consideration for instructional implications, the conflict between instruction and research as competing paradigms within higher education, a simple lack of historical understanding, and so forth. The sources of confusion are so numerous as to suggest that perhaps there is no such thing as a single general education paradigm. The lack of a unifying vision has had a paralyzing effect on the curriculum. Changes in society demand that we take a new look at the curriculum and renew our concern for it. The issue is one not only of excellence but of relevance, both to society and to the individual students whose knowledge, skills, attitudes, and predispositions are the true "products" of education. We are called upon to develop a shared understanding of general education. If colleges and universities are to grapple seriously with the issue of general education, they must be able to arrive at a common understanding to which faculty and administrators can agree, one that can be articulated to students and can guide what happens in the classroom. This is essential to an effective general education program.

Differentiating General Education from Other Curriculum Concepts

Our purpose in these pages have been to explore how our assumptions about general education and our organized response to those assumptions—the collection of ideas, principles, and practices that constitute the general education paradigm—have been shaped by social and internal forces over the years. Our goal has been to discover common threads of meaning that will help reduce the confusion that so often surrounds the term *general education*. Too often it has been used loosely, with a meaning so vague that it blurs the necessary distinctions between general education and a number of other curriculum concepts. As a result, people have come to think of general education as being synonymous with something else. Therefore, before summarizing what general education *is*, a look at what it *is not* may help clear the air.

• *General education is not liberal education*. This is perhaps the most common point of confusion about general education, and it is so widespread that one writer chose not only to hyphenate the two terms but also to alternate their positions so that he could speak equally of "liberal-general education" and "general-liberal education." Unfortunately, the difference cannot be dealt with so easily: General and liberal education are separated not simply by a hyphen, but by fundamentally different assumptions.

The confusion stems from two circumstances: (1) the variety of meanings that people have ascribed to general education over the years and (2) the ways in which liberal education has changed in the twentieth century. For instance, to some people the primary purpose of general education initially was to insure coherence in the structure of the curriculum and in the delivery of a core of knowledge common to all students. To people who continue to use this limited definition, there can be a great deal of overlap between liberal and general education, since both share these two goals. As Flexner (1979) points out, general education initially was simply a reform movement; under the influence of Dewey and the instrumentalists, however, general education eventually took on other goals and other assumptions and became not a reform of liberal education, but a replacement for it.

Similarly, liberal education has evolved in the twentieth century. While traditional liberal education centered around the classical humanist traditions passed down by the writers of ancient Greece and Rome, the advent of naturalistic humanism led to a humanistic approach to general education. This, like the instrumentalist approach, focused on the present and future rather than the past; it emphasized skills (problem solving and values development, for instance) rather than abstract knowledge, and it found its authority in the contemporary needs and interests of students and society rather than in the ideas of classical authors. The naturalist humanist element within the liberal education community adopted some of the procedures and methods of general education but kept the basic assumptions of liberal education. While there is an overlap between certain elements of general education and certain elements of liberal education, there remain essential differences. These differences in basic assumptions and goals are most evident at the extremes, as when traditional or classical liberal education is compared to the instrumentalist vision of general education (Flexner, 1979).

The differences can be described in several ways. Flexner (1979) cites Taylor's distinction between the *rationalist* assumptions of liberal education and the *instrumentalist* assumptions of general education, as well as Morse's contrast of the *logical* methods of liberal education and the *psychological* methods of general education. James Rice (1972) distinguishes between the *essentialist* orientation of liberal education and the *existentialist* orientation of general education. Liberal education, founded on rationalist assumptions, oriented toward essentialism, and based in the methods of logic, is concerned with ideas in the abstract, with the conservation of universal truths handed down through the years, and with the development of the intellect. General education, founded on instrumentalist assumptions, oriented toward existentialism, and based in psychological methods, is concerned with experimentation and problem solving for individual and social action, with the problems of the present and future, and with the development of the individual. The differences between the two are fundamental.

Meiklejohn's experiment at Wisconsin and Harvard University's attempt at general education testify to the problems that inevitably occur when these fundamental differences are not recognized. While the failure of the Experimental College at Wisconsin was partly due to organizational and political problems, an equally basic problem was that Meiklejohn failed to see that general education goals could not be accomplished solely through the development of the intellect, a belief that was a holdover from his liberal education roots. Harvard consciously tried to reconcile the two paradigms. It attempted to reach general education goals through liberal education methods without taking into account the conflicting assumptions involved; the result was a curriculum that was more concerned with paper goals and with organizational structure than with what happened in the classroom.

The confusion between liberal and general education, then, rests on two basic problems. One is a tendency to define both general and liberal education too superficially, for instance, to look only at the structure of the curriculum or only at the subject matter in making one's definition. The other is the wide variety of practice that exists within both paradigms. However, there is evidence that, while college and university curricula often fail to reflect a difference, individual faculty do distinguish between the two. Flexner and Berrettini (1982) surveyed 500 faculty in more than 235 colleges and universities nationally. They discovered that "some 60 percent of the respondents *personally* believed that there are important conceptual, substantive, and procedural differences between general and liberal education" (p. 11), even though the majority believed that their institutions saw no difference between liberal and general education. This supports the notion that, ultimately, general education is insured not simply by shaping the structure of the curriculum, but by shaping what happens between students and instructors in the classroom. Methods and procedures—what individual faculty do—are as important to the success of a program as are the goals listed in the catalog. Faculty involvement and development become key to the long-term success of a general education curriculum.

• *General education is not synonymous with interdisciplinary study.* From Columbia's Contemporary Civilization program to the thematic curriculum at the University of Wisconsin at Green Bay, general education has long been associated with interdisciplinary study (Flexner, 1979). Historically, interdisciplinary study was a natural alternative for those to whom general education was primarily a tool for reforming an overspecialized and fragmented curriculum. The more complex instrumentalist approach to general education saw interdisciplinary activity in a more philosophical light; it was one way to insure that the means of education were in accord with the ends. Since discipline-based education was inconsistent with the instrumentalist goals of general education, interdisciplinary work was a necessity. The increased popularity of interdisciplinary studies over the last two decades has been important in keeping general education concepts alive in higher education.

However, all this does not mean that interdisciplinary study and general education are the same thing. Interdisciplinary study is a means toward the goals of general education, but it is not the goal itself. In fact, it is quite possible to have an interdisciplinary program that, in its orientation and methods, runs counter to the goals of general education. Such a program can be, in its own way, as specialized, as knowledged based, and as authority centered as any course based in a classical discipline. The relationship between general education and interdisciplinary activity rests not with the content itself, but with the treatment of the content and with the purpose of studying a given collection of subject matter.

• *General education is not synonymous with undergraduate instruction.* General education is commonly associated with the undergraduate curriculum. In fact, as we have noted elsewhere, Arthur Levine (1978) defined general education simply as "the breadth component of the undergraduate curriculum" (p. 3). Such a definition, however, ignores much that is essential to the general education paradigm. While it is true that many general education programs have focused on the first two years of the undergraduate curriculum and that they can be contrasted with the vocational instruction that is usually identified with the latter two years of undergraduate study, this structure does not, by itself, define general education. Dewey saw general education as a lifelong activity. The upside-down curriculum at California Polytechnic and the postdoctoral component of general education at Columbia University both illustrate the comprehensive nature of general education.

• *General education is not synonymous with a prescribed curriculum.* The tendency to identify general education with prescribed education is tied to the confusion between general and liberal education and is rooted in the methods associated with the humanistic approach to general education. The notion of a prescribed curriculum dates back to the Yale Report (Yale University Faculty, 1829/1961) and beyond, to the medieval European universities. Prescription is based on the assumption that the ultimate goal of education is the transfer of *knowledge*—the "furniture of the mind" (p. 278)—to young men and women. Since the goal is accumulation of knowledge, a prescribed curriculum insures that every student receives the same knowledge. The free elective system was an attempt to allow individual students to frame educational experiences to suit their own future plans. In this respect, the elective system helped prepare the way for a student-oriented general education.

The early humanistic approach to general education tended to combine the liberal education assumption about the value of universal knowledge and the general education assumption about the importance of applying knowledge to the solution of contemporary problems. Columbia's Contemporary Civilization program and Meiklejohn's Experimental College are examples of these programs, which retained an element of prescription.

The instrumentalists, however, worked from two different assumptions. One was that education should focus on the interests and needs of the individual student rather than on particular subject matter. The other was that education *for* democracy must be education *by* democracy. The first of these assumptions made prescription unnecessary in an instrumentalist general education. The second made it wrong.

While prescription plays a role in some humanist general education programs, it is certainly not common to all general education and, for that matter, runs counter to the basic assumptions on which the general education paradigm is built.

The confusion between liberal and general education arises from philosophical differences over the nature and goals of education. The tendency to identify general education with prescription or interdisciplinary study or the first two years of undergraduate education reflects an incomplete conception of general education that takes into account only the structure of the curriculum. These areas of confusion point to a basic lack of understanding about the one factor that is central to the general education paradigm, namely, that general education is concerned first with the student and the student's relationship with her or his community. This, ultimately, dictates the subject matter and the structure of the curriculum.

The Attributes of General Education

General education is not defined around a single structure. Unlike, for example, Hutchins's Great Books program, it is not based on a collection of readings that can be easily transplanted from institution to institution. However, our historical analysis of general education reveals common threads in the weave of a curriculum, key assumptions and organizing principles that have been associated with general education since its inception and that give a general education program its distinctive mark. These principles define the *concept* upon which different structural approaches to general education can be developed.

• *General education is self-conscious.* To put it another way, general education is *purposeful.* This can be said of any curriculum, of course, but general education takes special note of purpose. The ends—the stated purposes—of general education guide every aspect of the curriculum. General education began as a movement to reform a curriculum that had become too specialized, too professionalized, and too removed from the personal needs of individual students and from the community needs of a democratic society. Its roots are in a philosophy of self-consciousness or pragmatism or, to use Dewey's phrase, instrumentalism. This philosophy calls for one constantly to test and evaluate one's assumptions against reality and to set new goals to reflect changes in one's situation. Moreover, general education has developed under the influence of educational psychology, most recently, developmental psychology; this influence has encouraged a commitment to ongoing self-study and evaluation of both goals and procedures.

The sense of self-consciousness and self-evaluation is an important organizing principle for general education. It insures that other assumptions and principles are not reduced to the level of rhetoric and that objectives are supported by relevant practices and procedures. It also insures that general education remains focused on the needs of students and their future. The self-consciousness of general education keeps it from becoming a "paper curriculum" that states objectives but provides no means for reaching those objectives. It is what, in part, separates the "general education" of Harvard's Redbook from general education at Bennington or Columbia.

• *General education is comprehensive.* The self-consciousness of general education contributes to its comprehensiveness. *Comprehensive* is a risky term to use in talking about curriculum. While general education is comprehensive, the term does not mean comprehensive in the sense usually associated with survey courses or baccalaureate degree distribution requirements or other terms that suggest "a comprehensive survey of knowledge." The issue is not breadth versus depth.

General education is often thought of as comprehensive in contrast to the narrowness of specialized education; that is one aspect of the matter, but the comprehensiveness of general education does not relate simply to knowledge, but to the entire environment in which learning takes place. General education is comprehensive in part because it gives equal weight to the goals, the procedures or methods, and the content of the curriculum. Moreover, each of these individual components contributes to the comprehensiveness of a general education curriculum.

Three examples will illustrate the nature of comprehensiveness in general education. The first relates to the content of the curriculum. In the early days of the general education movement, Alexander Meiklejohn (1932) talked about general education in terms of a "scheme of reference." In the 1960s, Daniel Bell (1966) described general education as method versus knowledge. This concern with *context* is a continuing thread in the development of general education. In one sense, then, general education is comprehensive in that it deals with basic contexts, methods, attitudes, values, and skills that can be arrived at from many different experiences and areas of study and that are valuable to all individuals regardless of their academic or professional interests.

General education is also comprehensive in that its procedures are not limited to classroom activity. From the beginning, general education curricula have been concerned with the student's total learning environment; the entire community is considered a resource for general education. At Bennington, for instance, extracurricular activities, student governance, advising, and the structure of dormitory life all were considered part of general education. The importance of involvement in community affairs—from Sarah Lawrence College's idea of a community laboratory, to the commitment of community colleges to evaluate and respond to community needs, to the University of Wisconsin at Green Bay's emphasis on environmental issues—reflects this type of comprehensiveness.

A third aspect of comprehensiveness lies with the goals of general education and with the scope of learning that is implied by those goals. Dewey (1916/1944) saw general education as a lifelong process whose only real goal was to enable and motivate the student to continue the learning process. To Dewey, this process was intimately tied to the process of democratic living and thus to the vitality of a democratic society. This kind of comprehensiveness, too, is evident in the objectives of general education programs. However, its real impact is in practice. Columbia's four-tiered general education program, the upside-down curriculum at California Polytechnic, and others illustrate that general education is comprehensive in that it is not confined to a particular corner of the curriculum but, in fact, applies to all levels of education. Columbia's postdoctorate general education seminars provide an excellent proof of this particular pudding.

• *General education is intimately concerned with democratic processes and with the needs of a democratic society and always has been.* It begins with the individual and his or her relationship to society, rather than knowledge, as its organizing goal. Virtually every other aspect of general education revolves around the relationship of general education to society. As noted earlier, Dewey (1916/1944) put the implications of the relationship succinctly when he observed that education *for* democracy must be education *by* democracy. Thus, it is the relationship with the democratic process as much as educational psychology that creates the unity of goals and methods in general education and that puts the student at the center of the curriculum.

The view of democracy that historically has guided general education is one based in the instrumentalist philosophy. Its concern is with the basic processes by which democratic society—and, specifically, the American brand of democracy—is maintained. The instrumentalists saw the individual as the fundamental building block of a democratic society. They saw the basic process of democracy as one that looks to the future and one in which individuals, working as part of a community, solve specific, immediate problems by transforming their environment through a process of continually creating new futures. General education, then, is designed to enable individuals to perform this basic democratic function within their communities.

From this fundamental vision of the role of education in American society flow the basic defining characteristics of general education. An education for and by democracy is, by definition, student-centered and future-oriented. It is concerned more with processes—the skills of inquiry, hypothesizing, and problem-solving—and with values and attitudes than with specific areas of knowledge. It is concerned with the immediate realities of daily life rather than with abstractions. And it is valuable in its own right, rather than as preparation for something else.

This emphasis on process as both the goal and means of general education does not deny a role for subject matter or content, nor does it dictate the specific subject matter to be taught. Instead, it presents some implications—some standards—for the selection of subject matter in a general education curriculum. The most basic implication is that knowledge, for its *own* sake, is not a part of general education. Knowledge is, instead, selected because it contributes to the goals of general education, that is, because it will be valuable in helping the student deal with current and future problems. This affects both the selection of subject matter and the treatment of that subject matter in an individual course or program.

A Final Observation

As some of the programs reviewed in this book suggest, developing a successful general education program is no easy task. It requires a truly concerted effort among faculty and administrators and a shared understanding of—and willing participation in—goals and methods, on the part of students. It also tends to run against the grain of habits of mind, which, though they themselves are not very many years older than general education, are nevertheless now sacred traditions.

This is not to suggest, however, that the current interest in general education is somehow misplaced. It is hard to imagine a time and a set of circumstances more naturally amenable to the general education paradigm. American higher education is surrounded by issues that demand a response: the incredibly swift transformation from an industrial to a technological society and all of the implications that entails, the increasingly rapid obsolescence of knowledge and the need for an education that will prepare students to live in a future that can in no way be forecast safely, the strains on democratic processes brought about by these revolutionary changes in society, the recent outcry over the devaluation of a college education, the rise of new students and new technology-based instructional tools, and the changing position of the United States in the world. All these and many more factors make it essential that colleges and universities tackle the issue of general education and try to arrive at a community of shared understanding that will make possible the development of coherent general education curricula that respond to the needs of both individuals and democratic society in a time of change.

References

Allen, Frederick Lewis. (1965). *The big change: 1900–1950.* New York: Bantam.

American Colleges Committee's Project on Redefining the Meaning and Purpose of Baccalaureate Degrees. (1985, February 13). "Integrity in the college curriculum: A report to the academic community." *The Chronicle of Higher Education, 29*(22), 12–16, 18–22, 24, 26–30.

Babbitt, Irving. (1930). "Humanism: An essay at definition." In Norman Foerster (Ed.), *Humanism and America* (pp. 25–51). New York: Ferrar and Rinehart.

Belknap, Robert L., & Kuhns, Richard. (1977). *Tradition and innovation: General education and the reintegration of the university.* New York: Columbia University Press.

Bell, Daniel. (1966). *The reforming of general education.* New York: Columbia University Press.

Benezet, Louis. (1943). *General education in the progressive college* (Contributions to Education 884). New York: Bureau of Publications, Teachers College, Columbia University.

Bennett, William J. (1985, November 28). "To reclaim a legacy." *The Chronicle of Higher Education, 29*(11), 16–21.

Ben-David, Joseph. (1972). *American higher education: Directions old and new.* New York: McGraw-Hill.

Berle, Adolf A., Jr. (1960). "The irrepressible issues of the 1960s." In G. Kerry Smith (Ed.), *Current issues in higher education* (pp. 3–8). Washington, DC: Association for Higher Education.

Boorstin, Daniel. (1974). *The Americans: The democratic experience.* New York: Vintage Books.

Boyer, Ernest L., & Kaplan, Martin. (1977). *Educating for survival.* New Rochelle, NY: Change Magazine Press.

Brockway, Thomas P. (1981). *Bennington College: In the beginning.* Bennington, VT: Bennington College Press.

Brubacher, John S., & Rudy, Willis. (1958). *Higher education in transition.* New York: Harper and Brothers.

Buchler, Justus. (1954). "Reconstruction in the liberal arts." In *A history of Columbia College on Morningside* (pp. 48–135). New York: Columbia University Press.

Butler, Nicholas Murray. (1919). "Education after the war." In *Proceedings of the 32d Annual Convention of the Association of Colleges and Preparatory Schools of the Middle States and Maryland* (pp. 7–21). Philadelphia: Association of Colleges and Preparatory Schools of the Middle States and Maryland.

Carnegie Foundation for the Advancement of Teaching. (1986, November 5). "Excerpts from the prologue and recommendations of 'Colleges: The undergraduate experience in America.'" *The Chronicle of Higher Education, 33*(10), 16–22.

Childs, John L. (1950). *Education and morals*. New York: Appleton-Century-Crofts.

———. (1956). *American pragmatism and education*. New York: Henry Holt and Co.

Commager, Henry Steele. (1950). *The American mind*. New Haven, CT: Yale University Press.

———. (1978). *The empire of reason*. Garden City, NY: Anchor Books.

Committee on the Objectives of a General Education in a Free Society. (1945). *General education in a free society: Report of the Harvard Committee*. Cambridge, MA: Harvard University Press.

Coon, Horace. (Ed.). (1947). *Columbia: Colossus on the Hudson*. New York: E. P. Dutton.

Cornell, Ezra. (1978). "Charter address." In A. Levine (Ed.), *Handbook on Undergraduate Education* (pp. 559–561). San Francisco: Jossey-Bass. (Original work published 1869).

Coss, John J. (Ed.). (1931). *Five college plans*. New York: Columbia University Press.

Cremin, Lawrence A. (1961). *The transformation of the school*. New York: Vintage Books.

Crosen, Robert G. (1952). "Contributions of general education toward strengthening the moral and spiritual foundations of modern society." In Francis H. Hess (Ed.), *Seventh annual conference on higher education* (pp. 125–126). Washington, DC: Association for Higher Education.

Cross, K. Patricia. (1981). *Adults as learners*. San Francisco: Jossey-Bass.

Dennis, Lawrence J., & Eaton, Eilliam E. (Eds.). (1980). *George S. Counts: Educator for a new age*. Carbondale, IL: Southern Illinois University Press.

Dewey, John. (1938). *Experience and education*. New York: Macmillan.

———. (1944). *Democracy and education*. New York: The Free Press. (Original work published 1916)

———. (1975). *Philosophy of education: Problems of man*. Totowa, NJ: Littlefield, Adams. (Original work published 1946, as *Problems of men*)

———. (1975). *Moral principles in education*. Carbondale, IL: Southern Illinois University Press. (Original work published 1909)

Doerschuk, Beatrice. (1933, March). "Statement." *Bulletin of the Association of American Colleges, 19*, 10.

Dykhuizen, George. (1973). *The life and mind of John Dewey*. Carbondale, IL: Southern Illinois University Press.

Eckert, Ruth. (1943). *Outcomes of general education: An appraisal of the General College program*. Minneapolis: University of Minnesota Press.

Eliot, Charles. (1978). "A turning point in higher education." In A. Levine (Ed.), *Handbook on undergraduate education* (pp. 562–574). San Francisco: Jossey-Bass. (Original work published 1869)

"The Experimental College of the University of Wisconsin." (1929, July 6). *School and Society, 30*(758), 15.

"The Experimental College of the University of Wisconsin." (1930, June 21). *School and Society, 31*(808), 834.

Ferguson, Marilyn. (1980). *The Aquarian conspiracy: Personal and social transformation in the 80s.* Los Angeles: J. P. Tracher.

Flexner, Hans. (1972, Fall). "General education and academic innovation." *Journal of Research and Development in Education, 6*(1), 46–57.

———. (1979). "The curriculum, the disciplines, and interdisciplinarity." In Joseph Kockelmans (Ed.), *Interdisciplinarity and higher education* (pp. 93–122). University Park: Pennsylvania State University Press.

Flexner, Hans, & Berrettini, Robert. (1981, March). "General education: Concept and practice." Paper presented at the annual meeting of the Eastern Educational Research Association, Philadelphia.

Flexner, Hans, & Hauser, Gerald A. (1979). "Interdisciplinary programs in the United States: Some paradigms." In Joseph Kockelmans (Ed.), *Interdisciplinarity and higher education* (pp. 328–350). University Park: Pennsylvania State University Press.

Frankel, Charles. (1970). "The happy crisis: 1961." In G. Kerry Smith (Ed.), *Twenty-five years: 1945–1970* (pp. 117–130). San Francisco: Jossey-Bass.

Gaff, Jerry. (1982). "Curricular imperatives for renewing general education." *The Journal of General Education, 39*(3), 189–197.

Godbey, Gorden. (1978). *Applied andragogy.* University Park: The Pennsylvania State University.

Goldman, Eric. (1966). *The crucial decade—and after: America, 1945–1960.* New York: Alfred A. Knopf.

Gould, Stephen Jay. (1981). *The mismeasure of man.* New York : W. W. Norton.

Grantham, Dewey W. (1976). *The United States since 1945: The ordeal of power.* New York: McGraw-Hill.

Guth, William. (1921, April). "The post-war curriculum." *Association of American Colleges Bulletin, 7*(3), 237–241.

Hahn, Milton E. (1940, May). "Vocational orientation." *Journal of Higher Education, 11*(5), 237–241.

Halliburton, David. (1977). "Perspectives on the curriculum." In Gary H. Quehl (Ed.), *Developing the college curriculum: A handbook for faculty and administrators* (pp. 35–74). Washington, DC: Council for the Advancement of Small Colleges.

Hawkes, Herbert E., et al. (1931). *Five college plans.* New York: Columbia University Press.

Heffner, Richard. (1962). *A documentary history of the United States.* New York: New American Library.

Henderson, Algo D. (1960). *Policies and practices in higher education.* New York: Harper and Brothers.

——. (1970). *The innovative spirit.* San Francisco: Jossey-Bass.

Henderson, Algo D., & Henderson, Jean. (1974). *Higher education in America.* San Francisco: Jossey-Bass.

Henry, Nelson. (Ed.). (1952). *The fifty-first yearbook of the National Society for the Study of Education: Part I, General education.* Chicago: University of Chicago Press.

Hofstadter, Richard. (1961). *Academic freedom in the age of the college.* New York: Columbia University Press.

——. (1962). *Anti-intellectualism in American life.* New York: Vintage Books.

Hofstadter, Richard, & Smith, Wilson. (Eds.). (1961). *American higher education: A documentary history.* Chicago: University of Chicago Press.

Hutchins, Robert Maynard. (1936a). *The higher learning in America.* New Haven, CT: Yale University Press.

Hutchins, Robert Maynard. (1936b). *No friendly voice.* Chicago: University of Chicago Press.

Jencks, Christopher, & Riesman, David. (1968). *The academic revolution.* Garden City, NY: Doubleday.

Johnson, B. Lamar. (1952). *General education in action: A report of the California study of general education in the junior college.* Washington, DC: American Council on Education.

Jones, Barbara. (1946). *Bennington College: The development of an educational idea.* New York: Harper and Brothers.

Kennedy, Gail. (Ed.). (1952). *Education for democracy: The debate over the report of the President's Commission on Higher Education.* Boston: D. C. Heath.

Kerr, Clark. (1982). *The uses of the university.* Cambridge, MA: Harvard University Press.

Kiester, Sally V. (1978). "It's student and computer, one on one." *Report on Teaching (Change Magazine), 10*(1), 56–58.

Kilpatrick, William Heard. (1926). *Foundations of method.* New York: Macmillan.

——. (Ed.). (1933). *The educational frontier.* New York: D. Appleton-Century.

Kirkland, J. H. (1922, March). "College objectives and ideals." *Association of American Colleges Bulletin, 8*(3), 57–74.

Kolbe, Parke R. (1919, April). "The college in the war and after." *Association of American Colleges Bulletin, 5*(3), 144–154.

Lamont, Corliss. (1949). *Humanism as a philosophy.* New York: Philosophical Library.

Lee, Calvin B. T. (1970). *The campus scene, 1900–1970: Changing styles in undergraduate life.* New York: David McKay.

Levine, Arthur. (1978). *Handbook on undergraduate curriculum.* San Francisco: Jossey-Bass.

MacLean, Malcolm S. (1934). "Reorganization at the University of Minnesota." *The Junior College Journal, 4,* 441–449.

——. (1951). "The general college: Its origins and influence." In H. T.

Morse (Ed.), *General education in transition: A look ahead* (pp. 29–44). Minneapolis: The University of Minnesota Press.

Malone, Dumas. (1981). *Jefferson and his times: The sage of Monticello.* Boston: Little, Brown.

McGrath, Earl J. (1974, October). "Careers, values, and general education." *Liberal Education, 15*(3), 19–22.

———. (1976). *General education and the plight of modern man.* Indianapolis: The Lilly Endowment.

McGrath, Earl J., Blommers, Paul J., Corben, John C., Goetsch, Walter R., Jacobs, James A., Longman, Lester D., Olson, Paul R., Smith, Goldwin, Stroud, James B., & Van Dyke, L. A. (1949). *Toward general education.* New York: Macmillan.

McGrath, Earl J., & Meeth, L. Richard. (1965). "Organizing for teaching and learning: The curriculum." In Samuel Baskin (Ed.), *Higher education: Some newer developments* (pp. 27–48). New York: McGraw-Hill.

Meiklejohn, Alexander. (1920). *The liberal college.* Boston: Marshall Jones Company.

———. (1923). *Freedom and the college.* New York: The Century Company.

———. (1932). *The experimental college.* New York: Harper and Brothers.

———. (1965). *Education between two worlds.* New York: Atherton Press.

Metzger, Walter P. (1961). *Academic freedom in the age of the university.* New York: Columbia University Press.

Meyers, Marvin. (1968). *The Jacksonian persuasion.* Stanford, CA: Stanford University Press.

Mortimer, Kenneth P., et al. (1984, October 24). "Involvement in learning: Realizing the potential of American higher education." *The Chronicle of Higher Education, 29*(9), 35–49.

Mourant, John A., & Freund, E. Hans. (Eds.). (1964). *Problems of philosophy.* New York: Macmillan.

Naisbitt, John. (1984). *Megatrends.* New York: Warner Books.

National Commission on the Role and Future of State Colleges and Universities. (1986, November 29). "To secure the blessings of liberty: The text of Report on State Colleges' Role." *The Chronicle of Higher Education, 33*(11), 29–36.

Quehl, Gary H. (Ed.). (1977). *Developing the college curriculum: A handbook for faculty and administrators.* Washington, DC: Council for the Advancement of Small Colleges.

Raines, Howell. (1977). *My soul is rested: Movement days in the Deep South remembered.* New York: G. P. Putnam's Sons.

Ravitch, Diane. (1983). *The troubled crusade: American education, 1945–1980.* New York: Basic Books.

Rice, James G. (1972, October). "General education: Has its time come again?" *Journal of Higher Education, 43*(7), 531–543.

Robertson, James Oliver. (1980). *American myth, American reality.* New York: Hill and Wang.

Rockfish Gap Commission. (1961). "Report of the Rockfish Gap Commission appointed to fix the site of the University of Virginia." In Richard Hofstadter & Wilson Smith (Eds.), *American higher education: A documentary history* (Vol. 1, pp. 193–199). Chicago: University of Chicago Press. (Original work published 1818)

Roosevelt, Theodore. (1962). "The new nationalism." In Richard Heffner (Ed.), *A documentary history of the United States* (pp. 220–225). New York: New American Library. (Original work published 1910)

Rudolph, Frederick. (1962). *The American college and university: A history*. New York: Vintage Books.

———. (1977). *Curriculum: A history of the American undergraduate course of study since 1636*. San Francisco: Jossey-Bass.

Rudy, Willis. (1960). *The evolving liberal arts curriculum: A historical review of basic themes*. New York: Bureau of Publications, Teachers College, Columbia University, 1960.

Ryder, Kenneth G. (1985, Winter). "Tradition and the learning society: A university perspective." *The Journal of Continuing Higher Education, 33*(1), 2–7.

Sagan, Carl. (1977). *The dragons of Eden*. New York: Random House.

Sanford, Nevitt. (1968). *Where colleges fail*. San Francisco: Jossey-Bass.

———. (1970). "The goal of individual development: 1962." In G. Kerry Smith (Ed.), *Twenty-five years: 1945–1970* (pp. 131–146). San Francisco: Jossey-Bass.

Scheffler, Israel. (1974). *Four pragmatists*. New York: Humanities Press.

Schilpp, Paul D. (Ed.). (1930). *Higher education faces the future*. New York: Horace Liveright.

Schneider, Herbert W. (1946). *A history of American philosophy*. New York: Columbia University Press.

Scully, Malcolm G. (1984, October 24). "U.S. colleges not realizing their full potential, panel says; Urges a national debate on quality." *The Chronicle of Higher Education, 29*(9), 1, 34.

Showerman, Grant. (1931, April 11). "A most lamentable comedy." *School and Society, 33*(880), 482.

Simmons, Adele Smith. (1982). *Hampshire College report of the president to the board of trustees, 1977–1982*. Amherst, MA: Hampshire College.

———. (1983). *Report of the president to the board of trustees, 1982–1983*. Amherst, MA: Hampshire College.

"Sisters in progressivism: Sarah Lawrence and Bennington educate by planless plan." (1939, December 25). *Newsweek, 14*(52), pp. 34–35.

Smith, John E. (1978). *Purpose and thought: The meaning of pragmatism*. New Haven, CT: Yale University Press.

Spafford, Ivol. (1940, June). "Home-life orientation." *Journal of Higher Education, 11*(6), 299–303.

Spero, Samuel K. (1973). "A computer course for educators." *Journal of Educational Technology Systems, 2*(1), 51–56.

Starrak, James A., & Hughes, Raymond M. (1954). *The community college in the United States.* Ames: Iowa State College Press.

Stickler, W. Hugh, Stoakes, James Paul, & Shores, Louis. (Eds.). (1950). *General education: A university program in action.* Dubuque, IA: Wm. C. Brown Company.

Students for a Democratic Society. (1972). "The Port Huron statement." In Robert D. Marcus & David Burner (Eds.), *America since 1945* (pp. 176–193). New York: St. Martin's Press. (Original work published 1962)

Taylor, Harold. (Ed.). (1950). *Essays in teaching.* New York: Harper and Brothers.

————. (1960). "The American idea." In G. Kerry Smith (Ed.), *Current issues in higher education* (pp. 43–46). Washington, DC: Association for Higher Education.

Thornton, James W., Jr. (1940, May). "Individual orientation." *Journal of Higher Education, 11*(5), 233–237.

Tocqueville, Alexis de. (1980). *Democracy in America.* New York: Alfred A. Knopf. (Original work published 1840)

Toffler, Alvin. (1970). *Future shock.* New York: Bantam Books.

Turner, Frederick Jackson. (1962). "The frontier in American history." In Richard Heffner (Ed.), *A documentary history of the United States* (pp. 178–186). New York: New American Library. (Original work published 1893)

Veysey, Laurence. (1965). *The emergence of the American university.* Chicago: University of Chicago Press.

Vine, Phyllis. (1976, Winter). "The social function of eighteenth century higher education." *History of Education Quarterly, 16*, 409–410.

Warren, Constance. (1930, November 19). "On the college frontier: The Sarah Lawrence plan." *The Nation, 131*(341), p. 550.

————. (1938, January). "What actually educates?" *Journal of the American Association of University Women, 31*(1), 72–74.

————. (1940). *A new design for women's education.* New York: Frederick A. Stokes.

Wayland, Francis. (1961a). "Report to the Corporation of Brown University, on changes in the system of collegiate education, read March 28, 1850." In Richard Hofstadter & Wilson Smith (Eds.), *American higher education: A documentary history* (Vol. 2, pp. 478–487). Chicago: University of Chicago Press. (Original work published 1850)

Wayland, Francis. (1961b). "Thoughts on the present collegiate system in the United States." In Richard Hofstadter & Wilson Smith (Eds.), *American higher education: A documentary history* (Vol. 1, p. 334). Chicago: University of Chicago Press. (Original work published 1842)

White, Morton. (1973). *Pragmatism and the American mind.* New York: Oxford University Press.

"Why the Wisconsin experiment was bound to fail." (1931, August 1). *School and Society, 34*(886), 152.

Wilson, E. C., & Ylvisakas, Hedvig. (1940, June). "Socio-Civic Orientation."
    Journal of Continuing Higher Education, 2(6), 293–298.
Wilson, Woodrow. (1962). "The new freedom." In Richard Heffner (Ed.), *A
    documentary history of the United States* (pp. 226–232). New York: New
    American Library. (Original work published 1913)
Wilson, Woodrow. (1962). "War message to Congress." In Richard Heffner
    (Ed.), *A documentary history of the United States* (pp. 238–242). New York:
    New American Library. (Original work published 1917)
Yale University Faculty. (1961). "Original papers in relation to a course of
    liberal education." In Richard Hofstadter & Wilson Smith (Eds.),
    American higher education: A documentary history (Vol. 1, pp. 275–291). Chi-
    cago: University of Chicago Press. (Original work published 1829)
Yoffe, Emily. (1984, November 4). "The chosen few." *The Washington Post
    Magazine*, pp. 8–9, 16–21.
Zwerling, L. Steven. (1984, Summer). "Continuing education in the liberal
    arts: Some alternatives." *Journal of Continuing Higher Education, 32*(3), 2–4.

About the Author

Gary E. Miller is Executive Director of the International University Consortium at the University of Maryland's University College. He earned a B.A. and an M.A. in English and a Ph.D. in higher education from the Pennsylvania State University. Dr. Miller is on the editorial board of the *American Journal of Distance Education,* to which he is a regular contributor.

Index